Family Book of Values

Character-Strengthening Lessons and Stories for Youth

Paula Noble Fellingham

Family Book of Values
Character-Strengthening Lessons and Stories for Youth

Solutions for Families, Inc.
Saratoga Springs, UT 84045
SolutionsForFamilies.com

In Association with:

Elite Online Publishing
63 East 11400 South
Suite #230
Sandy, UT 84070
EliteOnlinePublishing.com

Library of Congress Number - 2020925106

ISBN - 979-8582458432 (Amazon)

ISBN - 978-1735956008 (Paperback)

Dedication

With all the love in my heart I dedicate this book to my children - Melissa, Angela, Joy, Elise, Danny, David, Benjamin, and Heidi - and to their children, and their children…

My precious posterity brings me profound joy and they take my breath away as I watch them live, and teach through their examples, the values in this book. I am blessed beyond measure to be their Mom and Grammie.

My darling ones, I love you…all the world.

Table of Contents

INTRODUCTION 7

ACHIEVEMENT 9

APPRECIATION 13

ATTITUDE 19

BELIEF 25

CARING 29

CHARITY 33

CHEERFULNESS 37

CLEANLINESS 41

COMMITMENT 47

COMPASSION 53

CONFIDENCE 59

COOPERATION 63

COURAGE 69

COURTESY 73

CREATIVITY 77

DEPENDABILITY 85

DETERMINATION 89

EMPATHY 95

ENCOURAGEMENT 99

ENDURANCE 105

ENTHUSIASM 109

EXCELLENCE 113

FAIRNESS 121

FLEXIBILITY 127

FORGIVENESS 131

FRIENDSHIP 137

GENEROSITY 143

GENTLENESS 147

GRATITUDE...151

HELPFULNESS..157

HONESTY..163

HONOR..169

HOPE..175

HUMILITY..181

HUMOR..185

IMAGINATION..189

INDIVIDUALITY..195

INTEGRITY..199

JOYFULNESS..205

KINDNESS..209

LEADERSHIP..215

LEARNING..219

LISTENING..225

LOVE..229

LOYALTY..235

MERCY..239

MODERATION..246

MODESTY..254

OBEDIENCE..258

OPTIMISM..264

OVERCOMING ADVERSITY..270

PATIENCE..276

PEACE..282

PERSEVERANCE..286

PREPARATION..290

RELIABILITY..296

RESPECT..302

RESPONSIBILITY..310

SELF-DISCIPLINE..316

SELF-RELIANCE..322

SERVICE..328

STEADFASTNESS..334

TACT..338

TEAMWORK 342

THRIFT 348

TOLERANCE 354

TRUSTWORTHINESS 358

UNDERSTANDING 364

UNSELFISHNESS 370

WISDOM 376

WORK 382

ABOUT THE AUTHOR 386

Introduction

Has a story ever changed your life? You may be familiar with the famous French tale *The Little Prince*, by Antoine deSaint Exupery. Here's the part that deeply touched me:

The Little Prince's best friend, a fox, must leave him forever. Before the fox departs he promises to tell the Prince the most wonderful secret in the world if he'll meet certain conditions. The Little Prince agrees, does what is expected, and then asks for the secret. This is what the fox reveals: "Only that which is invisible is essential."

After re-reading the fox's secret three times, I set the book down and reflected on my life. I knew in that moment that I'd spent far too much time worrying about things that are visible and very little time contemplating that which is not.

Values are invisible. Although they can't be seen, touched, tasted, or smelled, they are without a doubt, the essentials of life. Adults who consistently live the moral values they believe in give children gifts of priceless worth. Those who teach these valuable, life-changing concepts - through explanation and stories - empower children to make wise choices and to live honorably.

Ideally, children should be well-grounded in a firm understanding of, and unswerving commitment to, noble values. Then they can more easily live in ways that are consistent with their beliefs.

And yet, how will our youth learn these essential principles if we don't teach them? I fear that too many children haven't stood for *something*, so they've fallen for *anything*. They've listened to alluring voices that point them down destructive paths. And our children, because they want leadership and guidance so desperately, will follow any leader, no matter where he's going.

Let's be bold in what we stand for and how we lead today's children. Let us show them through our example and instruction that living moral values brings happiness and that choosing the right is not old fashioned. Let us touch the future by teaching children that learning and living noble values prepares them to love and lead their fellowmen.

May I suggest that as you teach you may consider enlarging and expanding each value with your own explanation and experience. Additionally, highly effective teaching also includes applying the principles to children's personal, everyday lives and circumstances. Finally, and most importantly, remember that the very most effective way to teach children is by our example.

May you be blessed in your efforts to strengthen today's youth as you use the *Family Book of Values*.

Paula Noble Fellingham

ACHIEVEMENT

Achievement

Definition Achievement: A successful action or praiseworthy accomplishment.

Quotes

"It is time for all to stand and cheer for the doer, the achiever—the one who recognizes the challenge and does something about it."

Vince Lombardi[1]

"Nothing stops the man who desires to achieve. Every obstacle simply develops his achievement muscle."

Thomas Carlyle

Explanation

Achievement is accomplishing a goal. As you grow older, your goals change. When you're very young, achievements are like learning how to tie your shoes and ride a bicycle. Later, you learn to read and do math. As you get older perhaps you'll learn how to play a sport or a musical instrument. There are countless opportunities for achievement in high school, college, and in a career.

It's wonderful to know that if you learn and work hard enough you can achieve nearly anything you want to. J.A. Widstoe said, "Decide what you want to be, pay the price, and be what you want to be."

Your greatest achievements are sometimes unseen by others. For example, learning how to control a bad temper or learning how to quickly forgive others are remarkable achievements. Also, setting goals to improve relationships is always a good idea.

For example, perhaps you have a brother or sister, or a friend, who sometimes teases you and makes you angry. You might set two goals: first, to learn how to firmly and kindly tell that person that his teasing hurts your feelings; second, to not allow his teasing to upset you. To become more kind, loving, patient, cheerful, or helpful are the types of goals that, when you achieve them, bring long-lasting happiness and will help you in every relationship throughout your life.

---

[1] Glenn Van Ekeren. *Speaker's Sourcebook II*. 1994. Paramus, New Jersey: Prentice Hall, 9

Story for Young Children

<u>The Story of Shelly Mann</u>

In 1956, the Olympics were held in Melbourne, Australia. There on the winner's platform in the spotlight one day stood a beautiful, tall, blonde American girl. She was presented with a gold medal, symbolic of a first place in worldwide competition. As she stood there, some boys whistled and others were heard to say, "There's a gal who has everything."

Tears ran down her cheeks as she accepted the recognition. Many thought she was touched by the victory ceremony. The thing most of the audience did not know was the story of her determination, self-discipline, and daily action. At the age of five she had polio. When the disease left her body, she couldn't use her arms or legs. Daily, her parents took her to a swimming pool where they hoped the water would help hold her arms up as she tried to use them again. When she could lift her arm out of the water with her own power, she cried for joy. Then her goal was to swim the width of the pool, then the length, then several lengths.

She kept on trying, swimming, enduring, day after day after day, until she won the gold medal for the butterfly stroke – one of the most difficult of all swimming strokes.[2]

Shelly's determination helped her achieve her dream.

Learning Questions

1. What did Shelly achieve?
2. How does it make you feel when you do something well?
3. What is one thing you would like to achieve in your life?

Story for Older Children

It was a Friday morning, 400 years ago, in Rome, Italy. A famous sculptor and painter named Michelangelo was on his way to the Sistine Chapel to work on his ceiling painting. Only this day was different because it was his last day of work at the famous church. Michelangelo had been painting the ceiling of that magnificent building for seven long years, and today he would finish the painting!

As the artist slowly climbed the scaffolding, Michelangelo could barely see. He was nearly blind from the paint that had dripped into his eyes as he lay on his back on the hard, wood scaffolding - painting a ceiling - for seven years.

Yes, it took Michelangelo seven years – one brush stroke at a time – to paint his Biblical scenes in the Sistine Chapel. It took Brahms twenty years – one note at a time – to compose his First Symphony. It took Edmund Hillary and Tenzing Norgay eighty days – one step at a time – to

---

[2] Marvin J. Ashton, "The Time is Now," *Ensign,* May 1975, 85

climb the 29,000 feet of Mount Everest. Word by word, brush stroke by brush stroke, note by note, step by step, problem by problem, prayer by prayer – this is the secret of achievement.[3]

Learning Questions

1. How do people accomplish great things?
2. What are you working to achieve right now?
3. What is one thing you can do today that will bring you closer to achieving your goal?

You Show Achievement When You:

- Accomplish a goal.
- Understand that as you get older your goals will change.
- Realize that your greatest achievements are sometimes unseen by others.
- Learn that you can decide what you want to be, pay the price, and be what you want to be.

---

[3] Paula Noble Fellingham

APPRECIATION

Appreciation

Definition Appreciation: Thankfulness for the good things in your life.

Quotes

"The deepest hunger of human nature is the craving to be appreciated."

William James[4]

"As we express our gratitude, we must never forget that the highest appreciation is not to utter words, but to live by them."

John F. Kennedy[5]

Explanation

Appreciation is being thankful. There are many, many things we should be thankful for. We should notice and appreciate our beautiful world — the sun, the mountains, trees, and flowers. We should appreciate our eyes, ears, legs, and our good health. Also, we should be thankful for our families and friends. If we made a list of all the things we should appreciate it would take a long time, wouldn't it?

How should we show our appreciation for the good things in our lives? Some of the ways are to take care of the world around us and take care of our bodies. We should also help our family and friends.

We can take care of our world by never littering, and by being kind to all living things, like animals and plants. We can take care of our bodies by eating right, getting enough sleep, and being active. We can show appreciation for the good people in our lives by being kind and loving to them.

We can also show our appreciation by thinking good thoughts. Instead of thinking about what we *don't* have, we should focus on all the things we *do* have and be grateful for them. Also, we should *tell* people how much we appreciate them and the nice things they do for us.

Story for Young Children

---

[4] William James, *The Letters of William James*, ed. Henry James (Boston: The Atlantic Monthly Press, 1920), 2:33

[5] https://www.shutterfly.com/ideas/thank-you-quotes/

<u>The Lunch Bag: The True Story of Robert Fulghum and his 7-year-old Daughter Molly</u>

It was Molly's job to give her father his brown paper lunch bag each morning before he left for work. One morning, in addition to his usual lunch bag, Molly handed him a second paper bag. This one was worn and held together with duct tape, staples, and paper clips. "Why two bags?" Fulghum asked. "The other is something else," Molly answered with a smile.

"What's in it?" Molly's father questioned. "Just some stuff," Molly replied. "Please open it in your office at lunchtime."

Fulghum agreed, stuffed both sacks into his briefcase, kissed Molly and rushed off.

At midday, while hurriedly eating his lunch, he tore open Molly's bag and shook out the contents: two hair ribbons, three small stones, a plastic dinosaur, a pencil stub, a tiny sea shell, two animal crackers, a marble, a used lipstick, a small doll, two chocolate kisses, and 13 pennies. Fulghum smiled, finished eating, and swept the desk clean – into the wastebasket – leftover lunch, Molly's junk and all.

That evening, Molly ran up behind him as he read the paper. "Where's my bag?" she asked. "What bag?" said her father. "You know, Daddy, the one I gave you this morning." "I left it at the office. Why?" he replied. "I forgot to put this special note in it! And, besides," Molly continued, "those are my things in the sack, Daddy, the ones I really like – I thought you might want to play with them at work, to make you happy. You didn't lose the bag, did you?" "Oh, no," her father answered untruthfully. "I just forgot to bring it home, honey."

While Molly hugged her father's neck, he unfolded the note that had not made it into the sack: "I love you, Daddy" was written in large, careful scrawl. Molly had given him her treasures; everything in the world that a 7-year-old held dear. Love in a paper sack, and he missed it – not only missed it, but he threw it away!

When Molly went to bed, Mr. Fulghum hurriedly returned to the office. Just minutes ahead of the night janitor, he picked up the wastebasket and poured the contents onto his desk. After washing the mustard off the dinosaurs and spraying the whole thing with breath-freshener, he carefully smoothed out the wadded ball of brown paper and put the treasures inside. Fulgham carried it home gently. The bag didn't look very good, but the stuff was all there and that's what counted.

In the morning Mr. Fulgham asked Molly to tell him about the stuff in the sack. It took a long time to tell. Everything had a story or a memory or was attached to dreams and imaginary friends. Fairies had brought some of the things. He had given her the chocolate kisses, and she had kept them for when she needed them.

"Sometimes I think of all the times in this sweet life," Fulghum reflected, "when I must have missed the affection I was being given. A friend calls this 'standing knee deep in the river and dying of thirst.'" We should all remember that it's not the destination that counts in life – it's the journey. Like little girls' smiles, dinosaurs and chocolate kisses, old paper bags that we throw away too thoughtlessly… each day, each a tiny treasure. The journey with the people we love is all that really matters. Such a simple truth, so easily forgotten.[6]

Learning Questions

1. What did Molly's father not notice at first?
2. How can we show appreciation to others?
3. What are you thankful for in your life?

Story for Older Children

True Benevolence

A university student took a walk one day with his professor, often called the students' friend because of the kind way he treated them. While the young man and professor were walking together, they saw a pair of old shoes lying in the path. The shoes belonged to a poor man employed in the field nearby who had nearly finished his day's work. The student turned to the professor and said, "Let's play a trick on that man. We'll hide his shoes and conceal ourselves behind the bushes and watch to see his perplexity when he can't find them!"

"No," said the professor, "we must never use ourselves at the expense of the poor. But you are rich and may give yourself a greater pleasure than amusement by means of this poor man. Put a dollar in each shoe, and then we will hide."

The student did so, and then hid with the professor in the bushes nearby, where they could easily watch the laborer. The man finished his work and crossed the field to the path where he had left his coat and shoes. While he put on his coat, the man slipped one foot into a shoe -- but, feeling something there, he stooped down and found the dollar. Astonishment and wonder swept across his face. He gazed at the dollar, turned it over in his hand, and looked at it again and again. He looked around him but could see no one. Finally, he put the money in his pocket, and proceeded to put on his other shoe. How great was in one his surprise and he found the other dollar!

His feelings overcame him; he fell upon his knees and uttered aloud a fervent thanksgiving, in which he spoke of his wife -- sick and helpless -- and his children -- without bread -- whom this timely bounty from an unknown hand would save from suffering. The young student stood there, deeply affected, and tears filled his eyes. "Now," said the professor, "aren't you much more pleased than if you had played your intended trick?"

"You have taught me a lesson I shall never forget," answered the youth, "for I know now it is more blessed to give than to receive."[7]

Learning Questions

---

[6] Author Unknown, http://www.inspirationalstories.com
[7] Author Unknown, Especially for M, V 5, p. 156

1. How do you think the student felt when he saw the man's face?
2. What good example did the poor man set?
3. How can you show appreciation for the good things in your life?

You Show Appreciation When You:

- Are thankful for what you have.
- Focus on what you *do* have instead of worrying about what you *don't* have.
- Notice, with gratitude, the people in your life who love and help you.
- Take care of the things in your world, and take care of your body.
- Are kind to all living things.
- Think good thoughts.
- Help others.
- Tell your friends and family how much you appreciate and love them.

ATTITUDE

Attitude

Definition Attitude: Your state of mind; how you think about things.

Quotes

"A happy person is not a person in a certain set of circumstances, but rather a person with a certain set of attitudes."

Hugh Downs[8]

"There is very little difference in people. But that little difference makes a big difference. The little difference is attitude. The big difference is whether it is positive or negative."

Napoleon Hill[9]

Explanation

Your attitude is how you think about things. People with a good attitude are cheerful and happy, and others like to be around them. People with bad attitudes are cranky and upset most of the time. No one likes to be around them.

Many years ago U.S. President Abraham Lincoln said, "Most folks are about as happy as they make up their minds to be."[10] This means that you can choose your attitude. You can choose to either look on the bright side of things or you can complain about what's wrong.

Dale Carnegie said, "Happiness doesn't depend on outward conditions. It depends on inner conditions. It isn't what you have or who you are or where you are or what you are doing that makes you happy or unhappy. It is what you think about it. For example, two people may be in the same place, doing the same thing; both may have about an equal amount of money and prestige - and yet one may be miserable and the other happy. Why? Because of a different mental attitude."[11]

How is your attitude? When you see a glass partly filled with water, do you see it as half full or half empty?

---

[8] Glenn Van Ekeren. *Speaker's Sourcebook II*. 1994. Paramus, New Jersey: Prentice Hall, 45
[9] Glenn Van Ekeren. *Speaker's Sourcebook II*. 1994. Paramus, New Jersey: Prentice Hall, 46
[10] http://www.quotationspage.com
[11] *How to Win Friends and Influence People,* Dale Carnegie, Pocket Books, 1936, p. 71

We should try to have good attitudes about everything, even things that are sometimes difficult, like work. Each day there are things that have to be done in our families. For example, houses need to be cleaned and food needs to be prepared. Do you help your family cheerfully or do you complain?

Another challenge is to not let other people's bad attitudes affect our good attitudes. One evening a man named Sydney J. Harris was walking with his friend, a Quaker, to the newsstand. He bought a paper, thanking the newsie politely. The newsie didn't even acknowledge it.

"A sullen fellow, isn't he?" Harris asked.

"Oh, he's that way every night," shrugged his friend.

"Then why are you always so kind to him?" Harris asked.

"Why not?" said his friend. "Why should I let him decide how I'm going to act?"

That's right! It's a good idea to never let people with bad attitudes change your good attitude.

Positive Attitude

If you think you are beaten, you are.
If you think you dare not, you don't.
If you'd like to win but think you can't,
It's almost a cinch you won't.
Life's battles don't always go
To the stronger or faster man.
But soon or later the man who wins
Is the one who thinks he can.[12]

Story for Young Children

Your Point of View

A kind philosopher went into the hills each day to enjoy nature and learn the lessons nature can teach us. Each evening on his return he gathered the people of the village about him to impart unto them the lesson he had learned. One morning before he departed, one of his friends asked him to bring back a hawthorn twig. Another asked him to bring back a rose, and a third asked him to bring a lily. The kind philosopher agreed to the requests of the three friends.

As the day wore on and the evening let down her curtain, the three stood by to receive their gifts from nature. As they took them in their hands, the first said: "Here is a dead leaf on my hawthorn twig!" The second murmured: "Here is a thorn on my rose!" And the third cried out, "Yes, and here is some dirt on the root of my lily!"

---

[12] Author Unknown, *Especially for M,* V 2, p. 112

The kind philosopher took the gifts back. He removed the dead leaf from the hawthorn twig and placed it in the first friend's hand. Likewise, the thorn and the dirt from the rose and lily. Then he said, "You have what attracted you first. I will keep the hawthorn twig, the rose and the lily for the beauty I see in them."

Those who grow and develop the very best in life are the men and women who find only that which is good in
others.[13]

Learning Questions

1. What three gifts from nature did the philosopher bring back?
2. How was the philosopher's point of view different from his friends'?
3. What does it mean to have a positive attitude?
4. What is one thing you can do to show a positive attitude?

Story for Older Children

Michael J. Dowling was a young man who fell from a wagon during a blizzard in Michigan when he was 14 years of age. Before his parents discovered that he had fallen from the rear of the wagon, he was severely frostbitten. Consequently, his right leg was amputated almost to the hip, his left leg above the knee; his right arm was amputated; and his left hand was amputated. Not much future for a young lad like that was there? Do you know what he did? Michael went to the local Board of County Commissioners and told them that if they would educate him he'd pay back every penny.

During World War I, Mr. Dowling, who was at that time president of one of the largest banks in St. Paul, went to Europe to visit the soldiers -- to visit those who were wounded. Upon one occasion he was in a large hotel in London, and before him were the wounded soldiers in their wheelchairs. They were in the lobby, and he went up on the mezzanine floor above them. As he started to speak, he minimized the seriousness of their wounds. Michael explained that because one had lost an eye, another had lost an arm, etc., they shouldn't complain and be negative. Mr. Dowling got those fellows so wrought up that they started to boo him. Then he walked over to the stairway and down the stairs toward the lobby, telling them as he walked how fortunate they were. They continued booing.

Finally, Michael Dowling sat down on one of the steps and took off his right leg. And he kept on talking and telling them how fortunate they were. Well, they calmed down a little bit, but they still resented his remarks. Then he took off his left leg. Well, the booing stopped then. But before he arrived at the bottom of the stairs, he had taken off his right arm and flipped off his left hand, and there he sat -- just the stump of a body.

---

[13] Author Unknown, *Especially for M*, V2, p. 326

Michael Dowling was the president of one of the biggest banks in St. Paul. He had married and was the father of five children. He died as the result of the strength he gave as he traveled and encouraged the wounded soldiers of World War I.[14]

Learning Questions

1. How hard do you think it would be to keep a positive attitude if you were Michael Dowling?
2. How do you think Michael Dowling succeeded in life despite his troubles?
3. What do you think you can learn from his example?

You Show a Good Attitude When You:

- Are cheerful and happy.
- Are as happy as you make up your mind to be.
- Choose to look on the bright side of things.
- Help your family cheerfully.
- Don't let people with bad attitudes change your good attitude.

---

[14] Matthew Cowley, *Especially for M*, V2, p. 296

BELIEF

Belief

Definition Belief: Accepting something to be true.

Quotes

"Believe in yourself! Believe in your capacity to do great and good and worthwhile things."

Gordon Hinckley[15]

"Our beliefs about what we are and what we can be precisely determine what we will be."

Anthony Robbins[16]

"Believe that you will succeed. Believe it firmly, and you will then do what is necessary to bring success about."

Dale Carnegie[17]

Explanation

When you think something is true, you believe it. In other words, a belief is an idea that you think is right.

People create their beliefs from things they learn from others, and from their own life experiences. Do you think that everything you hear and read is true? No, it isn't. There are some people in your life you can trust to tell you the truth, and there are some people who don't always tell you the truth. It's sometimes hard to know the difference, but as children grow older they usually learn for themselves what is true. They learn what they *should* and *should not* believe.

People's beliefs often change as they grow older and learn more.

Beliefs are very important because what you believe determines how you act. For example, if you believe you are a kind person you'll probably have kind thoughts, say kind words, and do kind things for others. If you believe you aren't a very good singer, you probably won't want to sing in front of others. Or if you don't believe you're a good athlete you probably won't want to be in sports.

---

[15] Gordon B. Hinckley, *Stand a Little Taller,* 2001. Deseret Book Co.

[16] Glenn Van Ekeren. *Speaker's Sourcebook II*. 1994. Paramus, New Jersey: Prentice Hall, 52

[17] Glenn Van Ekeren. *Speaker's Sourcebook II*. 1994. Paramus, New Jersey: Prentice Hall, p. 53

Here is a very important thought about belief: if you believe something is wrong—like using drugs or lying or cheating—you shouldn't let other people change your mind, no matter who they are or what they say. Once you learn correct principles, you should always hold firmly to those beliefs and then teach others, to help them be happy.

Many years ago, a young woman named Joan of Arc lived in France. She was put to death because of her beliefs. Before she died, Joan of Arc wrote,

> "I know this now. Every man gives his life for what he believes. Every woman gives her life for what she believes. Sometimes people believe in little or nothing yet they give their lives to that little or nothing. One life is all we have and we live it as we believe in living it. And then it is gone. But to sacrifice what you are and live without belief, that is more terrible than dying."[18]

Story for Young Children

The Song of a Bird

A man found an eagle's egg and put it in the nest of a barnyard hen. The eagle hatched with the brood of chicks and grew up with them. All his life, the eagle did what the barnyard chicks did, thinking he was a chicken. He scratched the earth for worms and insects. He clucked and cackled. And he would thrash his wings and fly a few feet in the air. Years passed and the eagle grew very old. One day he saw a magnificent bird above him in the cloudless sky. It glided in graceful majesty among powerful wind currents, with scarcely a beat of its strong golden wings. The old eagle looked up in awe. "Who's that?" he asked. "That's the eagle, the king of the birds," said his neighbor. "He belongs to the sky. We belong to the earth—we're chickens." So the eagle lived and died a chicken, for that's what he believed he was.[19]

Learning Questions

1. What did the eagle believe he was?
2. Do you think that the eagle would have believed he was a chicken if he had grown up with other eagles?
3. Did you ever believe something that was not really true?

Story for Older Children

It Couldn't Be Done

Somebody said that it couldn't be done,
But he with a chuckle replied,
"Maybe it couldn't," but he would be one
Who wouldn't say so till he tried.

---

[18] http://www.famous-quotations.com

[19] Anthony DeMello, http://www.dobhran.com/inspire

So he buckled right in with the trace of a grin
On his face. If he worried, he hid it.
He started to sing as he tackled the thing
That couldn't be done, and he did it!
Somebody scoffed, "Oh, you'll never do that;
At least no one has ever done it;"
But he took off his coat and he took off his hat,
And the first thing we knew he'd begun it!
With a lift of his chin and a bit of a grin,
Without any doubting or quiddit,
He started to sing as he tackled the thing
That couldn't be done, and he did it!
There are thousands to tell you it cannot be done,
There are thousands to prophesy failure;
There are thousands to point out to you, one by one,
The dangers that await to assail you.
But just buckle in with a bit of a grin,
Just take off your coat and go to it;
Just start to sing as you tackle the thing
That "cannot be done" and you'll do it![20]

Learning Questions

1. What did the man in the poem believe?
2. Do you believe in yourself as much as he did?
3. How can believing in good things help you become a better person?

You Show Belief When You:

- Have an idea that you think is true.
- Learn from others and from your own life experiences.
- Are careful to believe only those things that trustworthy people teach you.
- Grow older and learn for yourself what is true.
- Understand that what you believe determines how you act.
- Refuse to let other people change your beliefs if they are principles of truth and goodness.
- Help others strengthen and improve their lives by sharing your good beliefs.

---

[20] *Little Book of Inspirational Stories*. (2000). Ed. R. Dale Jeffrey, Covenant Communications, American Fork: Utah. Edgar A. Guest, "It Couldn't Be Done," 45-46

CARING

Caring

Definition Caring: Showing love and concern for people and things.

Quotes

"No one can develop freely in this world and find a full life without feeling understood by at least one person."

Paul Tournier[21]

"Live so that when your children think of fairness, caring, and integrity, they think of you."

H. Jackson Brown, Jr.[22]

Explanation

Caring begins with showing love and respect to yourself. You do this by taking good care of yourself physically, mentally, and emotionally.

When you care about yourself
<u>Physically</u>:   You eat healthful foods, exercise, and keep yourself clean and neat.
<u>Mentally</u>:   You continue learning.
<u>Emotionally</u>:   You love and help other people, and you take care of your own needs.

Caring is also helping others; showing you're concerned about them. Caring about someone or something is a way to show your love.

For example, when you care for an animal, you feed him, give him water and attention. You carefully watch over him, protect, and love him. When you care for a possession, like a bicycle or a phone, you are careful not to break it.

When you do a careful job on your homework or on any task, you give it your best effort.

When you care about people, you smile at them. You are sincerely interested in their lives and how you can help them be happy. When you care about a person you look for ways to make his or her life easier and better.

---

[21] Glenn Van Ekeren. *Speaker's Sourcebook II*. 1994. Paramus, New Jersey: Prentice Hall, 360
[22] https://www.brainyquote.com/topics/caring

When you care about things you own, or that belong to others, you handle them gently.

For example, Jenny and her sister Kate were going to a dance, and Kate wanted to wear Jenny's new sweater.

Jenny had never worn her new sweater and didn't really want to lend it to her sister. Jenny was afraid that her new sweater would get stained or snagged while Kate was wearing it.

Kate promised that she'd take very good care of the sweater, so Jenny agreed. While Kate was getting dressed, she took off her jewelry so she wouldn't snag the sweater. While Kate was at the dance she didn't drink any of the red punch because she didn't want to stain her sister's sweater. She was careful all night and was pleased that she could return her sister's sweater looking just like new.

Jenny learned she could trust Kate to take care of her things.

Story for Young Children

<u>The Boy Who Cared</u>

Will was hurrying to get to baseball practice because the coach had said only those who went to practice could play in the game. He passed a little girl named Terri, sitting on the sidewalk. She was crying. Will wanted to run on, but he couldn't leave Terri there crying.

Will asked what was wrong and Terri told him she was lost. Will knew where the little girl lived, but he knew she wouldn't be able to get there alone.

If Will took Terri home, he'd surely be late to baseball practice. His coach would be angry and the other boys wouldn't understand. As Will looked into the little girl's eye's he realized that he cared about her and wanted her to get home safely. Will knew what he should do.

When they reached Terri's house, her parents were delighted and relieved to have their daughter home safely. They were so grateful to Will for his kindness. Terri's father then drove Will to his baseball practice and he was right on time! No one else would ever know what he had given up to help Terri, but he cared about the little girl, and about doing the right thing.[23]

Learning Questions

1. Why was it hard for Will to stop and help Terri?
2. Why do you think he helped Terri even though it was a difficult choice?
3. How do you think Terri felt when Will helped her find her way home?

Story for Older Children

---

[23] Paula Noble Fellingham

Coincidence

In 1945, there was a young boy who was 14 years old, living in a Nazi concentration camp, in Germany. He was tall and thin, but he had a bright smile. Every day, a young girl came by on the other side of the fence. She noticed the boy and asked him if he spoke Polish. He said yes. She said he looked hungry, and he said he was. The girl reached in her pocket and gave him her apple. He thanked her and she went on her way. The next day she came by again, bringing with her another apple, which she gave him. Each day the girl walked along the outside of the fence, hoping to see the young man. When she did, she happily gave him an apple and they talked.

One day he told her not to come by anymore because he was being shipped to another concentration camp. As the boy walked away with tears streaming down his face, he wondered if he'd ever see her again. She was the only kind person he had ever known.

The young man was eventually released from the concentration camp and immigrated to America. In 1957, he went on a blind date, having no idea who the woman was. During dinner she talked about her life in Poland, and they talked about the concentration camp. The girl told about a boy who she gave apples to. He asked if this boy was tall and skinny, and if he had told her that she shouldn't come back because he was leaving. She said yes, and they realized that after twelve years, and in another country, they had met again. He proposed that very night, and they are still happily married today.[24]

Learning Questions

1. How did the girl show she cared?
2. Why do you think he wanted to marry her?
3. Who are some of the people who care about you?

You Show Caring When You:

- Love and respect yourself and other people.
- Take care of yourself physically, mentally and emotionally.
- Take special care of animals and possessions.
- Find ways to help people.
- Give your heart and best effort to the things you do.
- Handle the property of others carefully and gently.

---

[24] http://www.cyberquotations.com/stories

CHARITY

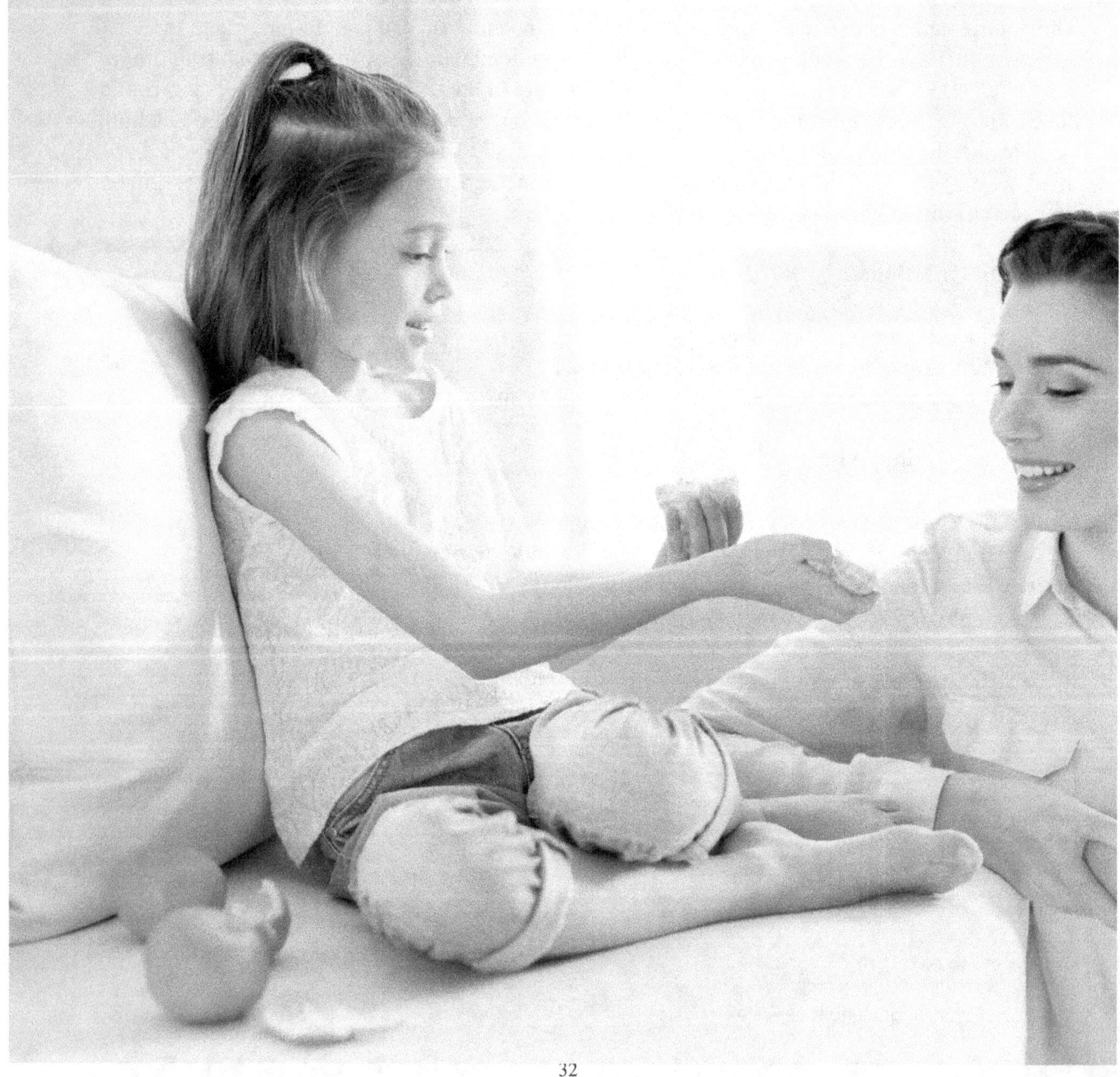

Charity

Definition Charity: Love; giving unselfishly; overlooking people's faults.

Quotes

"If you haven't got charity in your heart, you have the worst kind of heart trouble."

Bob Hope[25]

"Love (charity) is a fruit in season at all times, and within the reach of every hand."

Mother Teresa[26]

Explanation

Charity is love. Charity is kindness in *action*. When you have charity you look at people - <u>all</u> people - with kindness and love in your heart. You think kind thoughts. Even when someone is unkind to you, if you have charity, you think good thoughts about him or her.

Charity also means *speaking* kindly. When you speak to others kindly, it makes both of you happy and your kind words are remembered long after you say them.

Using a loving, gentle tone of voice when you speak is also part of charity. It's not always *what* you say, but *how* you say it that makes people happy or unhappy. When you speak unkindly, people don't want to be around you, and they sometimes get upset. When you speak kindly people want to be with you because you make them happy.

When you have charity you do kind things for people without expecting a reward. Kind actions always bring joy to both the giver and the receiver. And do you know what? The more kind things you do, the *easier* it is to *be* kind, and the more you <u>want</u> to be kind! And, another wonderful fact is that the more loving you are, the more people love <u>you</u>.

Story for Older Children

<u>**Beggar at the Door**</u>

---

[25] Glenn Van Ekeren. *Speaker's Sourcebook II*. 1994. Paramus, New Jersey: Prentice Hall, p. 169

[26] *Saint and Sinner*, as quoted by Russ Hauck, *The Orlando Sentinel*, Sept 12, 1997, A14.

It was a cold Sunday in winter. The church parking lot was filling up quickly. I noticed as I got out of my car that fellow church members were whispering among themselves as they approached the church. As I got closer, I saw a man leaning against the wall just outside the church. He was lying down, looking very sad. The man wore an old trench coat that was almost in shreds and a hat pulled down over his forehead. He wore old worn-out shoes. They were too small for his feet, and with so many holes that his toes stuck out.

I assumed this man was homeless, and perhaps asleep, so I walked on by through the church doors. We all fellowshipped for a few minutes, and then someone mentioned the man outside. People snickered and gossiped but no one asked the poor man to come in, including me. A few moments later church began. We all waited for the preacher to take his place and to give us the Word when the doors to the church opened. In came the homeless man. He walked down the aisle with his head lowered. People gasped and whispered and made faces. The shabbily dressed man made his way down the aisle and climbed up to the pulpit. When he took off his hat and coat my heart sank. There stood our preacher... he was the "homeless man." No one said a word. The preacher took out his Bible and laid it on the stand. "Folks, I don't think I have to tell you what I am preaching about today. I am talking about charity." Then he softly started singing the words to a song. "*If I can help somebody as I pass along. If I can cheer somebody with a word or song. If I can show somebody that he's traveling wrong. Then my living shall not be in vain.*"[27]

Learning Questions

1. Why didn't anyone invite the 'homeless' man to come inside the church?
2. What could they have done to show charity?
3. Do you know someone you can show more love to? Who?

Story for Young Children

Father's Charity: A True Story

For my eighth birthday, I wanted to have a party. My parents agreed, and so a week before my birthday, I took the invitations to school. On the school bus, I kept thinking about Alice. I was hoping that she wouldn't be there that day, so my parents couldn't blame me for not inviting her. You see, Alice's clothes were old and worn, her hair was seldom combed, and she was very quiet. She always played by herself at recess, and as far as I could see, she had no friends. I didn't want to invite her to my party.

When I got to school, much to my dismay, Alice was there. I handed out the invitations, and everyone was very excited.

The morning of my birthday party my parents asked. "Will Alice be coming?" I was surprised. I didn't think that they even knew Alice. "I don't know if she's coming," I mumbled. My father suggested that we take a ride over to her house and see. My father was a very kind man, but he was also very firm. If he suggested we do something, we did it.

---

[27] Author Unknown

Alice's mother answered the door, and my father told her why we were there. "She won't be coming," Alice's mother said. "She doesn't have a present for your daughter. You see, my husband lost his job and…" My father gestured that he understood, then said, "We would still like Alice to come. It doesn't matter if she has a present or not." *No present*? I thought. *What kind of a birthday party is that*? But, of course, I just stood there and smiled.

When we were in the car again, my father told me that after he took me home, he was coming back to take Alice to the store to buy a present for her to give to me. *This isn't turning out so bad after all*! I thought.

I can't remember what presents I got that day, but I do remember that Alice seemed to laugh a lot and was actually quite fun to be with. When it was time to take her home, I got in the front seat, and she got in the back seat. As we visited on the way home, I looked back at her once – and to my amazement – sitting right next to Alice was the prettiest doll I had ever seen! In my eight-year-old mind, I knew that my father had bought that doll for my friend Alice. I felt like my heart grew two sizes that day!

My father is not a rocket scientist. He has never invented anything or found a cure for a disease. But that day he did something just as important; he showed charity to a little girl and set a wonderful example for his daughter.[28]

Learning Questions

1. What did the father do to show charity towards Alice?
2. What did the father teach his daughter about charity?
3. What could you do to make someone feel important and/or loved?

You Show Charity When You:

- Look at all people with kindness and love in your heart.
- Think good thoughts, even when people are unkind to you.
- Speak kindly.
- Use a gentle tone of voice when you speak.
- Make people happy.
- Do kind things without expecting a reward.

---

[28]Johansen, Jackie. "Father's Charity," *Friend*, February 1997, 40-41.

CHEERFULNESS

Cheerfulness

Definition Cheerfulness: Being happy; smiling.

Quotes

"When we give cheerfully and accept gratefully, everyone is blessed."

Maya Angelou[29]

"The best way to cheer yourself up is to try to cheer somebody else up."

Mark Twain[30]

Explanation

Cheerfulness is an attitude of happiness.

When you are cheerful, you smile and your heart is happy. You look on the bright side of things. No matter what is happening around you, you are positive.

For example, pretend that two people are outside, on their knees in the grass pulling weeds. One person is grumpy and complains. He unhappily mutters, "I hate pulling weeds! My back aches, my fingers are sore, and the stupid weeds will grow right back anyway!" The other person is cheerful and says, "I don't mind it. When I'm outside I like breathing the clean air…and this work makes me feel like I'm helping my family. Even though the weeds grow back, this yard looks much better than it did!"

Everyone likes being around cheerful people. When you smile and talk positively, soon other people are smiling and cheerful too. Have you noticed that?

A man named Harold Abbott learned that lesson. He told this experience to his friend Dale Carnegie:

> I used to worry a lot but one spring day in 1934, I was walking down the street when I saw a sight that banished all my worries. It all happened in ten seconds, but during those ten seconds I learned more about how to live than I had learned the previous ten years.

---

[29] https://www.shutterfly.com/ideas/thank-you-quotes/

[30] http://quoteland.com/search.asp

Because of debt, I closed my grocery store the previous Saturday and now I was going to the bank to borrow money so I could go out of town to look for a job. I walked like a beaten man. I had lost all my fight and faith. Then suddenly I saw coming down the street a man who had no legs. He was sitting on a little wooden platform equipped with wheels from roller skates. He pushed himself along the street with a block of wood in each hand.

I met him just after he had crossed the street and was starting to lift himself up a few inches over the curb to the sidewalk. As he titled his little wooden platform to an angle, his eyes met mine. He greeted me with a grand smile. "Good morning, sir! It is a fine morning, isn't it?" he said cheerfully.

As I stood looking at him, I realized how rich I was. I had two legs. I could walk. I felt ashamed of my self-pity and said to myself, "If he can be happy, cheerful and confident without legs, I certainly can with legs!" I could already feel my chest lifting.

I had intended to ask the bank for only one hundred dollars. But now I had the courage to ask for two hundred. I had intended to say that I wanted to <u>try</u> and get a job. But now I announced confidently that I wanted to go <u>get</u> a job.

I now have the following words pasted on my bathroom mirror:

> "I had the blues because I had no shoes,
> Until upon the street I met a man who had no feet."[31]

Part of cheerfulness is recognizing how many things you have to be thankful for. When you're grateful for everything you *do* have instead of worrying about things you *don't* have, you'll be more cheerful.

Story for Young Children

<u>A Pessimistic Dog</u>

There was once a farmer who devised a competition between his dog and his rabbit. He made a hole in one of his biggest fields and hid a carrot and a bone in it. He wanted to see which animal would find them first.

The rabbit was very cheerful and optimistic, and he threw himself into looking for the carrot, digging here and there, totally convinced that he would find it. But the dog was pessimistic, and after sniffing around for a bit, he lay down on the ground and began to complain how difficult it was to find one bone in such a big field.

The rabbit dug for hours, and with every new hole the dog complained even more about how difficult this was, even for the rabbit. The rabbit, on the other hand, thought that each hole dug was one hole less that needed digging. When there was no place in the whole field left to dig, the rabbit dug a tunnel to right under where the dog had been lying all that time. There he found the carrot and the bone.

---

[31] Dale Carnegie, *How to Stop Worrying and Start Living*, Simon and Schuster, 1944.

And this is how it was that the dog lost due to his pessimism. Because, thanks to his great instinct, he had already found the right place at the very beginning! [32]

Learning Questions

1. Who had a better attitude – the dog or the rabbit?
2. Why did the dog lose the competition?
3. What have you done today to help others be more cheerful?

Story for Older Children

<u>Can One Person Really Make a Difference?</u>

One New Yorker thought so. He was determined to be complementary to every person he saw, every day. A friend asked him, "Do you even compliment cab drivers?" The man said, "Certainly! If I'm nice to one cab driver, he's likely to be nice to his next twenty fares, at a minimum. If they, in turn, show more kindness to the shopkeepers, waitresses, and their own families, that one gesture of goodwill might influence at least a thousand people!"

"Now, if only three people whom I talk to today have a happier day because of what I say to them, I might indirectly influence the attitude of 3,000 people. If a few of those I talk to are teachers, or people who have contact with more than the usual number of people…why my good mood might touch more than 10,000 lives. No other thing I do today is likely to have that kind of impact!"

Pass on a portion of cheerfulness today. Even if you have nothing but your own smile, goodwill, and joy – pass it on! You *can* make a difference! [33]

Learning Questions

1. Is smiling the easiest thing you can do to make a difference in the world?
2. Will you be more cheerful when you think about all your blessings?
3. What is one thing you have that makes you happy; that makes you smile?

You Show Cheerfulness When You:

- Look at the bright side of things.
- Smile.
- Have a happy heart.
- Talk and act positively no matter what is happening around you.
- Think about the many things you have to be thankful for.
- Show gratitude for things you *do* have and don't worry about what you *don't* have.

---

[32] https://freestoriesforkids.com/children/stories-and-tales/pessimistic-dog
[33] *God's Little Devotional Book for Leaders*, p. 47

CLEANLINESS

Cleanliness

Definition Cleanliness: Neat and tidy, clean mind, clean body, and clean surroundings.

Quotes

"Better keep yourself clean and bright; you are the window through which you must see the world."

George Bernard Shaw[34]

"I will not let anyone walk through my mind with dirty feet."

Gandhi[35]

Explanation

Let's talk about having a clean mind, a clean body, and clean surroundings (the place where you live).

Having a clean mind means that you think good thoughts. You try to allow only good, uplifting thoughts to fill your mind.

When thoughts come into your mind that you know you shouldn't be thinking, you can say to yourself, "That isn't like me. I usually don't think unclean thoughts like that." Then quickly replace the bad thought with a good one. You can replace bad ideas with happy thoughts about your friends, a fun vacation, someone you love, etc. Since all bad words and actions begin as thoughts, keeping your thoughts clean is the first step toward living a good life.

When you have a clean body, you keep your body washed and you wear clean clothes. You should brush your teeth at least twice every day. You should also shampoo your hair regularly and wash your hands often.

When you keep yourself clean, you feel good, you're more protected from disease, and people like being around you.

––––––––––––––––––––––––––

[34] https://www.happypublishing.com/blog/cleanliness-quotes/
[35] http://www.quotationary.com

Keeping your surroundings clean means putting things away after you use them, and helping your family keep your house tidy and orderly. When you help keep your house clean, you contribute to the beauty and peace in your home.

Story for Young Children

<u>**Mike's Messy Room**</u>

Mike and his friend Jerry liked to play with toy race cars and soldiers. One day, Jerry had to go home before they were finished playing.
"What a mess you boys made!" Mom said. "You'd better clean your room before dinner."
Mike frowned. He didn't think he could ever put away all the toys that he and Jerry had played with. Mike started to pick them up one by one, but there were so many! He went to the kitchen, where Mom was cooking. "It's too hard to clean my room," Mike complained.
His sister, Kimberly, was setting the table. "Cleaning is easy," she said.
Mom kept slicing vegetables. "Try a little harder," she said.
Mike went back to his room and picked up a few race cars, but there were many more still on the floor. "I'll be cleaning forever!" he thought. He went back to the kitchen and said, "It's too hard to clean my room."
"Cleaning is easy," Kimberly said again. She finished setting the table and disappeared down the hall.
Daddy was stirring juice. "You can do it," he said. "You made the mess, so cleaning it up is your special job."
Mike went back to his room and picked up several soldiers. But there were still many more on the floor, and he was getting tired. "Jerry helped make this mess, and he went home and no one is helping me clean it up," he thought. "It isn't fair!"
He ran back to the kitchen. "The mess is too big to clean up by myself," he wailed.
Mom's eyes twinkled. "Maybe you have too many toys," she teased. "Would it be easier to clean your room if we gave some of them away?"
"No!" Mike stomped back to his room in tears.
When he opened the door, he could hardly believe his eyes! There were no more toys on the floor. He wiped away his tears and peeked into the toy box. Like magic, race cars and soldiers were stacked neatly inside. Then he saw Kimberly hiding in the corner.
"Surprise!" she yelled.
"How did you clean my room so fast?" Mike asked.
"Cleaning is easy," Kimberly said. "I'm older than you, so some chores are easier for me. Next time I'll show you a game I learned that helps me clean faster."
Mike was happy because Kimberly had helped him. He gave Kimberly a big hug and said, "Thank you so much, sister!"[36]

Learning Questions

1. What did Mike learn about cleaning?
2. Have you ever helped someone clean a room like Kimberly helped Mike?

---

[36] Kimberly Webb, "Carl's Messy Room," *Friend,* Sept. 2003, 20

3. What is something you could help clean right now?

Story for Older Children

<u>A Gentleman's Game</u>

There once was a boy named Roy. He was very good at sports and played for several of his school's teams. Roy's mother was very proud of him, but she was worried about one habit of his - being dirty. Even though she reminded him often, Roy never bothered to create clean habits like brushing his teeth twice a day, taking baths and showers frequently, and wearing clean clothes. When he got dressed each day, Roy would often choose dirty clothes off of his dirty bedroom floor and make them even dirtier.

Roy had been preparing vigorously for the Cricket team tryouts at school, and when the day arrived, he performed very well. He was confident that he would be chosen for the team when the team selection day arrived. The morning that the team results were posted, Roy awoke early and rushed out the door. He had chosen some dirty clothes from the day before, didn't take a shower, and completely forgot to brush his teeth before leaving.

When he arrived, the list was posted on the door of the school gym, and the team coaches were beginning to hand out equipment to the new team members. Roy confidently approached the door, but when he caught a glimpse of the list, his name was not there. He scanned it multiple times, only to find that he was not on the list. Shocked, he rushed into the gym to speak to the coaches. There had to be a mistake!

"Coach! Coach!" he said anxiously. "My name was not on the list! Did I do something wrong?"

The coach turned and calmly replied, "The attitude of the game is as important as the skill of each player. Cricket is a gentleman's game, and a gentleman is always clean and presentable."

Roy stood stunned, but after a moment of reflection, he understood exactly what the coach meant. Roy learned a valuable lesson that day about the importance of cleanliness. [37]

Learning Questions

1. Why didn't Roy make the team?
2. In what ways can we keep our bodies clean?

You Show Cleanliness When You:

*   Think good thoughts.
*   Replace bad thoughts with good thoughts.
*   Brush your teeth at least twice a day.
*   Wash your hands often.
*   Wear clean clothes.

---

[37] https://www.quora.com/What-are-some-short-stories-for-kids-on-cleanliness-is-next-to-godliness

- Shampoo your hair regularly.
- Put things away after using them.
- Help your family keep your home clean and orderly.

COMMITMENT

Commitment

Definition Commitment: Agreement; promise.

Quotes

"Commitment is the serious promise to press on, to get up, no matter how many times you are knocked down."

David McNally[38]

"There's a difference between interest and commitment. When you're interested in doing something, you do it only when it's convenient. When you're committed to something, you accept no excuses; only results."

Kenneth Blanchard[39]

Explanation

Commitment means two similar things. Commitment means to make a promise, and it also means to give your heart to something. An example of a promise is this: your brother asks you to promise that you won't tell anyone at school that it's his birthday. When you agree and make a promise to your brother, you make a commitment to him that you won't tell anyone.

The second kind of commitment is when you commit your heart to something, like your family. Commitment to family means that you give family members your love and your time.

Families are like teams — they work together to reach the same goals. Both parents and children have very important positions on the team, and everyone is needed to make it work well. What happens to an athletic team when they don't work together? Usually, they don't win. On the other hand, each player on a winning team is committed to the success of the whole team. They each give of themselves, they support and help one another, and they usually do it enthusiastically. Those are good ingredients for families, too. As we commit our time and hearts to our family, we can reach our goals and "win" in the game of life.

The first step to achieving anything worthwhile is a commitment to do whatever is necessary to reach your goals. If you're really committed to something, you keep trying, even when you fail.

---

[38] Glenn Van Ekeren. *Speaker's Sourcebook II*. 1994. Paramus, New Jersey: Prentice Hall, 64
[39] Glenn Van Ekeren. *Speaker's Sourcebook II*. 1994. Paramus, New Jersey: Prentice Hall, 65

President Dwight D. Eisenhower told this story:

> "A neighboring farmer had a cow that he wanted to sell. We went over to visit the farmer and asked him about the cow's pedigree. The old farmer didn't know what pedigree meant, so he asked him about the cow's butterfat production. He told us he didn't have any idea what it was. Finally, we asked him if he knew how many pounds of milk the cow produced each year. The farmer said, 'I don't know. But she's an honest cow, and she'll give you all the milk she has.'
>
> President Eisenhower said, "I'm like the cow. I'll give everything I have."[40]

That's a good example of commitment.

Charles Dickens, a famous writer, said, "Whatever I have tried to do in life, I have tried with my heart to do well."[41] When you have commitment, you do your very best — you give 100% effort — to everything you agree to do.

Story for Young Children

<u>Nothing Important</u>

Cindy looked at her watch… it was nearly 1 o'clock.

She lifted her tennis racket and tossed the ball in the air for her final serve of the game. Donna, her opponent, hit a cross-court return that caught Cindy unprepared.

"I win!" Donna, called. "I beat you for once!"

Cindy smiled as she wiped the back of her hand across her damp face and began picking up the tennis balls.

"Let's have another game," Donna invited. "That last one was really an accident. You could easily win this time."

"I can't," Cindy replied. "There's just time for me to run home and shower before I go to the hospital to help Mrs. Holt with the story and craft activities."

"Oh nuts!" Donna scoffed, pulling a face. "That's some way to spend a summer! Two afternoons a week with sick kids."

"Those children have to spend a long time in the hospital. They do get awfully lonely, and I promised," Cindy began.

---

[40] Glenn Van Ekeren. *Speaker's Sourcebook II*. 1994. Paramus, New Jersey: Prentice Hall, 58
[41] http://www.cute-quote.com

"Well, just this once I'd think you could play another game," Donna insisted. It's not like you are really that important. You said yourself that you don't do very much."

Cindy had thought about this a number of times. All she ever did was pass out paper and crayons or scissors or whatever supplies were needed. And she also helped the children with their wheelchairs and crutches.

"Maybe I wouldn't be missed," she said to herself. "Maybe I've been building up the importance of what I'm doing because I want to feel like I'm helping someone."

"Come on, Cindy, and serve," Donna said impatiently.

Cindy rolled the ball across her racket a few times, but then she shook her head. "Donna, I can't. I really did promise, and it wouldn't be fair!"

Cindy knew that Donna thought she was being foolish, but she couldn't help that – even if Donna found someone else to play tennis with the rest of the summer.

Cindy hurried to shower and get ready to go to the hospital. She was afraid she would be late, so she ran most of the eight blocks to the hospital.

Her legs ached as she hurried up the steps and down the long corridor toward the room where the children were waiting. As she opened the door, Cindy paused a moment to catch her breath.

"Mrs. Holt hasn't started the story yet," she said to herself. "So maybe I'm not as late as it seems."

"Cindy's here!" Dennis called as he caught sight of her. Dennis was in a cast from his hips down, but he wouldn't think of missing the stories.

The others turned too. "Cindy! Cindy!" They called. It was almost like a chorus.

Mrs. Holt smiled, but Cindy saw that something was wrong with the gray-haired woman who was usually laughing with the children.

"Don't you feel well?" Cindy asked quietly.

Mrs. Holt shook her head. "I've been a bit dizzy all day. I didn't know if I could wait until you came. But now that you're here, I know everything will be alright."

Cindy felt her face grow warm, remembering how tempted she had been when Donna coaxed her to stay and play another game of tennis.

"I don't like to leave you, Cindy," Mrs. Holt sighed. "But all the children love you so much that I can go home and not worry. It's good to know I can depend on you. Since you'll be alone today, maybe you could read some stories."

A shiver of doubt ran through Cindy, but she nodded. "I — I'll do my best."

Reluctantly Cindy watched Mrs. Holt walk away. At the door the older woman turned back. "I hope I'll feel better by Friday, but if not, I'll depend on you again."

Cindy had never read stories to children before. At first her voice sounded shaky and small to her, but gradually her confidence grew. "You read good," Dennis announced. "Good as anybody!"

Cindy laughed and patted the little boy's arm. "That's because you're all my friends."

The afternoon went quickly -- -- almost too quickly.

"You'll come back, won't you?" Dennis asked as Cindy was leaving. "You said we were friends," he added wistfully.

Cindy turned and gave him a hug. "We are friends. And I'll come back, I promise."

As Cindy left the hospital, she knew she would keep her promise -- just as often as she was needed.[42]

Learning Questions

1. What was Cindy's commitment?
2. How did Cindy keep her promise?
3. What does it mean to keep a commitment?

Story for Older Children

The Story of Milton Hershey: Commitment to His Dream

Almost every kid in this country has at one time or another eaten a Hershey chocolate bar. Hershey chocolate has become famous around the world. But did you know that the Hershey chocolate factory is less than one hundred years old? And did you know that the founder of Hershey Chocolate, Milton Hershey, had many failures in business before he started his famous company?

Milton Hershey grew up in the rolling farm country of Pennsylvania. Before he became interested in making chocolate, Milton Hershey trained to become a printer. He worked for a small newspaper at first, and then decided that printing was not the right profession for him.

Before long, Milton got a job at a candy factory in Lancaster, Pennsylvania, a few miles from his home. After working a few years at the candy factory, he decided to open his own little candy

---

[42] Lucy Parr, "Nothing Important," Friend, June 1973, p. 43

business near Philadelphia. His first business had to close down because it was not making enough money. After closing his first store Milton traveled to Denver, Colorado, to learn how to make caramels. He took his new skills back to New York and worked selling candies on the street. But this second business also failed.

Finally, Milton Hershey moved back to the farm hills where he grew up. He then experimented with all sorts of different candies and chocolates. The area where he lived had lots and lots of dairy farms, so he had a large and easy supply of fresh milk.

And he could get other supplies, such as sugar, from nearby Philadelphia. By 1893, Milton was selling a million dollars' worth of caramel candy a year. Since his chocolate-dipped and chocolate-flavored caramels were the best-selling, he decided to make chocolate himself.

By experimenting, Milton Hershey discovered how to make delicious chocolate by using fresh, sweet, condensed milk. His milk chocolates were so popular that he sold his caramel factory and focused his business on making chocolate only.

In 1903, the same year the Wright Brothers flew the first airplane at Kitty Hawk, Milton Hershey built a huge chocolate factory and an entire town to support it. The town of Hershey, Pennsylvania, had a streetcar line, schools, library, sports arena, community center, and a special school for needy children.

Today, the town of Hershey is still the home of the factory that Milton Hershey built. And if you ever visit, you can smell delicious chocolate as you drive through the town.

The factory isn't hard to find. Just travel down Cocoa Avenue until you get to East Chocolate Avenue, turn right at the light and just follow your nose. [43]

Learning Questions

1. Have you ever failed and felt like giving up? Did Mr. Hershey give up on his idea and desire to make chocolate?
2. If Mr. Hershey had not remained committed to his wish to make chocolate, and quit after the first failure, what could have happened?
3. Name one thing you have promised to do; one commitment you have made in your life.

You Show Commitment When You:

- Make a promise.
- Give your heart and effort to something.
- Follow through and keep your promise.
- Keep trying, even when you fail.
- Do your very best.

---

[43] http://www.his.com/~pshapiro/stories.menu.html

COMPASSION

Compassion

Definition Compassion: Caring about people with problems; wanting to help them.

Quotes

"My mission in life is not merely to survive, but to thrive; and to do so with some passion, some compassion, some humor, and some style."

Maya Angelou[44]

"There never was any heart truly great and generous, that was not also tender and compassionate."

Robert Frost[45]

Explanation

Compassion is mentally putting yourself in another person's position. It is imagining what it would be like to *be* that person with their life experiences, their needs, and desires. And then, after you imagine what it would be like to be them, you try to help them in ways they need your help the most.

When you're compassionate, you understand and care about the heartaches of others. You quickly forgive people, and you are kind and gentle.

Compassionate people look for ways to help others feel good.

You should always try to show compassion to members of your family, to friends, and to everyone you meet, no matter if they look or talk differently than you.

A good thing to remember is the Golden Rule: *Do unto others as you would have others do unto you.* This means treating people the same way you want them to treat you.

Story for Younger Children

A Lesson on Compassion

---

[44] https://www.brainyquote.com/topics/compassion

[45] Edwards, Tyron. 1977. *The New Dictionary of Thoughts*. Stanbook, Inc., 100

At a fund-raising dinner for a school with learning-disabled children, the father of one of the school's students delivered a speech that would never be forgotten by all who attended.

The father said, "My handicapped son, Shay, cannot learn things as other children do. He cannot understand things as other children do."

Then, he told the following story: Shay and his father had walked past a park where some boys Shay knew were playing baseball. Shay asked, "Do you think they will let me play?" Shay's father knew that most boys would not want him on their team. But the father understood that if his son were allowed to play it would give him a much-needed sense of belonging. Shay's father approached one of the boys on the field and asked if Shay could play. The boy looked around for guidance from his teammates. Getting none, he took matters into his own hands and said, "We are losing by six runs, and the game is in the eighth inning. I guess he can be on our team, and I'll try to put him up to bat in the ninth inning."

In the bottom of the eighth inning, Shay's team scored a few runs, but they were still behind by three. At the top of the ninth inning, Shay put on a glove and played in the outfield. Although no hits came his way, he was obviously ecstatic just to be on the field, grinning from ear to ear as his father waved to him from the stands.

In the bottom of the ninth inning, Shay's team scored again. Now, with two outs and bases loaded, the potential winning run was on base. Shay was scheduled to be the next at-bat. Would the team actually let Shay bat at this juncture and give away their chance to win the game? Surprisingly, Shay was given the bat.

Everyone knew that this was all but impossible because Shay didn't even know how to hold the bat properly, much less connect with the ball. However, as Shay stepped up to the plate, the pitcher moved a few steps to lob the ball in softly so Shay could at least be able to make contact.

The first pitch came and Shay swung clumsily and missed. The pitcher again took a few steps forward to toss the ball softly toward Shay.

As the pitch came in, Shay swung at the ball and hit a slow ground ball to the pitcher. The pitcher picked up the soft grounder and could easily have thrown the ball to the first baseman. Shay would have been out and that would have ended the game.

Instead, the pitcher took the ball and threw it on a high arc to right field, far beyond reach of the first baseman.

Everyone started yelling, "Shay, run to first. Run to first." Never in his life had Shay ever made it to first base. He scampered down the baseline, wide-eyed and startled. Everyone yelled "Run to second, run to second!" By the time Shay was rounding first base, the right fielder had the ball. He could have thrown the ball to the second baseman for a tag.

But the right fielder understood what the pitcher's intentions had been, so he threw the ball high and far over the third baseman's head.

Shay ran towards second base as the runners ahead of him deliriously circled the bases towards home. As Shay reached second base, the opposing shortstop ran to him, turned him in the direction of third base, and shouted, "Run to third!"

As Shay rounded third, the boys from both teams were screaming, "Shay! Run home." Shay ran home, stepped on home plate and was cheered as the hero, for hitting a "grand slam" and winning the game for his team.

"That day," said the father softly with tears now rolling down his face," the boys from both teams taught everyone in that ballpark the true meaning of compassion."[46]

Learning Questions

1. Why do you think the boys let Shay play with them? For the other team, do you think helping Shay score was worth losing the game? Why?
2. How do you think Shay felt? How did Shay's father feel?
3. What have you learned from the boys' example of compassion?

Story for Older Children

First-Day Employee

My father had a small business, employing approximately fifteen people at any given time. We pasteurized and homogenized milk from farmers each morning and put it into bottles for home use and for restaurants. We also put the milk into small containers for the school kids every day. Additionally, we produced delicious homemade ice cream.

We sold all these milk products, and many more, in the front of a dairy building that had been fashioned into a small store with a large soda fountain. During the summer months there were rows and rows of eager tourists lined up at the ice cream counter, waiting for their daily indulgence of my father's most exquisite recipes and some twenty-seven flavors of homemade wonder.

Being such an extremely busy little store meant that the employees had to work very quickly for hours at a time, with little rest. The swarm never stopped and on hot days our "rush hour" lasted all day long.

I had worked for my father since I was young, as did all seven kids in our family. So, I had seen many new employees come and go due to the fast and furious work pace.

One day we had a new employee, Debbie, who wanted to work in the store for the summer. She had never done this type of work before, but she planned to give it her all.

---

[46] http://www.rogerknapp.com/inspire/shay.htm

On her first day, Debbie made just about every mistake in the book. She added the sales wrong on the cash register, she charged the wrong prices for items, she gave the wrong bag of food to the wrong customer, and she dropped and broke a half gallon of milk. The torture of watching her struggle was too much for me. I went into my father's office and said, "Please go out there and put her out of her misery." I expected him to walk right into the store and fire her on the spot.

Since my father's office was situated within view of the sales counter, he had no doubt seen what I was talking about. He sat, thoughtful, for a moment. Then he got up from his desk and walked over to Debbie, who was standing behind the counter.

"Debbie," he said, as he put his hand gently on her shoulder. "I have been watching you all day, and I saw how you treated Mrs. Forbush."

Debbie's face began to flush, and tears began to well in her eyes as she struggled to remember Mrs. Forbush from the many women she had given the wrong change to or spilled milk on.

My father continued, "I've never seen Mrs. Forbush speak so politely to any one of my employees before. You really knew how to handle her. I am sure that she is going to want you to wait on her every time she comes in. Keep up the good work."

In return for being a kind and compassionate employer, my father got a loyal and hardworking employee for sixteen years, and a friend for life.[47]

Learning Questions

1. How did the father show compassion to Debbie?
2. How do you think Debbie would have responded if her employer had fired her on that first day? What difference did he make with his choice to respond in a compassionate way?
3. Have you ever had the chance to show compassion to someone in trouble? What did you do?

You Show Compassion When You:

- Think kind thoughts about other people, no matter how different they may seem.
- Listen when someone wants to talk, even when it may be inconvenient for you.
- Forgive easily.
- Help people in need.
- Feel the pain of someone in trouble.
- Sincerely try to understand and empathize with others by putting yourself in their position, mentally "walking a mile in their shoes."

---

[47] Mary Jane West-Delgado, http://e365.cc163.net/topic/topic24.htm

-

CONFIDENCE

Confidence

Definition Confidence: Belief and trust in someone or something.

Quotes

"Believe in yourself! Have faith in your abilities! Without a humble but reasonable confidence in your own powers you cannot be successful or happy."

Norman Vincent Peale[48]

"The only thing that stands between a man and what he wants from life is often merely the will to try it and the faith to believe that it is possible."

Richard M. DeVos[49]

Explanation

Confidence in yourself means that you know you're a valuable, good person whether you succeed or fail. You have a feeling of assurance because you know that you're trying your best each day to live a good life. You know that when you make mistakes you'll learn from them and try again.

Confidence in others means that you trust people until they give you a reason not to. You think positively about people and rely on them to do what they say they'll do.

Confidence gives you peace of mind. When you're confident, doubts and worries don't keep you from doing the things you really want to do in life. You try new things. If you fail, you ask, "What can I learn from this?" Then you try again. For example, the great inventor Thomas A. Edison had confidence in his ability to create the electric light bulb. Although he failed over 1,000 times, he kept trying because he was confident he could do it. Mr. Edison said, "I am not discouraged, because every wrong attempt discarded is another step forward." Many people become successful because they are confident and never give up.

Confidence is one of the qualities of great leaders. Think about the great leaders you know. They are men and women who have confidence in their abilities to make good decisions. People usually follow and trust leaders with confidence.

---

[48] https://www.brainyquote.com/quotes/norman_vincent_peale_132560
[49] Glenn Van Ekeren. *Speaker's Sourcebook II*. 1994. Paramus, New Jersey: Prentice Hall, 52

Story for Young Children

<u>The Man Who Thinks He Can</u>

If you think you are beaten, you are.
If you think you dare not, you don't.
If you like to win, but think you can't,
It's almost a cinch you won't.

If you think you'll lose, you're lost.
For out in the world we find,
Success begins with a fellow's will.
It's all in the state of mind.

If you think you are outclassed, you are.
You've got to think high to rise.
You've got to be sure of yourself before
You can ever win the prize.

Life's battles don't always go
To the stronger and faster man,
But sooner or later the man who wins
Is the man who thinks he can.[50]

Learning Questions
1. Why is it important to live your life thinking you _can_ do things, not that you _can't_?
2. What is something you want to do but when you think about doing it you get worried or even frightened? What can you think or do that will help you be more confident?
3. What does being confident mean to you?

Story for Older Children

<u>Success Brings Confidence</u>

The famous architect, Sir Christopher Wren, once created a large church dome so unique that his competitors became fiercely jealous. They created such a stir that the authorities responsible for the building insisted that Wren add two supporting pillars to keep the dome from collapsing. Wren explained the integrity of his design and did his best to assure the officials that the dome would not collapse. However, the opposition won out. Wren added the pillars, against his will.

Fifty years later, the dome needed to be repainted. Workers built a scaffold to reach it, and they made an amazing discovery. The two pillars that had been added didn't even touch the ceiling. They were short by two feet! The authorities had only seen the pillars from the ground level, so

---

[50] *The Little Book of Inspirational Stories*. (2000) Ed. R. Dale Jeffery, Covenant Communications, American Fork, Utah. Walter D. Wingle, "The Man Who Thinks He Can," pg. 9

they assumed they reached the ceiling. The pillars were freestanding and supported nothing. Wren had won his point! The famous architect had confidence in his abilities, even when "experts" didn't.[51]

Learning Questions

1. Because Wren's competitors were jealous, they found a way to put obstacles in his way. How does having confidence help us overcome our obstacles?
2. What is one thing you have confidence that you can do well?
3. How can you develop greater confidence in yourself?

You Show Confidence When You:

- Think positive thoughts.
- Correct your mistakes quickly and try to learn from them.
- Try new things.
- Remember that you're valuable whether you win or lose.
- Trust other people.
- Act with strength, like a leader.

---

[51] *God's Little Devotional Book for Leaders*, p. 193

COOPERATION

Cooperation

Definition Cooperation: Working together peacefully.

Quotes

"You can do what I cannot do. I can do what you cannot do. Together we can do great things."

Mother Teresa[52]

"We should not only use all the brains we have, but all that we can borrow."

Woodrow Wilson[53]

Explanation

Cooperation is peacefully working or playing with another person. It is sharing your ideas or things you own.

When you work well with another person to reach a goal, you're cooperating. When you play with someone, or several friends, and kindly share things back and forth, you're cooperating.

When people cooperate and work together, they usually get jobs done more quickly and easily than when they work alone. Do you think it is more fun to work with people you like than to work alone?

In families, it's very important to cooperate because there are so many jobs to be done. There are meals to prepare, clothes to wash, a house or apartment to clean, and lots more. One person cannot do all the work, so family members need to cooperate and work together. The family is happiest when everyone does their part cheerfully.

Also, it's important to cooperate at school and in sports. In school, students need to cooperate with their teachers and other classmates. In sports, if team members don't cooperate the team doesn't win and the players don't have much fun.

Even in your neighborhood it is important to cooperate. For example, when one family goes on a vacation, other families in the neighborhood can watch over their house and yard to be sure it is kept safe.

---

[52] John C. Maxwell. 2001. *The 17 Indisputable Laws of Teamwork*. Nashville: Thomas Nelson Publishers, 184
[53] John C. Maxwell. 2001. *The 17 Indisputable Laws of Teamwork*. Nashville: Thomas Nelson Publishers, 7

Cooperation makes life easier and better for everyone.

Story for Young Children

Once upon a time there was a little red hen. She lived with a pig, a duck and a cat.

They all lived in a pretty little house which the little red hen liked to keep clean and tidy. The little red hen worked hard at her job all day. The others never helped. Although they said they meant to, they were all far too lazy. The pig liked to grunt in the mud outside, the duck swam in the pond all day, and the cat enjoyed lying in the sun, purring.

One day the little red hen was working in the garden when she found a grain of corn.

"Who will plant this grain of corn?" she asked.

"Not I," grunted the pig from his muddy patch in the garden.

"Not I," quacked the duck from her pond.

"Not I," purred the cat from his place in the sun.

So, the little red hen went to look for a nice bit of earth, scratched it with her feet and planted the grain of corn.

During the summer the grain of corn grew. First it grew into a tall green stalk, then it ripened in the sun until it had turned a lovely golden color. The little red hen saw that the corn was ready for cutting.

"Who will help me cut the corn?" asked the little red hen.

"Not I," grunted the pig from his muddy patch in the garden.

"Not I," quacked the duck from her pond.

"Not I," purred the cat from his place in the sun.

"Very well then, I will cut it myself," said the little red hen. Carefully she cut the stalk and took out all the grains of corn from the husks.

"Who will take the corn to the mill, so that it can be ground into flour?" asked the little red hen.

"Not I," grunted the pig from his muddy patch in the garden.

"Not I," quacked the duck from her pond.

"Not I," purred the cat from his place in the sun.

So, the little red hen took the corn to the mill herself, and asked the miller if he would be so kind as to grind it into flour.

In time the miller sent a little bag of flour down to the house where the little red hen lived with the pig and the duck and the cat.

"Who will help me to make the flour into bread?" asked the little red hen.

"Not I," grunted the pig from his muddy patch in the garden.

"Not I," quacked the duck from her pond.

"Not I," purred the cat from his place in the sun.

"Very well," said the little red hen. "I shall make the bread myself." She went into her neat little kitchen. She mixed the flour into dough. She kneaded the dough and put it into the oven to bake.

Soon there was a lovely smell of hot fresh bread. It filled all the corners of the house and wafted out into the garden. The pig came into the kitchen from his muddy patch in the garden, the duck came in from the pond and the cat left his place in the sun. When the little red hen opened the oven door the dough had risen up and had turned into the nicest, most delicious looking loaf of bread any of them had seen.

"Who is going to eat this bread?" asked the little red hen.

"I will," grunted the pig.

"I will," quacked the duck.

"I will," purred the cat.

"Oh no, you won't," said the little red hen. "I planted the seed, I cut the corn, I took it to the mill to be made into flour, and I made the bread, all by myself. I shall now eat the loaf all by myself."

The pig, the duck and the cat all stood and watched as the little red hen ate the loaf all by herself. It was delicious and she enjoyed it, right to the very last crumb. [54]

Learning Questions

1. Did the pig, the duck, and the cat cooperate well?
2. What are some ways you cooperate with the members of your family?

---

[54] http://www.hellokids.com/c_27875/reading-learning/stories-for-children/animal-stories-for-kids/the-little-red-hen?pos=0#top_page

Story for Older Children

<u>A Once-Told Story</u>

The story is told that once a young boy was invited to visit his uncle who was a lumberjack in the American Northwest where there are many forests. For months the boy had looked forward with anticipation to this trip as an exciting adventure.

Finally, the time for his journey to the vast timber empire came. His uncle met him at the train station and as the two pursued their way to the lumber camp the boy was impressed by the enormous size of the trees on every side. There was a gigantic tree that he observed standing all alone on the top of a small hill. The boy, full of awe, called out excitedly, "Uncle George," look at that big tree! It will make a lot of good lumber, won't it?"

Uncle George shook his head, then replied, "No, son, that tree will not make a lot of good lumber. It might make a lot of lumber, but not a lot of good lumber. When a tree grows off by itself, too many branches grow on it. Those branches produce knots when the tree is cut into lumber. The best lumber comes from trees that grow together in groves. Trees grow taller and straighter when they grow together."[55]

Learning Questions

1. Why do trees that grow together make better lumber?
2. How are people like trees?
3. What are some ways you cooperate with your family and friends?

You Show Cooperation When You:

- Work or play happily and cheerfully with others.
- Share your ideas or the things you own with others.
- Do your part to take care of your home cheerfully.
- Watch over your neighbors' property and help them when they need your help.

---

[55] Author Unknown, *Especially for M*, V 5, p. 15.

COURAGE

Courage

Definition Courage: Meeting danger and trouble calmly; making good choices when choosing the right is difficult.

Quotes

"Courage is not the absence of fear; rather it is the ability to take action in the face of fear."

Franklin D. Roosevelt[56]

"You gain strength, courage and confidence by every experience in which you really stop to look fear in the face. You are able to say to yourself, "I lived through this horror. I can take the next thing that comes along." You must do the thing you think you cannot do."

Eleanor Roosevelt[57]

Explanation

Courage is saying or doing something that seems difficult, even when you're afraid. Courage is not quitting when you feel like giving up.

When you have courage, you try new things and then, if you make a mistake, you try again and again. Courage is choosing the right when you are tempted to choose the wrong. Even if friends are doing something wrong, even if they laugh and call you names, if you have courage you'll do what is right.

Courage comes from knowing deep inside what is right and wrong and knowing that the people you love believe you can make good choices. Also, courage comes from knowing that your family or friends are there to help you be brave when you're afraid.

That's right. Those people in your life who teach and love you trust that you will have the courage to do what is right, even when they are not with you.

Part of courage is making good choices in the face of opposition. Even when others try their best to change your mind, when you have the courage of your convictions you choose the right – no matter what the consequences may be. You will always be blessed for courageously making good choices.

---

[56] Glenn Van Ekeren. *Speaker's Sourcebook II*. 1994. Paramus, New Jersey: Prentice Hall, 76
[57] Glenn Van Ekeren. *Speaker's Sourcebook II*. 1994. Paramus, New Jersey: Prentice Hall, 76

Story for Young Children

<u>Malala Yousafzai – The Bravest Girl in the World</u>

Malala Yousafzai was only ten years old when her beloved hometown in Pakistan began to change. The Taliban, a group of violent people in the Middle East, inched closer. Violence soon spread across the Swat Valley, and because these people did not want girls to be able to go to school and get an education, many girls had to stop attending their classes in order to stay safe.

Despite her young age, Malala knew that if she became afraid and stopped going to school like many girls already had, nothing would change. She didn't need to grow up to do it, she could make a change now.

In 2009, when she was only 11 years old, Malala began to write about her experiences during the Taliban's reign in her country. She wrote under a different name to keep her and her family safe, but she published her writing online so that many people could learn about what was going on in her part of the world. Even though her voice was little, she knew she could make a big impact if she just continued to speak out.

And she did make a big impact! Soon, an American reporter asked her to star in a documentary on television to talk more about the problems in her country. The whole world learned about her cause, and in 2011, she was awarded Pakistan's National Youth Peace Prize.

When Malala was only 15, the Taliban began to fear Malala's influence in the world. They threatened to hurt her and her family, but Malala's courage was stronger than her fear. She continued to write and tell the world her story, despite these evil people's threats. One day, Malala was on the school bus, and a member of the Taliban got on and shot her 3 times. Malala was badly hurt and had to receive surgery to save her life. However, she survived, and she was even more determined to make a difference after she recovered.

Malala went on to write a book all about her experiences, and in 2014, because of her bravery and hard work, Malala became the youngest person to be awarded the Nobel Peace Prize, which is one of the highest awards of bravery in the entire world. She was only 17 years old.

Malala still tells her story and fights for what is right today. She is a true example of how one little voice can make a big difference. [58]

Learning Questions
1. How did Malala show courage?
2. What things are you afraid of?
3. How can you show courage when you are afraid?

---

[58] https://www.goalcast.com/2018/03/07/malala-yousafzais-life-story/

Story for Older Children

<u>Courage</u>

We can all learn about courage from a man who overcame great defeat and eventually succeeded to become the 16th President of the United States. His name was Abraham Lincoln.

Death took the life of Lincoln's mother when he was just nine years of age. When he was but a young man, Abraham ran for the legislature in Illinois, but was badly defeated.

He entered business with a partner who proved to be dishonest. After the business failed, he spent seventeen years of his life working to pay the debts that his dishonest partner had left him.

Abraham became engaged to Ann Rutledge, a beautiful girl from New Salem, his first and only true love -- and she died. He proposed to Mary Owens a year later and was rejected.

After courtship and one broken engagement with Mary Todd, he finally married her, but Abraham was never completely happy in his marriage.

Of Lincoln's four children, all but one died when they were young.

Lincoln ran for Congress and was badly defeated. He tried to get an appointment to the United States Land Office but was unsuccessful. Lincoln was badly defeated when he became a candidate for the United States Senate. In 1858, he was defeated by Stephen A. Douglas. His associate, Stanton, as well as many others whom he regarded as friends, publicly ridiculed him.

Through all these losses and disappointments, Abraham Lincoln remained cheerful and carried on with quiet determination. He later became President of the United States and is today respected among all people.[59]

Learning Questions

1. Why is it so remarkable that Abraham Lincoln became the President of the United States?
2. What helped him overcome all his trials?
3. What is something in your life that you need courage for?

You Show Courage When You:

- Do what you know is right even when you are afraid.
- Try new things.
- Make a mistake and then try again.
- Choose the right even when friends laugh and call you names.
- Don't quit when you feel like giving up.
- Ask for help when you need it.

---

[59] Author Unknown, *Especially for M*, V 5, p. 57

COURTESY

Courtesy

Definition Courtesy: Polite, well-mannered behavior.

Quotes

"There is always time for courtesy."

Ralph Waldo Emerson[60]

"Small kindnesses, small courtesies, small considerations, habitually practiced give a greater charm to the character than the display of great talents and accomplishments."

M.A. Kelty[61]

Explanation

Courtesy is speaking and acting politely. Courtesy is using good manners.

Courteous people think about other people's needs before their own. They speak and act in ways that make others feel valued and important.

There are many courteous expressions. A few of them are: "Please," "Thank you," "You're welcome," "Excuse me," "Pardon me."

Courteous actions are: covering your mouth when you sneeze or yawn; opening doors for others; not interrupting when others are speaking; calling people by their names; smiling; being kind; allowing others to go first; being quiet in places where you should be quiet; listening and looking at people when they're speaking to you; waiting patiently in lines.

When you are courteous people usually treat you courteously and enjoy being around you.

You may think that you only need to be courteous when you're in public, away from home. You might believe that with your own family you can act any way you'd like and it's okay. That's not true. It is important to be courteous at home – to your parents, grandparents, and all other relatives. Your family deserves your courteous behavior. The habits you develop at home will determine how you act everywhere you go.

---

[60] Edwards, Tyron. 1977. *The New Dictionary of Thoughts*. Stanbook, Inc., 117
[61] Edwards, Tyron. 1977. *The New Dictionary of Thoughts*. Stanbook, Inc.,117

Most adults respect and sincerely appreciate courteous children.

Story for Young Children

The Drug Store

A few months after moving to a small town a woman complained to a neighbor about the poor service at the local drug store. She hoped the neighbor would repeat her complaint to the store's owner.

The next time she went to the drugstore the druggist greeted her with a big smile and told her how happy he was to see her again. He said he hoped she liked their town and to please let him know if there was anything he could do to help her get settled. He then filled her order promptly and courteously.

Later the woman reported the miraculous change to her friend. "I suppose you told the druggist how poor I thought the service was?" she asked.

"Actually," the woman said. "I told him you were amazed at the way he had built up his drug store and you thought it was one of the best you'd ever seen."[62]

Learning Questions

1. When the woman told her neighbor about the druggist, was she being courteous? Do you think she will be courteous from then on?
2. Why do you think the neighbor decided to be courteous instead of rude?
3. What are two things you can do to be more courteous?

Story for Older Children

The Most Important Question

During my second month of nursing school our professor gave us a pop quiz. I was a conscientious student and had breezed through the questions, until I read the last one: "What is the first name of the woman who cleans the school?" Surely this was some kind of joke. I had seen the cleaning woman several times. She was tall, dark-haired and in her 50's, but how would I know her name?

I handed in my paper, leaving the last question blank. Before class ended, one student asked if the last question would count toward her quiz grade. "Absolutely," said the professor. "In your career you will meet many people. All are significant. They deserve your attention and care, even if all you do is smile and say hello." I've never forgotten that lesson.[63]

---

[62] *The Little Book of Inspirational Stories.* (2000) Ed. R. Dale Jeffery, Covenant Communications, American Fork, Utah. "The Drug Store," Author unknown, pg. 8

[63] Author Unknown

Learning Questions

1. Why was it important to learn the cleaning lady's name?
2. Tell about a time when someone was courteous to you.
3. How do you feel when someone shows you courtesy?

You Show Courtesy When You:

- Use good manners.
- Speak politely.
- Treat others the way you'd like to be treated.
- Smile and be kind.
- Act in ways that make others feel important.
- Think about how your words and actions affect other people.

CREATIVITY

Creativity

Definition Creativity: Doing things in a new or different way.

Quotes

"The greatest enemy of your creative powers is being satisfied with less than what you are capable of doing."

Nido Qubein[64]

"Be brave enough to live creatively. The creative is the place where no one else has ever been. You have to leave the city of your comfort and go into the wilderness of your intuition. You can't get there by bus, only by hard work, risking, and by not quite knowing what you're doing. What you'll discover will be wonderful: yourself."

Alan Alda[65]

Explanation

Creativity is doing things in new and different ways. When you are creative you use your imagination to see old things in new ways. You do things that haven't been done before, in ways that no one else has done it. For example, instead of drawing a green tree with a trunk, branches and leaves, you might want to use your imagination and draw a red tree with lollipops on the branches instead of leaves.

When you are creative you do normal, familiar things a little bit differently. Sometimes you do things a little better than they've been done before. People who invent things are creative. They try to improve on what was done before. A man named Buckminster Fuller thought about new ways to do things and he created 170 inventions. Mr. Fuller wrote 24 books and made 57 trips around the world sharing his ideas with others.

Creativity is good because it helps mankind progress and improve. Without new ideas, we would keep doing things the same way—year after year, century after century. From original, new ideas, comes music that has never been played, paintings that have never been drawn, and books that have never been written.

---

[64] Glenn Van Ekeren. *Speaker's Sourcebook II*. 1994. Paramus, New Jersey: Prentice Hall, 80
[65] Glenn Van Ekeren. *Speaker's Sourcebook II*. 1994. Paramus, New Jersey: Prentice Hall, 80

Like many other values, the more you practice being creative, the more creative you become. The more you try, the better your imagination gets, and pretty soon you can easily think of interesting, new ways to do things.

It takes courage to be creative because it's easier to just do things the way others do them, or to do things the ways they've always been done.

Sometimes people laugh at those who try to do things creatively. That's alright, they can laugh and you can still be happy that you're creative. You can be glad that you're not copying other people; you're doing things your own special way.

Story for Young Children

<u>Lester's Leaf House</u>

Lester and his mother were in their backyard, raking leaves. Actually, Lester's mother was raking leaves. Lester was leaning on his rake.

"Lester," Mother said as she continued to add leaves to her large leaf pile, "when I was a little girl -–"

"I know, I know -- don't tell me, Mother." Lester loved to tease his mother. "When you were a little girl, you didn't have three maple trees in your backyard—you had three thousand, so there were zillions of leaves all over the place. But you never stopped raking. Not even for a minute. Not even if it started to rain. Nope, you didn't stop until every single leaf was in your pile."

Lester's mother smiled. "Three thousand maple trees! Goodness, Lester, I didn't grow up in the woods! No, what I was going to tell you was that when I was a little girl, I used to love jumping into leaf piles."

"What? Didn't that mess up the leaf piles?"

"Well, I suppose it did." Mother said. "But it was sure a lot of fun!"

"Fun?" Was this the same mother who ordered him to stay away from mud puddles and who wouldn't let him bring worms into the house? Was she teasing him?

"Yes, fun. Why don't you give it a try?"

"All right." Lester shrugged, trotted over to his mother's leaf pile, and took a half-hearted leap.

Scrunch! Crackle! Crunch! The leaf pile had become a king-size, autumn-scented pillow!

Lester giggled. His mother was right. Jumping into leaf piles was a lot of fun. In fact, it was so much fun that Lester kept jumping, and jumping, until Mother, who jumped in a couple of times herself, stopped and said, "Say, Lester, when I was a little girl-"

"I know, I know—don't tell me, Mother. When you were a little girl, the instant your mother told you to stop jumping into the leaf pile, you picked up your rake and started raking all over again. And you never stopped. Not even for a second. Not even when a hurricane blew through and you had to chase your leaves all over town. Nope, you didn't stop until you were absolutely sure that every single one of those leaves was in your pile."

Lester's mother smiled. "A hurricane! Goodness, Lester, I didn't grow up on the coast! No, what I was going to tell you was that when I was a little girl, I used to love making leaf houses."

"What? Lester scratched his head. "Didn't that mess up the leaf piles?"

Lester's mother laughed. "Well, I suppose it did." she said. "But it was sure a lot of fun!"

"Fun?" Where in the world was the mother who scolded him for playing with his food, the one who nearly hit the ceiling the last time he tried one of his original cake recipes? Why, she hadn't even let him put his mustard-marshmallow delight into the oven! She must be teasing him!

"Yes, fun. Watch."

Then, as Lester looked on in amazement, Mother began to rearrange her leaf pile. Before he knew it, the leaf pile had completely vanished, and his mother was standing in the center of four leaf-walls. Oh, the walls were no more than a foot high and a foot wide, but Mother seemed satisfied. "Well, Lester," she asked, "what do you think of the house?"

"Hmmmmm," Lester said. "I've never seen a leaf house before, so I suppose it's okay. Aren't you going to invite me in?"

"Why, how thoughtless of me!" Mother quickly raked an opening in the wall closest to Lester. "I thought someone was at the front door," she declared, smiling. "Won't you come in?"

"Thank you." Lester entered the leaf house.

"May I offer you something to drink?"

"Oh, yes," Lester said. "I'd love a chocolate milkshake. But where are you going to make it? I don't see a kitchen."

"A kitchen!" Mother said. "Why, Lester, you're absolutely right. I don't have a kitchen. Would you like to help me make one?"

Lester raced out the front door of the leaf house and grabbed his rake. Then he and Mother began to add on to the leaf house. They raked a kitchen, a dining room, a living room, two bedrooms, two bathrooms, a front porch, and a back door.

The leaf house sprawled across the entire backyard. Lester had never raked so hard or for so long in his life. "This is some kind of place!" he said as he drank his imaginary milkshake. "Don't you think so, Mother?"

"Lester, Lester," replied his mother, who was leaning on her rake, "did I ever tell you that when I was a little girl—"

"I know, I know—don't tell me, Mother. When you were a little girl, right after you finished building your leaf house, you started tearing it down. You had to because in your heart you knew that those leaves didn't belong all over your yard. They belonged in a nice, neat pile. So once again you began to rake. And you raked, and you raked, and you raked. You never stopped. Not even when it was after midnight and the worst blizzard of all time howled into your town, and two hundred polar bears wandered into your backyard and started fooling around with your leaves and you had to tell them to cut it out, because there was no way you were going to let perfect strangers mess things up, and the polar bears started blubbering, but you didn't give a hoot, you just told them to scram and kept right on raking until every single leaf was in your pile."

Lester was out of breath.

Mother smiled. "Two hundred polar bears! Goodness, Lester, I didn't grow up that close to the North Pole! No, what I was going to tell you was that when I was a little girl and it started to get dark and I started to get hungry, I'd rake shut the front door of my leaf house and head for the backdoor of my brick house."

"You'd just leave your leaf house?" Lester said, his eyes as big as full moons.

"Yes—I always liked to play in my leaf house the next day."

"Wow!"

"Well, of course," Mother said, "there was that one year when the strongest winds ever to blow across the face of the earth carried off one of my leaf houses while I was sound asleep. I couldn't find a trace of it the next morning, even though I looked everywhere. "But, she chuckled, "other than that time, I always enjoyed playing in my leaf house the next day."

Lester grinned. "You know, Mother, I think that I might have liked playing with you when you were little."

"Why, thank you, Lester."

Lester and mother shut the front door of their leaf house, put their rakes away, and walked in the back door of their other house, where their dinner just happened to be in the oven.[66]

---

[66] Renee Riede, "Lester's Leaf House," Friend, Oct. 1997, 16

Learning Questions

1. How did Lester's mother show creativity?
2. How was Lester creative?
3. What creative things have you done?

Story for Older Children

The Difference Between Ordinary and Extraordinary is That Little Extra

A family once moved into a new apartment and soon found themselves besieged by salesmen desiring to sign them up for everything from laundry service to life insurance. One day, a dairyman came to the door offering his services. The homemaker said, "No, my husband and I don't drink milk."

"I'd be glad to deliver a quart every morning for cooking," the dairyman persisted. "That's more than I need," she replied, trying to close the door.

"Well, ma'am, how about some cream? Berries comin' in now, and…" She answered curtly, "No! We never use cream."

The dairyman walked away slowly, and the woman congratulated herself on her sales resistance. The following morning, however, she answered a knock at the door only to find this same dairyman at the door, a bowl of ripe strawberries held carefully in one hand and a half pint of cream in the other.

"Lady," he said, as he poured the cream over the berries and handed them to her, "I got to thinkin'. If you've never used cream on berries, you sure have missed a lot in life." Needless to say, he delivered to her house every day thereafter!

When you meet with resistance, using creativity and kindness to overcome obstacles often works like magic.[67]

Learning Questions

1. Why do you think the dairyman was able to deliver to the lady "every day thereafter"?
2. Can you give an example of a time you tried using creativity to fix a problem?

You Show Creativity When You:

- Do things in new and different ways.
- Use your imagination to see old things in new ways.
- Do things that haven't been done before.
- Do normal, familiar things a little bit differently.

---

[67] *God's Little Devotional Book for Leaders*, p 307.

- Sometimes do things a little better than they've been done before.
- Are like many inventors who improve on what was done before.
- Don't copy other people; you do things your own way.
- Create new music, art, stories, inventions, etc.

DEPENDABILITY

Dependability

Definition Dependability: Doing what you say you will do when you say you'll do it.

Quotes

"The greatest ability is dependability."

Bob Jones[68]

"We must not be *nearly* dependable, but *always* dependable."

N. Eldon Tanner[69]

Explanation

Dependability means that people can count on you to do what you say you will do. They trust you.

For example, think about your mail carrier. Does your family depend on him or her to bring the mail each day? Companies depend on mailmen to bring their mail and deliver their products every day. We all depend on postal workers to do their jobs well, no matter how bad the weather is. Even when it rains and snows we trust they will dependably deliver our mail on time. When you do a chore, can people depend on you to do it well, in a timely manner?

When you are dependable you finish what you start no matter how hard it is. You don't blame others, you don't forget, and you don't have to be reminded.

When you're dependable you care about giving your best effort to everything you do. You want to do excellent work, every time.

Dependable people make agreements that they know they can keep. They also make reachable goals, create plans, and work their hardest. And people with dependability don't give up, no matter what.

When employers want to hire people for jobs they look for men and women who are dependable.

---

[68] http://www.quotationary.com

[69] N. Eldon Tanner, "Dependability," *Ensign,* Apr. 1974, 2

Story for Young Children

I Knew You Would Come

There were two childhood buddies who went through school and college and even joined the army together. War broke out and they were fighting in the same unit. One night they were ambushed.
Bullets were flying all over and out of the darkness came a voice, "Harry, please come and help me." Harry immediately recognized the voice of his childhood buddy, Bill. He asked the captain if he could go. The captain said, "No, I can't let you go, I am already short-handed and I cannot afford to lose one more person. Besides, the way Bill sounds he is not going to make it." Harry kept quiet. Again the voice came, "Harry, please come and help me."

Harry sat quietly because the captain had refused earlier. Again and again the voice came. Harry couldn't contain himself any longer and told the captain, "Captain, this is my childhood buddy. I have to go and help." The captain reluctantly let him go. Harry crawled through the darkness and dragged Bill back into the trench. They found that Bill was dead.

Now the captain got angry and shouted at Harry, "Didn't I tell you he was not going to make it? He is dead, you could have been killed and I could have lost a hand. That was a mistake." Harry replied, "Captain, I did the right thing. When I reached Bill he was still alive and his last words were 'Harry, I knew you would come.'"[70]

Learning Questions

1. How did this boy show that he was dependable?
2. What did the boy's captain say he should do instead of saving his friend?
3. What does it mean to be dependable?

Story for Older Children

The Real Test

Mr. Harper was trying to teach his students to be honest. He wanted to see who he could depend on, and who he couldn't depend on. So, at the end of the day the teacher gave his class a true or false quiz that they weren't expecting. When the bell rang the students handed in their papers and ran to catch their buses.

Mr. Harper took the quizzes home and graded them without putting any marks on the papers. When the students came to class, he handed the papers back and told the young people to take 5 points off for each wrong answer and subtract it from 100. When they had finished, he asked them to call their scores out as he put them next to the scores he had gotten when he had graded them. Every student in the class had changed his or her answers to get a higher score; every

---

[70] http://moralvaluebyrabi.blogspot.com/2013/11/be-dependable-and-practice-loyalty.html

student except one. Mary called hers out quietly as "45." Mr. Harper could see easily who could be depended on; only one student overcame the temptation to cheat. Mary passed the *real* test.[71]

Learning Questions

1. How did Mr. Harper know he could depend on Mary?
2. Have you ever been tempted to cheat?
3. What are some ways you show your dependability each day?

You Show Dependability When You:

- Can be counted on to do what you say you will.
- Finish what you start, even when it's difficult.
- Don't blame others.
- Don't forget.
- Don't have to be reminded.
- Give your best effort every time.
- Make agreements you can keep and goals you can reach.
- Don't give up, no matter what.

---

[71] Paula Noble Fellingham

DETERMINATION

Determination

Definition Determination: Focusing on a task and staying with it until finished.

Quotes

"I hope someday to have so much of what the world calls success, that people will ask me, "What's your secret?" and I will tell them, "I just get up again when I fall down.""

Paul Harvey[72]

"Be like a postage stamp. Stick to something until you get there."

Josh Billings[73]

Explanation

To be successful in anything worthwhile, you need determination. Alexander Graham Bell failed over 2,000 times and worked 18 years before he succeeded with his invention of the telephone. He said these powerful words: "What this power is I cannot say: all I know is that it exists, and it becomes available only when a man is in that state of mind in which he knows exactly what he wants and is fully determined not to quit until he finds it."[74]

People who achieve their goals usually learn that discouragement and doubt can be defeated—they will pass. Obstacles in life can be overcome; there are always obstacles. What we need to understand, really understand, is that opposition is part of life. All things worthwhile require effort, and nothing worthwhile comes easily.

Indeed, we need to *expect* opposition. When we understand that reaching our goals will probably be difficult, we won't be surprised or discouraged if we fail once, five times, or fifty times. Our determination, our sheer will to succeed, can help us get up each time we fall. If the way you're doing things isn't working, then study the problem and start again using a new method but stay on task.

Let's look at two wonderful examples of determination. An English woman, Florence Nightingale, was born into great wealth. However, she was determined to improve hospital standards and patient care; Florence knew she must leave her beautiful home to do so.

---

[72] Glenn Van Ekeren. *Speaker's Sourcebook II*. 1994. Paramus, New Jersey: Prentice Hall, 104

[73] Glenn Van Ekeren. *Speaker's Sourcebook II*. 1994. Paramus, New Jersey: Prentice Hall, 104

[74] Glenn Van Ekeren. *Speaker's Sourcebook II*. 1994. Paramus, New Jersey: Prentice Hall, 104

While just a young woman, Florence worked in dingy, dirty hospitals, and on the battlefield during the Crimean War. For many years Miss Nightingale arose at 4:30 a.m. and went to the battlefield where she cared for the bleeding and dying soldiers. By age 40 she was so ill herself that she had to return to England. Although restricted to her sick bed, she created the Nightingale School and Home for Nurses. With determination, Florence Nightingale taught others and blessed their lives until her death at age 90.

Another example of determination is Teddy Roosevelt. As a child he was bedridden with severe asthma, and he struggled for every breath. Teddy was so ill that some nights he didn't want to go to sleep, because the boy was afraid he'd never wake up.

Teddy Roosevelt had lots of determination. He wanted with all of his heart to be strong – both physically and mentally. So, every day, for hours, he exercised and lifted weights. Also, Teddy read books on every subject and became extremely knowledgeable. Largely because of his determination, Teddy Roosevelt became the 26th President of the United States.

Tommy Lasorda, former Manager of the Los Angeles Dodgers baseball team said, "The difference between the impossible and the possible lies in a man's determination."[75]

Story for Younger Children

Rachel's Determination

Rachel wanted to learn how to tie her shoelaces all by herself. Her older brothers Mark and Timothy knew how to tie their shoelaces, and Rachel wanted to be able to do it too. Rachel was five years old and would be going to kindergarten soon. She wanted to be able to show the other kids that she was old enough and smart enough to put on her own shoes!

Rachel's mom showed her how to tie her shoelaces. It seemed very easy, but when Rachel tried it seemed really hard. "Keep trying honey," said Rachel's mom. "I know you can do it." Rachel decided she would practice until she got it right, so she went out on the front porch and sat down with her shoes in her hand. She would get it right even if it took her all day! Rachel practiced and practiced.

Soon Megan, Rachel's best friend, came over to see if Rachel wanted to play. "Sorry Megan, I can't. I want to practice this until I get it right," said Rachel. "Okay," said Megan sadly as she walked away. Rachel tried and tried until her mother called her to dinner.

"I think I've almost got it Mom!" said Rachel proudly. "That's good honey, now go wash up so we can eat," said Rachel's mom. After dinner and all during the next day Rachel tried to tie her shoes. Her mom helped her and watched her as she did it. Megan came over again and Rachel told her she couldn't play until she had learned to tie her shoes. "You will never learn! You are taking so long!" yelled Megan. "You should just come and play with me!"

---

[75] Glenn Van Ekeren. *Speaker's Sourcebook II*. 1994. Paramus, New Jersey: Prentice Hall, 104

The next morning Rachel finally tied her shoes correctly for the first time. She yelled for her mom to watch her. When her mother remarked that she was very proud of Rachel, the little girl just smiled and said, "I knew I could do it if I just kept trying."[76]

Learning Questions

1. What did Rachel do to show determination?
2. Rachel said, "I knew I could do it if I just kept trying." Can we learn new things if we keep trying?
3. What is one thing you do that shows determination?

Story for Older Children

Power of Determination

The little country schoolhouse was heated by an old-fashioned, pot-bellied coal stove. A little boy had the job of coming to school early each day to start the fire and warm the room before his teacher and classmates arrived.

One morning they all arrived to find the schoolhouse engulfed in flames. They dragged the unconscious little boy out of the flaming building more dead than alive. He had major burns over the lower half of his body and was taken to a nearby county hospital.

From his bed the dreadfully burned, semi-conscious little boy faintly heard the doctor talking to his mother. The doctor told his mother that her son would surely die which was for the best, because the terrible fire had devastated the lower half of his body.

But the brave boy didn't want to die. He made up his mind that he would survive. Somehow, to the amazement of the physician, he did survive. When the mortal danger was past, he again heard the doctor and his mother speaking quietly. The mother was told that since the fire had destroyed so much flesh in the lower part of his body, it would almost be better if he had died, since he was doomed to be a lifetime cripple with no use at all of his lower limbs.

Once more the brave boy made up his mind. He would not be a cripple. He would walk. But unfortunately, from the waist down he had no motor ability. His thin legs just dangled lifelessly.

Ultimately, he was released from the hospital. Every day his mother would massage his little legs, but there was no feeling, no control, nothing. Yet his determination that he would walk was as strong as ever.

When he wasn't in bed, he was confined to a wheelchair. One sunny day his mother wheeled him out into the yard to get some fresh air. This day, instead of sitting there, he threw himself from the chair. He pulled himself across the grass, dragging his legs behind him.

---

[76] Holly Daley

He worked his way to the white picket fence bordering their lot. With great effort, he raised himself up on the fence. Then, stake by stake, he began dragging himself along the fence, resolved that he would walk. He started to do this every day until he wore a smooth path all around the yard beside the fence. There was nothing he wanted more than to develop life in those legs.

Ultimately, through daily massages, his iron persistence and his resolute determination, the boy developed the ability to stand up, then to walk haltingly, then to walk by himself, and then to run.

He began to walk to school, then to run to school. He ran for the sheer joy of running. Later, in college, he made the track team.

Still later in Madison Square Garden this young man who was not expected to survive, or walk, or run, broke a world track and field record. This determined young man, Dr. Glenn Cunningham, ran the world's fastest mile![77]

Learning Questions

1. Why did the doctors say the little boy should have died?
2. What would you have done if this was you?
3. Name one thing you can do to show determination in your life.

You Show Determination When You:

- Decide what you want to do and believe it is important.
- Focus your attention on reaching your goals.
- Learn how to avoid distraction.
- Keep trying after you fail, or when it gets difficult.
- Ask people for help if you need it.
- Finish what you start.

---

[77] http://www.cmfaq.com/sha/real_stories_02_determination.html by Burt Dubin

EMPATHY

Empathy

Definition Empathy: Sincerely caring about others and their challenges.

Quotes

"The great gift of human beings is that we have the power of empathy."

Meryl Streep[78]

"Some people think only intellect counts: knowing how to solve problems, knowing how to get by, knowing how to identify an advantage and seize it. But the functions of intellect are insufficient without courage, love, friendship, compassion and empathy."

Dean Koontz[79]

Explanation

Empathy is caring about people and trying to understand how they feel. Empathy is trying to mentally put yourself in another person's position. When you have empathy, you think like this: "What would it be like to be this person, with her life experiences, her needs and desires?" And you ask yourself, "How would I feel if I were her?" Then you really try to imagine how she's feeling and try your best to help that person be happy.

When you have empathy, you notice if people are sad, afraid, or discouraged, and you're kind and helpful. Sometimes being helpful is as easy as just listening, or sharing an experience you had that was like theirs. At school there are usually many opportunities to show empathy to struggling students. Sometimes young people are concerned because they're new in town, or they're hurt, or they're worried about a test, or they aren't popular. You can show empathy by being interested in them and by helping however they need you most. You will always be appreciated and more well-liked when you show empathy to others.

It may not always be easy or convenient to be empathetic, but it's always a good choice. Remember, what you send into the lives of others — kindness or unkindness — always comes back into your own. In other words, if you help someone who is sad, then when you are sad, they will probably show empathy and help you.

---

[78] http://www.quotationspage.com
[79] http://www.quotationspage.com

Story for Younger Children

Love thy Neighbor

One day I was visiting a second-grade elementary school classroom. The student teacher held the children captive with her storytelling skills. In great detail she told of a cross old man whose name was Mr. Black. In contrast, the account was given of a Mr. Brown who was kind and thoughtful and loved by everyone. At the conclusion of the story, the teacher asked the children, "How many of you would like to be a neighbor to Mr. Brown?" Every hand was raised high. Then, almost as an afterthought, she inquired if there was anyone who would like to have Mr. Black for a neighbor.

A little boy in a faded green shirt near the back of the room began to raise his hand, which brought a ripple of amusement from the children. When called on for an explanation to his single vote, he spoke in a soft tone. "Well," he said, "I'd like Mr. Black to be my neighbor, because if he was, my mom would make a cake for me to take to him, and then he wouldn't be cross anymore."

A hush fell over the room. Everyone felt something wonderful that they couldn't explain. Another student broke the silence: "Oh, I wish I'd said that!"[80]

Learning Questions

1. How did the little boy show empathy for Mr. Black?
2. How could you show empathy for Mr. Black if he was your neighbor?
3. Is it hard to show empathy to those who aren't nice to us? Should we still be kind and empathetic, even if it's difficult?

Story for Older Children

The Easter Bunny

When I was a little girl, every Sunday my family of six would put on their best clothes and go to Sunday School and then to church. The kids in elementary school would all meet together to sing songs, and then later divide into groups based on their ages.

One Easter Sunday, all the kids arrived with big eyes and exciting stories about what the Easter Bunny had brought. While all the kids shared their stories with delight, Bobby sat sullenly. One of the teachers, noticing this, asked Bobby, "And what did the Easter Bunny bring you?" He replied, "My mom locked the door on accident so the Easter Bunny couldn't get inside."

---

[80] Ardeth Greene Kapp, *Sunshine from the Child's Soul*, 2001, Deseret Book Company, Salt Lake City, Utah, pp. 199-200.

This sounded like a reasonable idea to all of us kids, so we kept telling the stories. My mom knew the true story, though. Bobby's mom was a struggling single parent who just couldn't afford the Easter Bunny.

After Sunday school everyone went off to church. When Dad came to meet us, Mom announced that we were going home instead. At home, she explained that to make Bobby feel better, we were going to be Easter Bunnies and make a basket of goodies for him and leave it at church. We all donated some of our candies to the basket chosen for Bobby, then headed back to church. There, mom unzipped his coat that was hanging on the coat rack, then zipped up the coat with the Easter basket hanging inside, and attached a note:

Dear Bobby,

I'm sorry I missed your house last night. Happy Easter!

Love,
The Easter Bunny [81]

Learning Questions

1. How did the family show empathy for Bobby?
2. How do you think it made Bobby feel when he found the basket?
3. Name one thing you can do to show empathy for someone you know.

You Show Empathy When You:

- Care about people.
- Try to understand how others feel.
- Mentally put yourself in another person's position.
- Ask yourself, "What would it be like to be her?"
- Try to help people be happy.

---

[81] Beth H. Arbogast, *Chicken Soup for the Christian Family Soul*, 177-178

ENCOURAGEMENT

Encouragement

Definition Encouragement: To inspire or help someone; to give courage and hope to others.

Quotes

"People love others not for who they are but for how they make us feel."

Irwin Federman[82]

"Three billion people on the face of the earth go to bed hungry every night, but four billion people go to bed every night hungry for a simple word of encouragement and recognition."

Cavett Roberts[83]

Explanation

Encouragement is words and actions that help people feel good about themselves. Encouragement helps people feel appreciated. We all want to feel good about ourselves, and we all enjoy encouragement.

Here are some encouraging words you can say to others:

1. To your friend when he's trying something difficult: "I know you can do it! You'll be great!"
2. To your mom or dad after dinner: "Thanks! That was a great dinner."
3. To the store clerk: "I appreciate your help!"

You are showing kindness when you offer encouragement and words of appreciation to others. Richard M. DeVos said, "Few things in the world are more powerful than a positive push. A smile. A word of optimism and hope. A 'You can do it' when things are tough."[84]

Giving encouragement to family members, friends, and even strangers is a good habit. We can all give more praise and encouragement to others each day. Cavett Roberts said, "Three billion people on the face of the earth go to bed hungry every night, but four billion people go to bed every night hungry for a simple word of encouragement and recognition."[85]

---

[82] Glenn Van Ekeren. *Speaker's Sourcebook II*. 1994. Paramus, New Jersey: Prentice Hall, 123

[83] Glenn Van Ekeren. *Speaker's Sourcebook II*. 1994. Paramus, New Jersey: Prentice Hall, 122

[84] Glenn Van Ekeren. *Speaker's Sourcebook II*. 1994. Paramus, New Jersey: Prentice Hall, 122

[85] Glenn Van Ekeren. *Speaker's Sourcebook II*. 1994. Paramus, New Jersey: Prentice Hall, 122

We should take every opportunity to make people happy and to lighten their loads. You never know when a few sincere words or a simple act of kindness will have a powerful impact on another person's life.

Story for Young Children

<u>A Miracle</u>

Like any good mother, when Karen found out that another baby was on the way she did what she could to help her 3-year-old son, Michael, prepare for a new sibling. When they found out that the new baby was going to be a girl, day after day, night after night, Michael sang to his sister in Mommy's tummy. The pregnancy progressed normally for Karen, until the labor pains came. Every five minutes…then every minute. Then there were complications during delivery.

Finally, Michael's little sister was born, but she was in serious condition. With sirens howling in the night, the ambulance rushed the infant to the neonatal intensive care unit at St. Mary's Hospital, Knoxville, Tennessee. The days inched by and the little girl grew worse. The pediatric specialist told the parents to prepare for the worst.

Karen and her husband contacted a local cemetery about a burial plot. Just weeks ago, they created a special room in their home for the new baby, and now they planned a funeral.

Michael begged his parents to let him see his sister. "I want to sing to her!" he pleaded. Michael kept nagging about singing to his sister, but children are not allowed in Intensive Care. Finally, Karen made up her mind. She decided to take Michael to the baby whether the hospital staff agreed or not. If he didn't see his sister now, Karen reasoned, he may never see her alive. She dressed the little boy in an oversized scrub suit and marched him into the ICU. The head nurse bellowed, "Get that kid out of here now! No children are allowed!" The mother in Karen rose up strong, and the usually mild-mannered lady glared steel-eyed at the nurse, her lips a firm line. "My son is not leaving until he sings to his sister."

Karen took Michael to his sister's bedside. He gazed at the tiny infant who was losing the battle to live.

Michael began to sing. With the sweet voice of a 3-year-old, Michael sang: "You are my sunshine, my only sunshine, you make me happy when skies are gray." Instantly the baby girl responded. The pulse rate became calm and steady. "Keep on singing, Michael!" his mother pleaded.

"You never know, dear, how much I love you. Please don't take my sunshine away."

And the baby's strained breathing became smoother.

"Go on, son," his mother urged.

"The other night, dear, as I lay sleeping, I dreamed I held you in my arms…"

Michael's little sister relaxed as healing rest swept over her.

"Keep on singing, Michael," the head nurse encouraged, as tears overcame her.

"You are my sunshine, my only sunshine. Please don't take my sunshine away."

Michael's baby sister was on her way to recovery. *Woman's Day Magazine* called *it "The Miracle of a Brother's Song."* The entire medical staff called it miraculous, and Karen referred to the experience as "a miracle of love." [86]

Learning Questions

1. What is the miracle in this story?
2. How did Michael give his little sister encouragement?
3. How do you show encouragement to members of your family?

Story for Older Children

A Special Teacher

Years ago, a professor at John Hopkins University gave a group of graduate students this assignment: Go to the slums. Take 200 boys, between the ages of 12 and 16, and investigate their background and environment. Then predict their chances for the future.

The students, after consulting social statistics, talking to the boys, and compiling much data, concluded that 90 percent of the boys would spend some time in jail.

Twenty-five years later another group of graduate students was given the job of evaluating and testing the previous prediction. They went back to the same area. Some of the boys – by then men – were still there, a few had died, some had moved away, but they connected with 180 of the original 200. The students discovered that only four of the group had ever been sent to jail.

Why was it that these men, who had lived in a breeding place for crime, had such a surprisingly good record? The researchers were continually told: "Well, there was a teacher…"

They pressed further and found that in 75 percent of the cases it was the same woman. The researchers went to this teacher, now living in a home for retired teachers. How had she exerted this remarkable influence over that group of children? Could she give them any reason why these boys should have remembered her?

---

[86] Author Unknown, http://www.cyberquotations.com/stories

"No," she said, "no, I really can't." And then, thinking back over the years, she said softly, more to herself than to her questioners: "Oh, how I loved those boys…"[87]

Learning Questions

1. What difference did this teacher make in the lives of her students?
2. Do you think she was an example of encouragement?
3. Who has made a difference in your life because they encouraged you?

You Show Encouragement When You:

1. Compliment others.
2. Tell people that you appreciate their accomplishments, work, or service.
3. Congratulate people when they are doing their best to achieve a goal.

---

[87] Bits and Pieces, http://www.cyberquotations.com/stories

ENDURANCE

Endurance

Definition Endurance: Continuing, even when in pain or distress.

Quotes

"What can't be cured must be endured."

English Proverb[88]

"Big shots are only little shots who keep shooting."

Chris Morley[89]

Explanation

Endurance means to keep trying and do your best, even when it's difficult. Enduring to the end means that you keep going until a job is finished, no matter what. You don't make excuses, complain, or whine…you just keep working until the job is done.

People quite often blame others, or what's happening around them, for their failure. They might say:

- "But it's not my fault…it's his fault that I couldn't finish!"
- "My friend — he didn't help me and I didn't want to do it alone!"
- "The weather was bad."
- "My leg hurt."
- "I forgot!"
- "I was too tired."

Most of the time, reasons like these are excuses. People with endurance don't make excuses, they have courage and keep going. You may have heard the saying, "When the going gets tough, the tough get going."

---

[88] *Five thousand Quotations for All Occasions.* 1945. Edited by Lewis C. Henry. Garden City, New York: Doubleday & Company, Inc., p. 73

[89] Glenn Van Ekeren. *Speaker's Sourcebook II.* 1994. Paramus, New Jersey: Prentice Hall, 278

People who are highly successful have endurance; they don't quit. H. Ross Perot said, "Most people give up just when they're about to achieve success. They give up at the last minute of the game, one foot from a winning touchdown."[90]

Dr. C.E. Welch, the founder of Welch's Grape Juice, agreed with Mr. Perot when he said, "Many men fail because they quit too soon. They lose faith when the signs are against them. They do not have the courage to hold on, to keep fighting in spite of that which seems insurmountable. If more of us would strike out and attempt the "impossible," we very soon would find the truth of that old saying that nothing is impossible…you can accomplish anything you wish."[91]

Story for Young Children

The Crow and the Pitcher

A crow, half-dead with thirst, came upon a pitcher that had once been full of water. But when the crow put its beak into the mouth of the pitcher, he found that only very little water was left in it, and he couldn't reach far enough down to get at it. He tried, and he tried, but at last he gave up in despair.

Then a thought came to him, and he took a pebble and dropped it into the pitcher. Then he took another pebble and dropped it into the pitcher. Then he took another pebble and dropped that into the pitcher. Again and again the crow dropped pebbles into the pitcher. At last, he saw the water mount up near him, and after casting in a few more pebbles he was able to quench his thirst and save his life.

Learning Questions

1. How did the crow endure and do his best to get the water he wanted?
2. Was it hard work?
3. Tell about a time when you really wanted something and you worked very hard and finally got it because you didn't give up.

Story for Older Children

Joshua Dennis: A Treasure of Faith

It was Joshua's Brown's tenth birthday, and his father promised him he could go with a Boy Scout troop from Midvale, Utah, to explore the Hidden Treasure Mine in Eureka, Utah. Joshua's father was the Scout leader and Joshua loved to hike and explore.

During the exploration of the mine, Joshua decided to follow some older Scouts back into the mine tunnel, and he gave his flashlight to his dad, who was leaving the tunnel with a visually handicapped boy. The older Scouts did not know that Joshua was behind them. They began to

---

[90] Glenn Van Ekeren. *Speaker's Sourcebook II*. 1994. Paramus, New Jersey: Prentice Hall, 277
[91] Glenn Van Ekeren. *Speaker's Sourcebook II*. 1994. Paramus, New Jersey: Prentice Hall, 277-278

run, but Joshua couldn't keep up with them and was soon left behind in total darkness. He couldn't even see his hand in front of his face.

Joshua turned around and tried to feel his way back to the entrance, but he made a wrong turn and slid down a slope. He climbed back up but went too far and ended up in an ore stope (a stope is a hole where ore has already been mined out). The stope was six feet wide and twenty-five feet deep. Because of the rocks, the stope was almost impossible to see from the main tunnel.

"I tried to find my way out for a long time," Joshua recalled. He yelled, but the stope muffled his cries, and no one heard him. By this time, he was tired and cold and his feet were wet. "I knew that I was lost, and I realized that I had better just sit down and wait," he said.

Joshua's wait turned out to be five days. He had no food or water and only his coat to keep him warm in the 50-degree temperature. He endured loneliness, hunger, and blackness, but he waited calmly for someone to find him. To pass the time he sang songs and prayed.

Not only was Joshua enduring, but the rescue team searching for him did not give up. When the search party came out of the mine after their unsuccessful attempt on the fifth day, one man decided to go back in…just one more time. When he came to an ore cavity he heard Joshua's faint cry.

Because there was no light in the mine, Joshua had lost track of time. Dehydrated, and suffering mild frostbite on his feet, he was flown to a hospital where he rested and recovered. Joshua and his family were forever grateful to that one member of the search team who didn't give up.[92]

Learning Questions

1. What did Joshua do when he was lost?
2. How did the man who found Joshua show endurance?
3. What did you learn about endurance in this lesson?

You Show Endurance When You:

- Keep trying and do your best, even when it's very hard.
- Finish the job — no matter what — with no excuses.
- Don't complain or blame others.
- Never quit.

---

[92] Shannon W. Ostler, Friend, November 1990, pp. 20-22

ENTHUSIASM

Enthusiasm

Definition Enthusiasm: Doing things wholeheartedly and cheerfully.

Quotes

"I have found enthusiasm for work to be the most priceless ingredient in any recipe for successful living."

Samuel Goldwyn[93]

"I feel sorry for the person who can't get genuinely excited about his work. Not only will he never be satisfied, but he will never achieve anything worthwhile."

Walter P. Chrysler[94]

Explanation

People with enthusiasm smile, laugh, and act happy. They are cheerful and fun to be around. Enthusiastic people bring joy to whatever they do because they are positive and look on the bright side of things. They enjoy life, and people enjoy being around them.

Enthusiasm isn't something you _do_, it's the way you _are_. In other words, enthusiasm isn't something you put on and take off – it's a way of being. When you're enthusiastic you wake up happy and look forward to events of the day, and you go to bed looking forward to the next day.

When you have enthusiasm, you bring fun into everything from going to school to washing the dishes. You do things wholeheartedly, with cheerfulness and 100% effort. People who are enthusiastic put all their energy into doing a superior job.

One of the best things about enthusiasm is that it's contagious. That's right! Enthusiastic, happy people spread good cheer and make others happy!

Have you noticed that amidst cheerfulness even the unhappiest person begins to smile? Also, enthusiasm reflects confidence, and others are drawn toward confident people.

---

[93] Glenn Van Ekeren. _Speaker's Sourcebook II_. 1994. Paramus, New Jersey: Prentice Hall, 129
[94] Glenn Van Ekeren. _Speaker's Sourcebook II_. 1994. Paramus, New Jersey: Prentice Hall, 129

Every person is enthusiastic at times. One might be enthusiastic for an hour, another for a week. However, those who are enthusiastic for a lifetime are usually extremely successful, happy human beings.

To create enthusiasm, you must not dwell on your troubles or the obstacles in your path. You shouldn't focus on what you don't have. Rather, notice the good things in your life, and look for ways to overcome your challenges with a cheerful "I can and will be successful!" attitude.

And remember, things of great worth are usually accomplished with enthusiasm.

Story for Young Children

<u>The Toy Rocket</u>

There once was a boy named Edgar who loved rockets. He dreamed of owning a shiny, new toy rocket, but his family was very poor and could not afford expensive toys. Even so, the boy dreamed of the day when he might have one.

One day, Edgar was walking home from school and noticed an old, beat-up cardboard box on the side of the road. It looked soggy and wet from the recent rain, but Edgar thought he could see the shape of a rocket on the front. Sure enough, upon opening the old box, he found an old toy rocket! The paint was faded and chipped, the stickers were peeled and pale, but it was a rocket, and Edgar was thrilled! Overjoyed, he ran the rest of the way home with the rocket.

For the next few days, Edgar worked tirelessly on making the rocket his own. He applied fresh paint to its body and shined it until it gleamed. He spent many hours cutting out paper planets and stars to stick to the walls of his bedroom. Soon, his bed had become a mission control center and his walls had become the windows into the universe. Edgar was transported whenever he played with his new rocket, and he was proud of the hard work he had put in.

The next weekend, Edgar invited a friend over to play. When his friend entered his room, he, too, was in awe of the amazing work that Edgar had done. Most of all, he noticed the toy rocket. With wide eyes, he asked, "Edgar, where did you get that incredible rocket?" Edgar replied, "I found it in an old box on the side of the road, and then I repainted it and polished it all by myself." "Whoa!" exclaimed his friend, almost giddy with excitement. "How did you do it?" Edgar, now grinning ear to ear, proudly said, "All it took was a little enthusiasm and a lot of hard work."[95]

Learning Questions

1. How did Ken and Eric show their enthusiasm?
2. Name one thing you're enthusiastic about.
3. When you're enthusiastic about something, what do you do to show it?

---

[95] https://freestoriesforkids.com/children/stories-and-tales/paper-rocket

Story for Older Children

<u>An Enthusiastic President</u>

About sixty years ago President Theodore Roosevelt went buffalo hunting with a man named Joe Ferris, in the Badlands of South Dakota. During the trip they encountered problem after problem. At one point they ran out of water and became extremely dehydrated. Later they lost their tent and they slept on the ground using only their saddles as pillows. One night, wolves caused their horses to bolt, and it took hours to recapture them. No sooner had the men fallen asleep than it began to rain heavily. When they awoke, they found themselves in four inches of water. Shivering with the cold and sopping wet, Joe Ferris reported that President Roosevelt exclaimed with great enthusiasm, "By Godfrey, but this is fun!"[96]

Learning Questions

1. Do you think you'd have enthusiasm if you woke up covered with water?
2. What are you enthusiastic about?

You Show Enthusiasm When You:

- Smile, laugh and act happy.
- Look on the bright side of things.
- Do your best at everything.
- Look forward to the next day expecting happiness and success.
- Enjoy life and help others enjoy it too.

---

[96] Glenn Van Ekeren. *Speaker's Sourcebook II*. 1994. Paramus, New Jersey: Prentice Hall, 130

EXCELLENCE

Excellence

Definition Excellence: Doing and being your very best.

Quotes

"Quality doesn't mean we have to be 100 percent better in any one thing; it means we strive to be 1 percent better in 100 things."

Jan Carlzon[97]

"Real excellence does not come cheaply. A certain price must be paid in terms of practice, patience, and persistence."

Stephen Covey[98]

Explanation

Excellence is _doing_ your very best in whatever you do and _being_ your best with the people in your life.

Excellence is trying your hardest with every task. For example, if you are asked to clean the kitchen, you thoroughly clean every part of the kitchen. If you are asked to do a school assignment you give 100% effort and try your very best to do it well.

In every area of your life, excellence means you act the best way you possibly can. For example, with your friends you are kind, loyal, and unselfish. You are the best friend possible.

Additionally, people who practice excellence don't give up. They understand that excellence comes little by little, not all at once.

For example, Thomas Edison was an excellent inventor. His inventions included the electric light bulb, phonograph, and motion pictures. However, Thomas Edison wasn't always an excellent inventor; he failed thousands of times before succeeding. However, his attitude was excellent. He said, "I am not discouraged because every wrong attempt discarded is another step forward."[99]

---

[97] Glenn Van Ekeren. _Speaker's Sourcebook II_. 1994. Paramus, New Jersey: Prentice Hall, 138
[98] Glenn Van Ekeren. _Speaker's Sourcebook II_. 1994. Paramus, New Jersey: Prentice Hall, 138
[99] http://www.quotedb.com/quotes

Successful people understand that excellence is a process. If you want to be excellent at something, keep trying to do your best. Often, people discover their special gifts this way.

Some of the most famous people in the world are well known because they did things in excellent ways. For example, the musician Wolfgang Mozart was an excellent composer; Rembrandt was an excellent artist; Abraham Lincoln was an excellent American President.

Others are well known because they had excellent character. Mother Teresa was one of these people. Mother Teresa was a Catholic nun who took good care of sick and dying people in Calcutta, India. She was a kind and loving woman who cared for people in excellent ways. Mother Teresa said, "Let no one ever come to you without leaving better and happier." It is just as important to *be* an excellent person than it is to *do* excellent things.

Story for Young Children

<u>The Five Dollar Job</u>

No one in our small Utah town knew where the Countess had come from; her careful precise English indicated that she was not a native American. From the size of her house and staff we knew that she must be wealthy, but she never entertained, and she made it clear that when she was at home, she was completely inaccessible. Only when she stepped outdoors did she become a public figure, and then chiefly to the small fry of the town who lived in awe of her.

The Countess always carried a cane, not only for support, but as a means of chastising any youngster she thought needed disciplining. And at one time or another most of the youngsters in our neighborhood seemed to display that need. By running fast and staying alert I had managed to keep out of her reach. But one day when I was about thirteen, as I was shortcutting through her hedge, she got close enough to rap my head with the stick.

"Young man, I want to talk to you," she said. I was expecting a lecture on the evils of trespassing, but as she looked at me, half smiling, she seemed to change her mind.

"Don't you live in that green house with the yellow trees in the next block?"

"Yes, Ma'am."

"Do you take care of your lawn? Water it? Clip it? Mow it?"

"Yes, Ma'am."

"Good, I've lost my gardener. Be at my house Thursday morning at seven, and don't tell me you have something else to do; I've seen you slouching on Thursdays."

When the Countess gave an order, it was carried out. I didn't dare not come on Thursday. I went over the whole lawn three times with a mower before she was satisfied, and then she had me down on all fours looking for weeds until my knees were as green as the grass. She finally called me up to the porch.

"Well, young man, how much do you want for your day's work?"

"I don't know. Fifty cents maybe."

"Is that what you figure you're worth?"

"Yes 'm'. About that."

"Very well, here's the fifty cents you say you're worth, and here's the dollar and a half that I earned for you by pushing you. Now I'm going to tell you something about how you and I are going to work together. There are as many ways to mow a lawn as there are people, and they may be worth anywhere from a penny to five dollars. Let's say that a three-dollar job would be just about what you have done today, except that you would do it all by yourself. A four-dollar job would be so perfect that you'd have to be something of a fool to spend that much time on a lawn. A five-dollar lawn is – well, it's impossible so we'll forget about that. Now then, each week I'm going to pay you according to your own evaluation of your work."

I left with my two dollars, richer than I remembered being in my whole life, and determined that I would get four dollars out of her the next time. But I failed to reach even the three-dollar mark. My will began to falter the second time around her yard.

"Two dollars again, eh? That kind of job puts you right on the edge of being dismissed young man."

"Yes'm, but I'll do better next week."

And somehow, I did. The last time around the lawn I was exhausted, but I found I could spur myself on. In the exhilaration of that new feeling, I had no hesitation in asking the Countess for three dollars.

Each Thursday for the next few weeks, I became more acquainted with her lawn; places where the ground was a little high or a little low, places where it needed to be clipped short or left long on the edges to make a more satisfying curve along the garden. Then I became more aware of just what a four-dollar lawn would consist of. And each week I would resolve to do just that kind of job. But by the time I had earned my three or three and one-half dollars I was too tired to remember even having had the ambition to go beyond that point.

"You look like a good consistent $3.50 man," she would say as she handed me the money.

"I guess so," I would say, too happy at the sight of the money to remember that I had shot for something higher.

"Well, don't feel too bad," she would comfort me. "After all, there are only a handful of people in the world who could do a four-dollar job."

And her words were a comfort to me at first, but then, without my noticing too much what was happening, her comfort became an irritant that made me resolve to do that four-dollar job, even if it killed me. In the fever of my resolve, I could see myself expiring on her lawn, with the Countess leaning over me, handing me the four dollars with a tear in her eye, begging my forgiveness for having ever thought I couldn't do it.

It was in the middle of such a fever, on Thursday night when I was trying to forget the day's defeat and get some sleep, that the truth really hit me – so hard that I sat upright, half choking in my excitement. It was the five-dollar job I had to do, not the four dollar one! I had to do the job that no one could do because it was impossible.

I was well acquainted with the difficulties ahead. I had the problem, for example, of doing something about the worm mounds in the lawn. The Countess might not have noticed them yet, they were so small; but in my bare feet I knew about them and had to do something about them. And I could go on trimming the garden edges with shears, but I knew that a five-dollar lawn demanded that I line up each edge exactly with a yardstick and then trim it precisely with the edger. And there were other problems that only I and my bare feet knew about.

I started the next Thursday by ironing out the worm mounds with a heavy roller. After two hours of that I was ready to give up for the day. Nine o'clock in the morning and my will was already gone. It was only by accident that I discovered how to regain it. Sitting under a walnut tree for a few minutes after finishing the rolling, I surveyed my job. The lawn looked so good, and felt so good under my feet, I was anxious to get on with the job.

I followed this renewal secret for the rest of the day, reviewing a few minutes every hour or so to regain my perspective. Between reviews I mowed four times, two times lengthwise, and two times across, until the lawn looked like a green velvet checkerboard. Then I dug around every tree, crumbling the big clods and smoothing the soil with my hands, then finished with the edger, meticulously lining up each stroke so the effect would be symmetrical. And I carefully trimmed the grass between the flagstones of the front walk. The shears wore my fingers raw, but the walk never looked better.

Finally, about eight o'clock that evening it was all completed. I was so proud I didn't even feel tired when I went up to the door.

"Well, what is it today?" She asked.

"Five dollars," I said, trying for a little calm and sophistication.

"Five dollars? You mean four dollars, don't you? I told you that a five-dollar lawn job was impossible."

"Oh, ma'm, it isn't. I just did it."

"Well, young man, the first five-dollar lawn in history certainly deserves some looking around."

We walked about the lawn together in the light of the evening, and even I was overcome by the impossibility of what I had done.

"Young man," she said, putting her hand on my shoulder, "What on earth made you do such a crazy, wonderful thing?"

I didn't know why, but even if I had, I could not have explained it in the excitement of hearing that I had done it.

"I think I know," she continued, "how you felt when the idea first came into your head, this idea of caring for a lawn that I told you was impossible to accomplish. It made you very happy when it first came, then a little frightened, am I right?"

She could see she was right by the startled look on my face.

"I know how you felt, because the same thing happens to almost everyone. They feel this sudden burst in them of wanting to do some great thing. They feel a wonderful happiness. But then it passes because they have said, 'No, I can't do that. It's impossible.' Whenever something in you says, 'It's impossible,' remember to take a careful look and see if it isn't really God asking you to grow an inch, or a foot, or a mile, that you may come to a fuller life."

Since that time some twenty-five years ago, whenever I have felt myself at an end with nothing before me, suddenly - with the appearance of the word "impossible" - I have experienced the leap inside me, and I know that the only *possible* way lies right through the middle of *impossible*.[100]

Learning Questions

1. What did the Countess challenge the boy to do?
2. Why do you think he was able to achieve the "impossible five-dollar job?"
3. Name one thing you do with excellence. *(Hint: It could be that you are excellent at being patient, or forgiving, or kind.)*

Story for Older Children

Excellence—The Story of Clifton E. Cushman

"Don't feel sorry for me. I feel sorry for some of you. You may have seen the U.S. Olympic Trials on television September 13, 1964. If so, you watched me hit the fifth hurdle, fall, and lie on the track in an inglorious heap of skinned elbows, bruised hips, torn knees and injured pride, unsuccessful in my attempt to make the Olympic team for the second time.

---

[100] Author Unknown

In a split second all the many years of training, pain, sweat, blisters, and agony of running, were simply and irrevocably wiped out. But I tried. I would much rather fail knowing I had put forth an honest effort than never to have tried at all.

This is not to say that everyone is capable of making the Olympic team. However, each of you is capable of trying to make your own personal 'Olympic team', whether it's a sports team, the glee club, the honor roll, or whatever your goal may be. Unless you reach and exceed your grasp, how can you be sure that you can attain?

Over fifteen years ago I set a goal—first place in the Olympic Games. I literally started to run after it. In 1960, I came within three yards of grabbing it; this year I stumbled, fell and watched it recede four more yards away. Certainly, I was very disappointed in falling flat on my face. However, there is nothing I can do about it now but get up, pick the cinders from my wounds, and take one more and one more step, followed by one more and one more, until the steps turn into miles and miles of success.

I know I may never make it. The odds are against me, but I have something in my favor. Desire and faith. Romans 5:3-5 has always had an inspirational meaning to me in this regard: "We rejoice in our sufferings, knowing that suffering produces hope, and hope does not disappoint us…" At least I am going to try.

How about you? Would a little extra effort on your part bring up your grade average at school? Or would you have a better chance to make the football team if you stayed an extra fifteen minutes after practice and worked on your blocking?

Let me tell you something about yourselves. You are taller and heavier than any past generation in this country. You are spending more money, enjoying more freedom, and driving more cars than ever before, yet many of you are very unhappy. Some of you have never known the satisfaction of doing your best in sports, the joy of excelling in class, the wonderful feeling of completing a job, any job, and looking back on it knowing that you have done your best.

I dare you to have your hair cut and not wilt under the comments of your so-called friends. I dare you to clean up your language. I dare you to honor your mother and father. I dare you to go to church without having to be compelled to go by your parents. I dare you to go unselfishly help someone less fortunate than yourself and enjoy the wonderful feeling that goes with it. I dare you to look up at the stars, not down at the mud, and set your sights on one of them, that up to now, you thought was unobtainable. I dare you to read a book that is not required in school. There is plenty of room at the top, but no room for anyone to sit down.

Who knows? You may be surprised at what you can achieve with sincere effort. So get up, pick the cinders out of your wounds, and take one more step!

I dare you.

Sincerely,

Clifton E. Cushman, Olympic Medalist[101]

Learning Questions

1. Even though Clifton failed twice to achieve his Olympic goals, what did he do that showed excellence?
2. Why do you think Clifton dares young people to be excellent in something?
3. What is one way you show excellence in your life?

You Show Excellence When You:

- Do your very best and try your hardest in everything you do.
- Act your very best with people.
- Understand that excellence comes little by little, not all at once.
- Don't give up; you keep trying.
- Discover your special gifts and work diligently to develop them.

---

[101] Author Unknown, *Especially for M*, V 12, p.37-39

FAIRNESS

Fairness

Definition Fairness: Everyone treated in a way that is good for all.

Quotes

"Everyone has a fair turn to be as great as he pleases."

Jeremy Collier[102]

"It is not fair to ask of others what you are not willing to do yourself."

Eleanor Roosevelt[103]

Explanation

Fairness means being just and fair. It means treating people the right way, whatever their size, color, nationality, religion, sex, or bank account happens to be.

Fairness means hearing all the facts – not just one side – and deciding the right thing that should be done. Fairness means showing justice.

Without justice or fairness our world would be a dangerous place, because there wouldn't be any punishment for wrongdoing. Without fairness, the people who hurt others would keep hurting them, and the people who don't do anything wrong would suffer.

With fairness, people get what they deserve. When they are evil, they're punished. Through punishment they are supposed to learn how to act better the next time. With fairness, when people are good, they are usually rewarded.

In your life you practice justice when you treat others fairly. For example, when you're fair, you take turns when playing; you are friends with everyone; and you never gossip. When you're fair, you are kind to everyone, no matter how different they are.

However, the fact is, life is not always fair. Bad things happen to good people and as you grow older you will notice that things are not always fair or equal. Sometimes you are required to do things that may seem unfair to you. No matter what happens in your life, you have choices regarding how fairly you treat other people, animals, and the world you live in.

---

[102] http://www.quotationspage.com
[103] http://quoteland.com/search.asp

Story for Young Children

<u>Fairness</u>

Phillip woke early and was excited to start playing. He hurriedly dressed and ate his breakfast. Then he ran outside when he heard Brady call him from outside the kitchen window.

Phillip and Brady loved playing outside, and today was especially clear and sunny. When they reached the playground one of the swings was broken, so there was only one. Phillip grabbed it and started swinging. Brady waited patiently and then asked, "Can I please swing now?"

"Sure!" Phillip answered and ran to the merry-go-round.

Soon Brady was tired of swinging and came to play with Phillip, but the merry-go-round was going too fast for him to get on. When Phillip saw Brady coming, he slowed down so that his friend could easily get on.

After a few minutes the two boys decided to play in the sand pile. Brady wanted the big sand bucket, so Phillip gave it to him and played with a smaller one. Both boys were building houses in the sand. After a few minutes, Phillip asked Brady if he could use the big bucket. "Yes, I guess it would be fair, if I can have it again in a little while."

At lunchtime both boys ran to Brady's to eat. They told Brady's mom all about the fun they had playing together that morning.

As Mom congratulated them on playing peacefully and fairly, she handed them the same size sandwich. Mom had learned about fairness when she was young, too![104]

Learning Questions

1. Do you think Phillip and Brady treated each other with fairness?
2. What did Brady's mom do for Brady and Phillip at lunch to be fair?
3. How do you show fairness when you play with your friends?

Story for Older Children

<u>A Fable: The Tiger in the Trap</u>

Once upon a time, there was a small town in the deep mountains. The people of this town were always afraid of the tigers that roamed in the surrounding mountains. One day, their fear and anxiety brought all the villagers together to discuss their problem and to find some ways of living peacefully without this constant fear.

---

[104] Paula Noble Fellingham

After much discussion, they came to an agreement: they decided to dig pits here and there to trap the tigers. Every able-bodied villager came out to dig deep pits around the village and, particularly, along both sides of the mountain pass leading to the village.

One day, a traveler was passing through the area and heard strange groaning sounds nearby. He approached the sounds and found a large tiger trapped in a pitfall and trying to jump out.

Seeing the traveler, the tiger begged him for help. "Please, help me out of this trap, and I will never forget your kindness." Out of mercy, the traveler dragged a felled tree and lowered it into the pitfall. And the tiger climbed out.

As soon as the tiger was out of the trap, he said to the traveler, "I am grateful for your help, but because humans made the trap to catch me, for that I will have to kill you." The traveler was utterly speechless and frightened.

Trying to be calm and mustering his courage, the traveler said, "Wait a minute, Mr. Tiger. It is unfair and outrageous to kill me. Fairness demands that we should have a few impartial parties to judge who is right." The tiger agreed and both of them went to see the ox.

After listening to their story, the ox said, "Well, it is the fault of humans. We, oxen, too, have a grudge against humans. They drive us hard for their own benefit and then they butcher us mercilessly. This is all very unfair!"

Next, they went to a pine tree. The pine tree listened to their story and said, "Humans are wrong. They cut us down for lumber and for their firewood. What have we done to them to deserve that? They just have no heart!"

Listening to the second opinion, the tiger was elated and ready to attack the traveler, when a hare came hopping toward them. "Phew, just in time, Mr. Hare. Please, judge our case," pleaded the traveler.

Then the traveler told the hare what had happened. The hare said, "Fine, but before I make any judgment, I must see the original scene."

So, the traveler, the tiger, and the hare all went to the pitfall where the tiger had been trapped. The hare said to the tiger, "I must see exactly how you were before this traveler rescued you. Where exactly were you?"

Eager to show where he was, the tiger jumped right into the pitfall. The hare asked, "Was this felled tree in the pitfall when you fell into it, Mr. Tiger?"

"No, it was not."

So, the hare and the traveler took the tree out of the pitfall. The hare, then, said to the traveler, "Mr. Traveler, be on your way. All is fair now." And the hare, too, hopped away.[105]

---

[105] *http://www.csun.edu/~hcedu004/*

Learning Questions

1. Why did the tiger want to kill the human after he had rescued him?
2. Why did the ox and pine tree agree with the tiger about the human?
3. Are you fair with the people in your life? Name one way you show fairness.

You Show Fairness When You:

- Choose the right.
- Treat others kindly, no matter how different they are.
- Take turns when you're playing with others.
- Are friends with everyone.
- Never gossip.
- Treat others as you would like to be treated.

FLEXIBILITY

Flexibility

Definition Flexibility: Being moveable without breaking; adapting easily to different conditions.

Quotes

"Change is the law of life, and those who look only to the past or the present are certain to miss the future."

John F. Kennedy[106]

"The ability to recognize opportunities and move in new - and sometimes unexpected - directions will benefit you, no matter your interests or aspirations."

Drew Gilpin Faust[107]

Explanation

Flexibility means being willing to change when necessary. Many times during our lives unexpected things happen that require us to be flexible and to do things differently. Sometimes the changes we make are just temporary – for a little while – and sometimes the changes last a long time.

Flexibility means being open to new ideas or other people's ways of doing things. When you are flexible you don't insist on doing things your own particular way, and you don't always require other people to do things your way. Instead, you are open to the ideas of others and you're willing to change your mind and do things their way, if their way is better.

Flexible people understand that if one way doesn't work, they should try another way. They can look honestly at themselves and their choices, then decide if their ideas are best, or if other ideas are better.

Flexible people are usually successful because they keep making positive changes. They adjust, adapt, and continue getting better and better. As they keep thinking of better ways to do things they accomplish more and they improve.

On the other hand, people who won't change just keep doing things in the same old ways; they aren't flexible and they don't improve their lives. A key to happiness is to accept things you

---

[106] Glenn Van Ekeren. *Speaker's Sourcebook II*. 1994. Paramus, New Jersey: Prentice Hall, 56
[107] https://www.brainyquote.com/quotes/drew_gilpin_faust_645247?src=t_flexibility

cannot change, to recognize things that need to be changed, and to be flexible as you keep moving forward.

Story for Young Children

Every day at school, Jack's class would do things in the same order. He liked that, because he liked to know what was going to happen next. First, they would all do morning work, then math. They did that every day: first their morning work, then math.

One day after morning work Jack's teacher, Mrs. Wheeler, told everyone to get out their science notebooks and jackets, then line up to go outside. She said they were going to do an experiment. Everyone else got their things and lined up, but Jack stayed at his desk and got his math book out.

Mrs. Wheeler told Jack that the class would do math later, and that he needed to line up. When he refused to move, she had Ms. Jensen, the principal, come and talk to him.

Ms. Jensen said, "Jack, you need to learn to be flexible."

Jack knew that when the gym teacher wanted him to be flexible, Jack had to move and touch his toes, but Jack didn't know what being flexible with his body had to do with changing math time.

Ms. Jensen said 'flexible' meant that if something changes, like a schedule, Jack needed to change with it. If Mrs. Wheeler changes math time, she probably has a good reason. "You need to trust Mrs. Wheeler, Jack. She won't let you down," said Ms. Jensen.

Jack learned that sometimes schedules can change suddenly. When they do, Jack decided that he would do his best to be flexible - to change with it.[108]

Learning Questions

1. Why was Jack upset?
2. After Jack understood flexibility, what did he decide to do?
3. Why is flexibility important?

Story for Older Children

<u>Hang In There</u>

Long ago, Nicolo Paganini was a famous violinist. He was also well known as a great showman with a quick sense of humor. His most memorable concert was in Italy with a full orchestra. He was performing before a packed house and his technique was incredible, his tone was fantastic, and his audience dearly loved him. Toward the end of his concert, Paganini was astounding his audience with an unbelievable composition when suddenly one string on his violin snapped and

---

[108] https://study.com/academy/lesson/social-stories-on-being-flexible.html

hung limply from his instrument. Paganini frowned briefly, shook his head, and continued to play, improvising beautifully. Then to everyone's surprise, a second string broke. And shortly thereafter, a third. Almost like a slapstick comedy, Paganini stood there with three strings dangling from his Stradivarius violin. But instead of leaving the stage, Paganini stood his ground and calmly completed the difficult number on the one remaining string.[109]

Learning Questions

1. Why did Paganini's performance require flexibility?
2. Have you ever had things go wrong and you had to be flexible?
3. What did you do?

You Show Flexibility When You:

- Understand that unexpected things in life sometimes require change.
- Are willing to change when necessary.
- Know that some changes are temporary and some changes are permanent.
- Are willing to consider other people's opinions and ideas.
- Can look at your ideas honestly and decide if your way is best, or if another way is better.
- Can change your mind and do things differently when necessary.
- Can continue adjusting and adapting; continue thinking of ways to improve.

---

[109] Author Unknown, http://www.inspirationalstories.com

FORGIVENESS

Forgiveness

Definition Forgiveness: To have no ill feelings, blame or resentment toward people who make mistakes.

Quotes

"They who forgive most shall be most forgiven."

William Blake[110]

"There is no love without forgiveness, and there is no forgiveness without love."

Bryant H. McGill[111]

Explanation

You show forgiveness when you do not stay angry at people who do things that are wrong or that you don't like. Even if you can still remember what they did that you didn't like, you let go of your anger.

In your heart you forgive a person by thinking, "I forgive you, and I'll give you another chance. I'll also try to forget what you did." Then you try sincerely to forget the mistake and act toward him (or her) as if it never happened.

Since we all make mistakes in our lives, we all need to be forgiven. It is very important that we learn how to quickly forgive one another.

It is also important to forgive yourself when you've done something disappointing or wrong. This is how you do it: first, you admit your mistake; you recognize that you were wrong. Second, you do whatever it takes to make it right, if possible. This includes apologizing to the person you wronged. Third, you try your best not to make the mistake again. Fourth, you don't think about your wrong-doing over and over again; you try to forget it and move on with your life.

Although you should try not to make mistakes, you can learn valuable lessons from mistakes. At the very least you learn what doesn't work, and you try not to do it that way again.

---

[110] Stevenson, Burton. 1934. *The Home Book of Quotations: Classical and Modern.* Binghamton, New York: Vail-Ballou Press, 709

[111] https://www.brainyquote.com/quotes/bryant_h_mcgill_168276?src=t_forgiveness

Story for Young Children

<u>Hand-Painted Tie</u>

As the school bus bumped along the rough road, Kathryn bounced with excitement.

"You should see my Father's Day gift!" she told Cheryl.

Kathryn said, "Mr. Hansen, my art teacher, stayed after school for a few days to help me. It's a hand-painted tie with all the nice colors my dad likes."

"Do you have it with you?" asked Cheryl.

"It's in my room, ready to be wrapped," Kathryn answered with a smile.

"What if your dad goes into your room and sees it?" Cheryl said.

"He won't. Dad left for work early this morning and he won't be home until after I get home from school."

The bus slowed for Kathryn's stop. Her spirits soared as she raced into her home and up the stairs. It was time to wrap her gift. But as soon as she reached the second floor, she knew something was wrong. Her bedroom door was wide open.

She ran into her bedroom and found her four-year-old brother sitting on the carpet, holding what was left of the treasured tie. Tie scraps surrounded the shiny scissors on the floor. Sammy's pudgy fingers worked to knot the ragged tie about his neck, and when he glanced up, a big smile creased his round face.

"See? I look like Daddy!" Sammy said happily.

Kathryn screamed, "How could you, Sammy? You've ruined it!"

She dragged herself downstairs, collapsed onto a kitchen chair, and sobbed. Her mother was speaking on the phone, jotting notes on a pad. When she saw Kathryn she said,

"Let me call you back. Something's come up."

In one movement, Mom was in a nearby chair. The story of the tie spilled out, and Mom nodded, her face serious.

"Now what am I going to do? cried Kathryn. "I have no gift for Dad. And I worked so hard on that tie!"

"I'm so sorry," Mom said. "This must be a terrible disappointment. And now you have even more hard work ahead of you."

"You mean making another tie?"

"No, I mean forgiving Sammy."

"After what he did? No way!"

"As I said, it's hard work. Forgiveness isn't just words. Forgiveness includes completely getting rid of your angry feelings."

Stunned, Kathryn left the kitchen. Forgive her brother for wrecking Dad's gift? How could she? Why should she?

Kathryn sat on the steps, trying to deal with her feelings. As she sat there, she argued silently with herself, "I shouldn't have left it on my desk…Sammy shouldn't have gone into my room, either—that was my private space- but four-year-olds don't understand privacy."

With a wince, Kathryn recalled the pride and innocent pleasure on Sammy's face as he showed her that he just wanted to be like Dad. He wasn't trying to hurt anyone, and Kathryn realized that Sammy must have been hurt by what she said.

With growing joy, Kathryn realized she had feelings of love not only for Dad and Mom but for Sammy too.

She hurried back to her room. Kneeling, she hugged Sammy tightly. "I wanted to give Dad a super gift," she explained. "That's why I was upset by what you did. But you're special to me too. Next time we'll make a gift from both of us."

"I think you just gave me a special gift," Dad said from the doorway.

Kathryn got to her feet, holding out the tie. "Sorry, Dad."

"Sorry that you're a kind person who puts people ahead of material things? Don't ever be sorry for that. I'm proud that you're my daughter."

Kathryn flew into his arms. The wonderful sense of joy that she had felt on the stairs returned stronger than ever. Her family was much more important than a piece of colored cloth.[112]

Learning Questions

1. What made forgiving Sammy so hard for Kathryn?
2. How did Kathryn's forgiveness affect her family?
3. Name one time you forgave another person.

---

[112] Arnold Madison, "Hand-Painted Tie," Friend, June 1994, 30

Story for Older Children

<u>Building Bridges</u>

Once upon a time two brothers who lived on adjoining farms had a quarrel. It was the first serious rift in 40 years of farming side by side, sharing machinery, and trading labor and goods as needed.

The long collaboration fell apart with a small misunderstanding that grew into a major difference. It finally exploded into an exchange of bitter words followed by weeks of silence.

One morning there was a knock on the older brother's door. He opened it to find a man with a carpenter's toolbox. "I'm looking for a few days of work" he said. "Perhaps you would have a few small jobs here and there. Could I help you?"

"Yes," said the older brother. "I do have a job for you. Look across the creek at that farm. That's my neighbor, in fact, it's my younger brother. Last week there was a meadow between us, and he took his bulldozer to the river levee and now there is a creek between us. Well, he may have done this to spite me, but I'll give him one better. See that pile of lumber curing by the barn? I want you to build me a fence – an 8-foot fence – so I won't need to see his place anymore. It'll cool him down, anyhow."

The carpenter said, "I think I understand this situation. Show me the nails and the post-hole digger and I'll be able to do a job that pleases you." The older brother needed to go to town for supplies, so he helped the carpenter get the materials ready and then he was off for the day.

The carpenter worked hard all that day measuring, sawing, and nailing. About sunset when the farmer returned, the carpenter had just finished his job. The farmer viewed the job with his eyes wide open and his jaw dropped. There was no fence there at all! It was a bridge – a bridge stretching from one side of the creek to the other! A fine piece of work with handrails and all. The neighbor, his younger brother, was coming across smiling, with his hand outstretched.

"You are quite a fellow to build this bridge after all I've said and done." The two brothers stood at each end of the bridge, and then they met in the middle, taking each other's hands. They turned to see the carpenter hoist his toolbox on his shoulder. "No, wait! Stay a few days," they exclaimed.

"I have a lot of other projects for you," said the older brother.

"I'd love to stay on," the carpenter said, "but I have many more bridges to build."[113]

Learning Questions

---

[113] Author Unknown, http://www.inspirationalstories.com

1. What do you think would have happened if the carpenter had built the fence as the older brother had asked?
2. Is there someone you can forgive right now?
3. How will forgiving them make you feel?

You Show Forgiveness When You:

- Don't stay angry when people make mistakes.
- Think, "I'll forgive you and give you another chance."
- Sincerely try to forget the mistake.
- Act toward the person who made the mistake as if it never happened.
- Forgive yourself.
- Try to learn lessons from mistakes.

FRIENDSHIP

Friendship

Definition Friendship: Caring, sharing, and concern between two or more people.

Quotes

"Be careful of the environment you choose for it will shape you. Be careful of the friends you choose for you will become like them."
W. Clement Stone[114]

"Friends in your life are like pillars on your porch. Sometimes they hold you up, and sometimes they lean on you. Sometimes it's just enough to know they're standing by."

Elizabeth Foley[115]

Explanation

Friendship means sincerely sharing with another person. Friends share their deep heartfelt thoughts and feelings. They share their time, compassion, interests, ideas, and love.

Friends share both the good times and the bad times in their lives. This sharing acts like a chain that ties two or more people together. The chain is created one link at a time as friends share more and more with one another. Through the years friendships usually become stronger as people continue to share their lives.

Friendship is also about making others feel comfortable and welcome. Especially when you are away from home you appreciate friendly people who smile, ask about you, and try to see that you're comfortable. Friendly people sincerely care about you and your well-being.

Friends are kind to one another. True friends only speak kindly about each other; they are loyal. True friends forgive one another quickly and always support and encourage each other through the good times and hard times.

Story for Young Children

<u>My Best Friend</u>

My name is Henry, and I want to tell you about my best friend. Sometimes my friend and I dress

---

114 Glenn Van Ekeren. *Speaker's Sourcebook II*. 1994. Paramus, New Jersey: Prentice Hall, 164
115 Glenn Van Ekeren. *Speaker's Sourcebook II*. 1994. Paramus, New Jersey: Prentice Hall, 164

alike and pretend we're great explorers. Then we discover new countries and conquer awful monsters to protect our people. Sometimes I'm the king, and sometimes my friend is the king. We always take turns.

I am learning to read, and I like books about dinosaurs. My friend is already a good reader. He likes books about faraway countries. We read all kinds of books together. It's lots of fun, and we learn a lot!

On Saturdays, my friend and I like to ride our bikes. We love the way the wind feels on our faces, especially when we go downhill. At the top of hills we sometimes stop to rest and look up at the clouds. We imagine they are flying alligators or giant ice-cream cones.

Sometimes my friend goes away on trips, and I always miss him when he's gone. But he always sends me a postcard. My favorite one is from Alaska. It has a picture of a big moose on the front. On the back my friend wrote a message. He said he likes having me for a friend. That made me feel happy.

My mom says I'm very lucky to have such a great best friend. I think she's right. My best friend is my dad.[116]

Learning Questions
1. What kind of fun things do you do with your best friend?
2. Are you friendly to other people?
3. What would you do if someone you knew didn't have any friends?

Story for Older Children

True Friendship

Darkness filled the corners of the dungeon under the castle. All about on the hard floor lay men who had been arrested by the ruler's soldiers. Most of them had been condemned to death. A hopeless silence filled the room so that the low words of the young man outside the barred door sounded loud and angry.

"What did you do, my good friend, Pythias?" the young man demanded. "What did you do that so displeased the king?"

The prisoner at the door sighed. His hand reached through the narrow bars and touched his friend's arm. Since early childhood these two had always been together. Now Pythias knew that he was going to leave his friend forever and his heart ached at the thought of this separation.

"I did nothing, Damon," he insisted, "but the King has claimed that I am a rebel. There is nothing that can be done about it."

------

[116] Lynnanne Eddington, "My Best Friend," *Friend,* Sep 1990, 30

"Then what can I do for you?" Damon asked. "Shall I go to your home and comfort your parents?"

Neither of the young men had heard the great outer door open. They did not see the ruler as he came near to them.

"I would like to see them myself once more," Pythias' voice was hopeless. "I would come back here and pay with my life if I could only say farewell to them."

A loud laugh startled the two young men. Damon whirled and found himself face to face with his king. Quickly he bowed and waited for the ruler to speak. Again, the king laughed as he looked at the prisoner.

"So, you would come back to die if I would let you go to your distant home?" he mocked Pythias and all the prisoners.

"I would come back," Pythias stated simply. "I promise."

"How do I know that you would keep your promise?" the king's eyes narrowed as he watched the man. "You are trying to cheat me. You cannot go."

"Then let me stay in prison in his place," Damon looked straight at the king as he made his request. "He has never broken a promise, but if he does not return, I will die for him on the day that is set for his execution."

The king was amused. This strange request would make a delightful story to tell his friends. A young man who offered to die for his friend! This was the best jest of the year and he and his courtiers would watch it with interest.

Soon the prison door closed behind Damon, and Pythias was on his way home. The days passed and the day of execution came nearer and nearer. Day by day the king came to the prison to taunt the foolish young man. Again and again his cruel laughter rang out.

"If Pythias does not come back, it will not be his fault," Damon stated calmly, "Something will have happened to him."

At last, the day for the execution arrived and Pythias had not returned. The king and his courtiers jeered at Damon as he was led from the cell.

"The man who dies for his friend, a false friend," they called out. "We told you that he would not return."

"He will come if he can," Damon said to himself as he walked straight and tall in the line of condemned men. "He will come if…"

"Here he comes! Here he comes!" a soldier ran shouting to the king.

Damon smiled as he saw his friend. Pythias was hardly able to breathe. Storms and misfortunes had beset him all of the way back. He had feared that Damon would die before he could arrive. His face beamed with happiness when he found his friend alive. Quickly he fell into the line of prisoners and gently pushed Damon aside.

"I came," Pythias panted.

"I knew you would!" responded Damon.

The king could hardly believe his eyes and ears. Never had he known that there could be such friendship. His heart softened before such a great love.

"Go!" he said to the two young men. "Go back to your homes."

Then he turned to his stunned courtiers and added, "I would give all my wealth to have one such friend!"[117]

Learning Questions

1. How do you show your friendship to your friends?
2. How do you show your friendship to your family?
3. How have others shown friendship to you?

You Show Friendship When You:

- Smile and greet others warmly.
- Share your heartfelt thoughts and feelings with your friends.
- Tell people your name and ask about them.
- Are sincerely interested in others and in their well-being.
- Show that you care about people by helping them to be comfortable and happy.
- Never talk about people unkindly.
- Forgive quickly.
- Are loyal, supportive and encouraging.

---

[117] A Greek myth adapted by Jewel Varnado, Especially for M, pp. 129-131.

GENEROSITY

Generosity

Definition Generosity: Giving and sharing happily.

Quotes

"What's mine is yours, and what is yours is mine."

William Shakespeare[118]

"I'd rather be a beggar and spend my last dollar like a king, than be a king and spend my money like a beggar."

Robert G. Ingersoll[119]

Explanation

Generosity is giving of yourself or giving away something without expecting anything in return.

Generous people understand that the most important things in life are not things. These people realize that when you have plenty, especially when you have more than you need, you should share with others.

It is a good idea to *look for ways to be generous* and share with others. Ask yourself, "What can I do to help my family?" Or, "How can I help my neighbors?" Ideas will probably come to you easily when you ask those questions.

Since there are many people in this world who need help, there are many opportunities to generously give. You can give many different things. You can share your time, knowledge, or money. You can share possessions, wisdom, compassion, and love. For example, you can lend your bike to a friend who doesn't have one. You can share your lunch or help someone who doesn't understand a math problem. You can visit a sick relative, or tend a baby (for free) while his or her mother goes shopping

You may think that you have very little to give, but *it's the way you give that counts.* If you give a gift because you think you have to, and you do it with a complaining, unhappy heart, then you

---

[118] *Five Thousand Quotations for All Occasions.* 1945. Edited by Lewis C. Henry. Garden City, New York: DoubleDay & Company, Inc., 152

[119] Stevenson, Burton. 1934. *The Home Book of Quotations: Classical and Modern.* Binghamton, New York: Vail-Ballou Press, 777

aren't being sincerely generous. And you won't enjoy the same happy feelings that come when you give cheerfully.

On the other hand, people with real generosity always feel good about themselves after they give, because they know they have unselfishly helped make another person happy.

Story for Young Children

You Can Share My Daddy

As I sat in the garden weeding, my four-year-old neighbor came over to the fence and settled down to supervise my activities. Since her mother had just had a baby the previous week, she was allowed more freedom to entertain herself and explore her world.

The little girl asked endless questions about what this was and why that was, and she finally asked about a metal object that had been fastened on the fence. I told her that I didn't know exactly what it was, but I thought it was something that my father had put there for some reason or another.

She looked around the yard carefully and said, "Where is your daddy? Is he at work?"

I explained to her that he had died several years ago, and that was how I came to live in the house.

She thought about this for a minute and then asked, "Well, then did you get a new daddy?"

I was not sure how to answer her, so I just went with the simple truth and said, "No, I didn't."

She thought about that for a moment, as if the prospect of not having a daddy was just too complex to embrace, and then she suddenly offered a solution that made sense to her. "You can share my daddy, if you want to. He is a very good daddy, and I don't think he would mind."[120]

Learning Questions

1. How did the little girl in this story show generosity in this story?
2. Tell about a time when you were generous with someone and shared something of yours.
3. How does it make you feel when you're sincerely generous?

Story for Older Children

The Circus

Once when I was a teenager, my father and I were standing in line to buy tickets for the circus. Finally, there was only one family between us and the ticket counter. This family made a big

---

[120] Linda L. Kerby, "You Can Share My Daddy," *Chicken Soup for the Father's Soul*, 126–127.

impression on me. There were eight children, all probably under the age of 12. You could tell they didn't have a lot of money. Their clothes were not expensive, but they were clean. The children were well-behaved, all of them standing in line, two-by-two behind their parents, holding hands. They were excitedly jabbering about the clowns, elephants and other acts they would see that night. One could sense they had never been to the circus before. It promised to be a highlight of their young lives.

The ticket lady asked the father how many tickets he wanted. He proudly responded, "Please let me buy eight children's tickets and two adult tickets so I can take my family to the circus." The ticket lady quoted the price. The man's wife let go of his hand, her head dropped, the man's lip began to quiver.

The father leaned a little closer and asked, "How much did you say?" The ticket lady again quoted the price. The man didn't have enough money. How was he supposed to turn and tell his children that he didn't have enough money to take them to the circus?

Seeing what was going on, my dad put his hand into his pocket, pulled out a $20 bill and dropped it on the ground. (We were not a wealthy family.) My father reached down, picked up the bill, tapped the man on the shoulder and said, "Excuse me, sir, this fell out of your pocket."

The man knew what was going on. He wasn't begging for a handout but certainly appreciated my father's generosity in a desperate, heartbreaking, embarrassing situation. He looked straight into my dad's eyes, took my dad's hand in both of his, squeezed tightly onto the $20 bill, and with tears in his eyes he replied, "Thank you, thank you, sir. This really means a lot to me and my family."

My father and I went back to our car and drove home. We didn't go to the circus that night, but I learned a wonderful lesson I'd never forget.[121]

Learning Questions

1. What was the lesson the boy learned that night?
2. How do you feel when you are generous?
3. Tell about someone in your life who was generous to you.

You Show Generosity When You:

- Share something without expecting anything in return.
- Look for ways to help others.
- Understand that many people need help.
- Look for ways to help others.
- Share parts of yourself like your time, knowledge, and love.
- Realize the importance of sharing with others and helping others, without expecting a reward.

---

[121] Dan Clark, *A 2nd Helping of Chicken Soup for the Soul*, pp. 3-4

GENTLENESS

Gentleness

Definition Gentleness: Speaking and acting kindly.

Quotes

"When you encounter difficulties and contradictions, do not try to break them, but bend them with gentleness and time."

Saint Francis de Sales[122]

"There is nothing stronger in the world than gentleness."

Han Suyin[123]

Explanation

Gentleness is thinking, speaking, and acting kindly and carefully.

Gentle people are considerate and thoughtful. They care about the possessions and feelings of others. They speak and act in ways that don't hurt people, animals, or things.

Gentle people talk without getting angry. They control their tones of voice, words, and actions.

When you are gentle, you think kind thoughts. When you speak you say kind words that make people feel good. You are careful not to hurt anyone's feelings. When you play you are careful and you try your best not to break things.

Animals and people aren't afraid when they're treated gently. Animals like to be touched softly and spoken to lovingly. Everyone likes to be spoken to lovingly.

Do you know someone who is gentle? Everyone who knew Mother Teresa said she was a gentle person. She was a Catholic nun who helped the sick and dying people in Calcutta, India. Mother Teresa was kind, loving, and soft-spoken. She once said, "Let no one ever come to you without leaving better and happier." Isn't that good advice? Gentle people help make this world a better place.

---

[122] http://www.quotationspage.com
[123] http://www.quotationspage.com

Story for Young Children

The Sun and Wind

A fable is told about a quarrel the North Wind had with the Sun about who was more powerful. They finally agreed to settle their argument with a wager: the first to cause a wayfaring man to strip away his clothing would be the victor.

The North Wind huffed and puffed and blew with all his might, but the more it blew, the closer the traveler wrapped his cloak around him. He finally gave up and the Sun moved in to have a turn.

The Sun happily shone with all its warmth. As the rays warmed the traveler, he took off first one garment and then the next. At last, nearly overcome by the radiant heat, he undressed completely and plunged himself into a stream for a cool and soothing swim.

The Sun turned to the North Wind and said, "Gentleness is better than force."

Criticism and harsh demands can turn a warm heart cold. Rebellion is more likely to be the result than improved performance. In contrast, praise and encouragement warm the heart. The person who feels appreciated not only follows the leader who gives such praise but turns in a better performance.[124]

Learning Questions

1. How did the sun win the competition?
2. Do you know someone who is gentle?
3. How can you show gentleness in your family and with your friends?

Story for Older Children

Cookies

While at summer camp, a small boy named Billy received a large package of cookies in the mail from his mother. He ate a few, then placed the remainder under his bed. The next day, after lunch, he went to get a cookie and the box was gone.

That afternoon a camp counselor, who had been told of the theft, saw another boy sitting behind a tree eating the stolen cookies. "That young man," he said to himself, 'must be taught not to steal."

He returned to the group and sought out the boy whose cookies had been stolen. "Billy," he said, "I know you stole your cookies. Will you help me teach him a lesson?"

---

[124] God's Little Devotional Book for Leaders, p. 171.

"Well, yes – but aren't you going to punish him?" asked the puzzled boy.

"No, that would only make him resent and dislike you," the counselor explained. " I want you to call your mother and ask her to send you another box of cookies."

The boy did as the counselor asked and a few days later received another box of cookies in the mail.

"Now," said the counselor, "the boy who stole your cookies is down by the lake. Go down there and share your cookies with him."

"But," protested the boy, "he's the thief!"

"I know. But try it – see what happens."

Half an hour later the camp counselor saw the two boys come up the hill, arm in arm. The boy who had stolen the cookies was earnestly trying to get the other to accept his jackknife in payment for the stolen cookies, and the victim was just as earnestly refusing the gift from his new friend, saying that a few old cookies weren't that important anyway.[125]

Learning Questions

1. How did the boy whose cookies were stolen show gentleness?
2. What do you think would have happened if he had not been gentle?
3. Why do you like to be treated gently?

You Show Gentleness When You:

- Think, speak, and act kindly and carefully.
- Show thoughtfulness and consideration for other people's things.
- Care about the feelings of others.
- Talk softly and lovingly.
- Carefully touch things, animals, and people.
- Control your thoughts, words, and actions.

---

[125] Author Unknown

GRATITUDE

Gratitude

Definition Gratitude: Being thankful.

Quotes

"He enjoys much who is thankful for little; a grateful mind is both a great and a happy mind."

Thomas Secker[126]

"Gratitude is not only the greatest of virtues, but the parent of all others."

Cicero[127]

Explanation

Gratitude is being thankful. Gratitude is being happy about things like your body, your home, your family, and the world you live in. For example, when you have gratitude for the beautiful world, you notice and appreciate the weather. When it's raining you think about how the flowers, grass, and trees grow better because of the rain. You think about how people and animals need rainwater. When it's warm you notice how good it feels to be warm, and you enjoy the sunshine.

When you notice and appreciate the good things in your life you have an attitude of gratitude. Our attitudes are very important. They help us stay happy, even when bad things happen. For example, if you fall and skin your knee, you can be grateful that you didn't break your leg. If you are hungry, you can think about how nice it will feel to eat again. You can always look on the "bright side of things" if you try hard enough.

When one little boy's father died, he was very sad. But he was grateful for the years he spent with his wonderful father, and the boy was grateful that his mother was still with him every day.

It is a good idea to count your blessings often. Think about all the things you *do* have instead of the things you *don't* have. Remember that there are always people who have less than you, and there will always be people who have more than you. One secret of happiness is to be grateful for the things that you have instead of wanting more and more.

Remember, the best things in life are not things. Happiness doesn't come from things that you own; happiness comes from loving other people and helping them be happy.

---

[126] Edwards, Tryon. 1977. *The New Dictionary of Thoughts.* Stanbook, Inc., 246
[127] http://www.quotationspage.com

Story for Young Children

<u>A Gratitude Lesson</u>

Jerry wasn't happy. Although he had everything he ever wanted, he was never satisfied. He complained about his clothes. He complained about his toys. And he especially complained about his food.

One day Mom made Jerry's favorite dish – macaroni and cheese. She served it to him in his favorite bowl, gave him his favorite spoon to eat it with, and expected him to say, "Thanks! This is my favorite!" But all Jerry said was, "It isn't cheesy enough."

Mom took a deep breath – what she usually did when she was upset.

"Jerry, I've had enough! You don't like Jell-O because it falls off your spoon. You won't eat apples because they have seeds. Now you're even complaining about macaroni and cheese! I give up! Starting tomorrow, you do the cooking! See if you can make something that's just right!"

When Jerry went downstairs the next morning, Mom, Dad, and Sarah were already at the kitchen table.

"We're waiting for breakfast! We would like some pancakes please," Mom said.

"I don't know how to make pancakes. How about cereal?" asked Jerry.

"I don't want cereal today," Mom said.

"Me neither," said Dad.

"I want pancakes!" Sarah shouted.

"Get the pancake mix out of the pantry and read the directions on the box," Mom said. "I'll help you if you don't understand them."

Jerry was upset. Why couldn't they just eat cereal? But everyone was staring at him, so he got out the pancake mix.

Mom helped him figure out what to do, but it still wasn't easy. As he put the pancake mix into a big bowl, he spilled some onto the counter. And when he cracked two eggs into the mix, pieces of shell fell into the bowl. It took a while to get them out – yuck! Finally, he added the milk and stirred everything together. Jerry scooped up some batter with a measuring cup and poured it on the hot, oiled griddle Mom had prepared for him.

"Remember, son," Dad said, "I like thin, little pancakes – lots of them."

"And I like fat, round pancakes," Sarah added.

"I want big, brown, crispy ones," Mom remarked.

After a few minutes, Jerry looked at the pancakes on the griddle. None of them were thin and little, or fat and round, or brown and crispy. One pancake was flat but big. Another was round but lumpy. And the biggest one was brown, all right, but it looked soggy in the center.

Jerry put the pancakes on the three plates. He gave one to Dad, another to Mom, and the last to Sarah. Then he got out the syrup and butter and put them on the table.

"This isn't thin and little," Dad said. "It's flat and big and not even round. And there's only one!"

"My pancake looks lumpy!" Sarah said.

"And mine looks soggy in the center," Mom said. "Maybe you'd better make some more for us."

"Maybe they'll be OK once you put on the butter and syrup," said Jerry hopefully.

Mom remarked, "We'll try them, but I like melted butter, and my pancake isn't hot enough to melt it."

"I like hot syrup," said Dad.

"I like blueberry syrup," said Sarah, "and this is maple."

Jerry was getting upset. They were such complainers!

"Oh, no," he thought. "They're acting just like I do every day."

"I'll melt the butter," Jerry told Mom. "And you'll have hot syrup in just a minute, Dad. Here's your blueberry syrup Sarah. Would you like it heated?"

While the rest of the family ate their pancakes, Jerry ate his favorite cereal in his favorite bowl with his favorite spoon. No one said anything more.

After breakfast Jerry helped Mom clean up the kitchen. As she was putting the last plate into the dishwasher, he was wiping off the table.

"Mom," he said softly, "will you make the sandwiches for lunch? Any kind will be OK."

Mom didn't take a deep breath this time. She just smiled. "I'll be happy to, Jerry. And, honey, thank you for a wonderful breakfast."

Jerry smiled and said, "You're welcome, Mom…and thanks for the lesson."[128]

Learning Questions

1. Was Jerry grateful in the beginning of the story? How do you know?
2. Why did his family complain about their pancakes?
3. What was Jerry's lesson?

Story for Older Children

The Glass of Milk

One day a poor boy who was selling goods from door to door to pay his way through school, found he had only one thin dime left, and he was hungry. He decided he would ask for a meal at the next house. However, he lost his nerve when a lovely young woman opened the door.

Instead of a meal, he asked for a drink of water. She thought he looked hungry and so she brought him a large glass of milk. He drank it slowly, and then asked, "How much do I owe you?"

"You don't owe me anything," she replied. "Mother has taught us never to accept pay for a kindness." He said, "Then I thank you from my heart."

As Howard Kelly left that house, he not only felt stronger physically, but his faith in God and man was strengthened also. He had been ready to give up and quit.

Years later, that young woman became critically ill. The local doctors were baffled. They finally sent her to the big city, where they called in specialists to study her rare disease.

Dr. Howard Kelly was called in for consultation. When he heard the name of the town she came from, he went down the hall of the hospital to her room. Dressed in his doctor's gown, he went in to see her. He recognized her at once. He went back to the consultation room determined to do his best to save her life. From that day, he gave special attention to her case.

After a long struggle, the battle was won. Dr. Kelly requested from the business office to pass the final billing to him for approval. He looked at it, then wrote something on the edge, and the bill was sent to her room. She feared to open it, for she was sure it would take the rest of her life to pay for it all. Finally, she looked, and something caught her attention on the side of the bill. She read these words:

PAID IN FULL WITH ONE GLASS OF MILK.

(Signed)
Dr. Howard Kelly.

---

[128] Suzanne Lieurance, "Picky Nicky," Friend, Feb. 1993, p. 40.

Learning Questions

1. What did the doctor do to show his gratitude?
2. Why is it important to show gratitude?
3. Name five things you are grateful for in your life.

You Show Gratitude When You:

- Are thankful.
- Are happy for the things you have, and the wonderful things in the world.
- Notice and appreciate the good things in your life.
- Have an attitude of gratitude.
- Count your blessings often.
- Think about things you do have instead of things you don't have.
- Don't always want more and more.
- Understand that the best things in life aren't things.

HELPFULNESS

Helpfulness

Definition Helpfulness: Doing things to make life easier for others.

Quotes

"In giving advice seek to help, not please, your friend."

Solon[129]

"You can't help someone get up a hill without getting closer to the top yourself."

H. Norman Schwarzkopf[130]

Explanation

Helpfulness is doing things for other people, or yourself, to make life easier and/or better.

If you are a helpful person, you look for ways to help other people, and you do it cheerfully.

There are many ways you can be helpful. You can listen when someone needs to share her or his heartfelt feelings. You can clean the house or tend a pet. You can do your chores without complaining or hug a sad friend.

Every day there are many opportunities to be helpful. One of the best things you can do is ask, "What can I do to help?"

Everyone appreciates helpful people, especially those who help without being asked.

A wonderful benefit of helping others is this: usually when you do something kind for another person, good things will happen to you, and you will be happier and well-liked. This is called the "Law of the Harvest." Whatever you sow, you shall reap. In other words, all that you send into the lives of others comes back into your own. So, when you kindly help others, usually they will kindly help you.

Story for Young Children

---

[129] http://www.quotationspage.com
[130] http://www.quotationspage.com

<u>Which Loved Best?</u>

"I love you, Mother," said Little John;
Then forgetting the work, his cap went on;
And he was off to the garden swing,
Leaving his mother the wood to bring.
"I love you, Mother." said Rosey Nell
"I love you better than tongue can tell."
Then she teased and pouted full half the day,
'Till her Mother rejoiced when she went to play.
"I love you, Mother," said Little Nan.
Today I'll help you all I can.
How glad I am that school doesn't keep."
So she rocked the baby till it fell asleep.
Then stepping softly, she fetched the broom
And swept the floor and tidied the room.
Busy and happy all day was she,
Useful and helpful as a child can be.
"I love you, Mother," again they all said.
Three little children going to bed.
How do you think that Mother guessed
Which of them really loved her best?[131]

Learning Questions

1. Which child showed her love best?
2. Name three ways you can be helpful at home.
3. How does your family feel when you are helpful?

Story for Older Children

<u>A Song in the Night</u>

One of the joys of my life centers in the songs I learned as a child in my home. Never a soloist, I have received great satisfaction in being a humble part of any chorus--in a school choir, in the church choir, and with the birds outside my kitchen window.

When I am discouraged or worried, I go out to my garden and pick up a watering hose and sing myself into a better mood.

Sometimes I have to sing loudly to give myself the courage to overcome my challenges. Never was the need more urgent than on a hot summer night several seasons ago when I went out into the dark while a loved one slept inside, recovering from illness.

---

[131] Joy Allison, Jack M. Lyon et al., eds., *Best-Loved Poems of the LDS People* (Salt Lake City: Deseret Book, 1996), 217-218

I was tired and discouraged, and the tension showed in my voice. How fortunate it was, I thought, that everybody within listening distance was away. One neighbor was at the beach, another at the nearby mountains, a third vacationing in another state. The little house on the side street was completely dark, so I supposed this neighbor, whom I knew but slightly, was away also.

Thus isolated, I started to sing, but my voice broke. Again, I tried and had to give it up as a bad job. Finally, with almost a yell, I made a third attempt and managed to stay on tune and sing brightly.

For over an hour I sang, totally undisturbed and feeling completely alone on my little island of depression. Then I went indoors, rested enough by the comfort of the songs, to fall into a deep but troubled sleep.

The next morning there was a knock at my door. There stood the slightly known neighbor, looking wan and pale. She moved shakily into a chair. "I came to thank you for singing those glorious songs last night. You will never know how much I needed them."

I told her I had thought I was singing to myself to keep up my own courage. "You strengthened me," she said. "I learned yesterday that I must have extensive medical care and must move from here to live with my daughter. I was lying in bed fighting the move with all my heart. Now it is all right, there is peace in my heart, and I can do what is necessary."

When she left, I reflected anew how we are a part of each other in this life and that it matters indeed how well we bear our own burdens, for unknown to us someone may be needing us for strength and courage.

Out of my temporary discouragement and heartache I had sung songs for my neighbor who needed their solace too, and she gained the courage she needed. I was determined to remember that there are special blessings when you face life with a song in your heart.[132]

Learning Questions

1. Has someone been helpful to you lately? What did they do?
2. How did it make you feel?
3. What can you do this week to be helpful?

You show helpfulness when you:

- Do things for people that make their lives easier or better.
- Serve others cheerfully.
- Look for ways to be helpful.
- Listen.

---

[132] Ruth C. Ikerman, "A Song in the Night," *Especially for M*, V 4, pp. 259-260.

- Clean the house.
- Tend a pet.
- Do your chores without complaining.
- Show love.
- Ask, "What can I do to help?"
- Help without being asked.

HONESTY

Honesty

Definition Honesty: Being truthful and trustworthy.

Quotes

"Honesty means having integrity in everything you do. Honesty means wholeness, completeness; it means being truthful in everything- in deed and in word."

Orison Swett Marden[133]

"The truth is incontrovertible, malice may attack it, ignorance may deride it, but in the end; there it is."

Winston Churchill[134]

Explanation

Being honest is acting in honest ways and telling the truth. Even when it is easier to be dishonest and lie, when you live your life honestly, you tell the truth no matter what the consequences may be.

People trust you when you're honest. They know that when you speak you will only tell them what is true and right. When you are honest and you make a mistake, you say so right away. You say, "I'm sorry. I made a mistake. This is what happened…" And you tell the truth.

Then you say, "I'll try to never do that again." People will be happy when you talk like that, and they will know you are trying to be honest.

Honest people don't cheat or steal. They never take things that don't belong to them.

Also, when you're honest you try your best to live the values you believe in. For example, if you really believe in patience, you kindly wait for others without getting upset. If you believe in obedience, then as soon as your parents call you, you obey quickly and cheerfully. If you say you believe in something and your actions don't show it, that's not being honest.

Additionally, when you're honest, you give your best effort to everything you do.

---

[133] Glenn Van Ekeren. *Speaker's Sourcebook II*. 1994. Paramus, New Jersey: Prentice Hall, 193
[134] Glenn Van Ekeren. *Speaker's Sourcebook II*. 1994. Paramus, New Jersey: Prentice Hall, 193

Also, honest people don't pretend they are something that they aren't. They don't say or do things to try and look good. Always remember that you don't need to make things up just to look good, because people love you just the way you are.

Marvin J. Aston wrote, "How great it is to resolve that we are going to be totally honest with ourselves, that we will have real integrity. Don't allow yourself to perform shabbily. Be proud of yourself, truly proud. Develop self-respect, poise, personality, and especially honesty in your total personal conduct. You don't know how many people are looking at you and copying you. It behooves each of us to be honest in our personal lives so others can follow someone who is sincere, who teaches well through his or her actions. Others are counting on you to have personal pride, patience, and performance. Others are watching you – often unannounced – and they don't want you to let them down. They're counting on you and your example so they in turn can go forward and have an influence on other people. To do this, you must be honest with yourself."[135]

Honesty always brings happiness.

Story for Young Children

<u>An Honest Boy</u>

Today I saw truth. For a moment I lived and breathed in the great presence of truth and felt its sweetness plunge deep into my soul.

I am a coach in a junior high school. I work with 500 boys each day. This has been my occupation for over 20 years. I enjoy it.

Traditionally, l am supposed to be rugged, tough, crusty; yes, even a little severe at times – and yet, underneath this exterior, feeling and understanding must exist if the job is to be done.

Today was test day in rope climbing. We climb from a standing start to a point 15 feet high. One of my tasks these past few weeks has been to train and teach the boys to negotiate this distance in as few seconds as possible.

The school record for the event is 2.1 seconds. It has stood for three years. Today this record was broken but this is not my story. How this record was broken is the important thing here, as it so often is in many endeavors in this life.

For three years Bobby Polacio, a 14 1/2-year-old ninth grade Mexican boy, has trained and pointed and, I suspect, dreamed of breaking this record. It has been his consuming passion; it seemed his whole life depended upon owning this record.

In his first of three attempts Bobby climbed the rope in 2.1 seconds, tying the record. On the second try the watch stopped at 2.0 seconds flat, a record! But as he descended the rope and the entire class gathered around to check the watch, I knew I must ask Bobby a question. There was

---

[135] Marvin J. Ashton, "We Believe in Being Honest," *New Era,* Sep 1983, 4

a slight doubt in my mind whether or not the board at the 15-foot height had been touched. If he missed, it was so very, very close – not more than a fraction of an inch – and only Bobby knew this answer.

As he walked toward me, expressionless, I said, "Bobby, did you touch?" If he had said, "Yes," the record he had dreamed of since he was a skinny seventh grader and had worked for almost daily would be his, and he knew I would trust his word.

With the class already cheering him for his performance, the slim, brown-skinned boy shook his head negatively. And in this simple gesture, I witnessed a moment of greatness.

Coaches usually do not cry. But as I reached out to pat this boy on the shoulder, there was a small drop of water in each eye. And it was with effort through a tight throat that I told the class: "This boy has not set a record in the rope climb. No, he has set a much finer record for you and everyone to strive for. He has told the simple truth."

I turned to Bobby and said, "Bobby, I'm proud of you. You've just set a record many athletes never attain. Now, in your last try I want you to jump a few inches higher on the takeoff. You're going to break this record."

After the other boys had finished their next turns, and Bobby was ready for his last try, a strange stillness came over the gymnasium. Fifty boys and one coach were breathlessly set to help boost Bobby Polacio to a record. He climbed the rope in 1.9 seconds! A school record, a city record. And perhaps close to a national record for a junior high school boy.

When the bell rang and I walked away, now misty-eyed, from this group of boys, I was thinking: "Bobby, little brown skin, with your clear, bright dark eyes and your straight trim, lithe body- Bobby, at 14 you are better man than I. Thank you for climbing so very, very high today."[136]

Learning Questions

1. Do you think it was hard for Bobby to tell the truth?
2. How do you think Bobby felt when he set the record honestly?
3. Name one way you can be honest.

Story for Older Children

George Jones began his career as a clerk in a crockery store. He soon gained a reputation as being a bright, ambitious employee — a young man known for good work habits, fine manners, and an easy-going personality. The foremost traits people referred to when praising George, however, were his honesty and trustworthiness.

It was this reputation that came to the attention of Henry Raymond, a renowned journalist, and together Raymond and Jones started the New York Times.

---

[136] "Come Listen to a Prophet's Voice: Honesty: A Moral Compass," *Friend*, Nov 2001, 2.

Mr. Jones continued to live up to his reputation. His loyalty to Raymond, and his honesty as a businessman, won him great repute in New York City.

Then the Times began a crusade against Boss Tweed and his corrupt dynasty. Jones received an under-the-table offer of $500,000 — a vast sum at the time — from associates of Tweed.

All he had to do was retire to Europe. "You can live like a prince the rest of your days," said the man making the offer. But Jones replied, "Yes, and know myself every day to be a rascal."

A clean conscience can't be bought. That is what makes it so highly valued. Keeping a clean conscience is as simple as deciding to. Decide not to let tempting offers influence you, and when you do, you'll gain the strength necessary to overcome other temptations.[137]

Learning Questions

1.   What kind of a reputation did George Jones have?
2.   How do people get good reputations?
3.   What kind of reputation do you think you have?

You Show Honesty When You:

- Tell the truth, even when it's hard.
- Live so that your actions match your beliefs.
- Never cheat or steal.
- When you make a mistake, admit it right away.
- Try your best not to make the same mistake again.
- Give everything you do your best effort.
- Don't pretend.
- Don't say or do things to look good.
- Do what you know is right, every day.

---

[137] God's Little Devotional Book for Leaders, p. 141

HONOR

Honor

Definition Honor: Living the values that you know are right.

Quotes

"No one can acquire honor by doing what is wrong."

Thomas Jefferson[138]

"Mine honor is my life; both grow in one. Take honor from me and my life is done."

William Shakespeare[139]

Explanation

When you act with honor you live the values you believe in. You are honest, obedient, kind, friendly, and respectful. You make good choices every day.

Honorable people are respected and admired. They set good examples for others.

When you are honorable, you are not ashamed of your good choices. You don't make excuses for your decisions or the way you live your life.

When you act with honor it can give others the courage to act that way too. For example, when you're honest, people see how honesty contributes to the joy and goodness in your life and they may want to be honest also.

However, even if other people don't choose to live honorable lives and if they don't make good choices, you would continue to do so – regardless of their decisions. If you are a person of honor, it doesn't matter what anyone else does; you do what is right.

Everyone has the capacity and the opportunity to live honorably, no matter what happens around them. Each day we choose whether or not we will develop this value in our lives.

Story for Younger Children

---

[138] Stevenson, Burton. 1934. *The Home Book of Quotations: Classical and Modern*. Binghamton, New York: Vail-Ballou Press, 917

[139] www.motivationalquotes.com

The New Emperor

The new Emperor called all the young people in the kingdom together one day. He said, "It has come time for me to step down and to choose the next emperor. I have decided to choose one of you." The children were shocked!

The Emperor continued, "I am going to give each one of you one seed. It is a very special seed. I want you to go home, plant the seed, water it and come back here one year from today with what you have grown from this one seed. I will then judge the plants that you bring to me. The person who grows the best plant will be crowned the next Emperor of this kingdom!"

There was one boy named Ling who was there that day and he, like the others, received a seed. He went home and excitedly told his mother the whole story. She helped him get a pot and some planting soil, and he planted the seed and watered it carefully. Every day he would water it and watch to see if it had grown.

After about three weeks, some of the other youths began to talk about their seeds and the plants that were beginning to grow. Ling kept going home and checking his seed, but nothing ever grew. Three weeks, four weeks, five weeks went by. Still nothing.

By now others were talking about their plants but Ling didn't have a plant, and he felt like a failure. Six months went by, still nothing in Ling's pot. He just knew he had killed his seed. Everyone else had trees and tall plants, but he had nothing. Ling didn't say anything to his friends, however. He just kept waiting for his seed to grow.

A year finally went by, and all the youth of the kingdom brought their plants to the emperor for inspection. Ling told his mother that he wasn't going to take his empty pot. But she encouraged him to go, and to take his pot, and to be honest about what happened. Ling felt sick to his stomach, but he knew his mother was right. He took his empty pot to the palace.

When Ling arrived, he was amazed at the variety of plants grown by all the other youth. They were beautiful, in all shapes and sizes. Ling put his empty pot on the floor and many of the other kids laughed at him. A few felt sorry for him and said, "Hey, nice try."

When the Emperor arrived, he surveyed the room and greeted the young people. Ling tried to hide in the back. "My, what great plants, trees, and flowers you have grown," said the Emperor. "Today one of you will be appointed the next Emperor!"

All of a sudden, the Emperor spotted Ling at the back of the room with his empty pot. He ordered his guards to bring him to the front.

Ling was terrified. "The Emperor knows I'm a failure! Maybe he will have me killed!"

When Ling got to the front, the Emperor asked his name. "My name is Ling," he replied.

The kids began laughing.

The Emperor asked everyone to quiet down. He looked at Ling, and then announced to the crowd, "Behold your new Emperor! His name is Ling!"

Ling couldn't believe it. Ling couldn't even grow his seed, so how could he be the new Emperor?

Then the Emperor explained. "One year ago today, I gave everyone here a seed. I told you to take the seed, plant it, water it, and bring it back to me today. But I gave you all boiled seeds which would not grow.

All of you, except Ling, have brought me trees and plants and flowers. When you found that the seed would not grow, you substituted another seed for the one I gave you. Ling was the only one with the courage and honesty to bring me a pot with my seed in it. Therefore, he is the one who will be the new Emperor!"[140]

Learning Questions

1. How did Ling show honor?
2. How does it make you feel when you honor your parents and leaders?
3. Can you think of a time when you showed honor?

Story for Older Children

The Scholarship

One day the principal of a boys' school received a message to call a certain small-town lawyer.

The lawyer stated that someone had anonymously given a scholarship, entitling one boy to a four-year education, completely free of charge. The lawyer needed the principal's help to determine which young man deserved it most.

"I have concluded to let you decide which boy in your school most deserves the scholarship," explained the lawyer.

"That will be difficult to decide," replied the teacher, thoughtfully. "Two of my pupils will complete their courses this year. Both desire a college education, and neither is able to obtain it without assistance. They are so nearly equal that I cannot tell which is the better scholar."

"How is their discipline?" asked the lawyer.

"They are both keen observers of all the rules of the school," was the answer.

---

[140] Author Unknown

"Well," said the lawyer, "if at the end of the year one boy has not gone ahead of the other, send them to me and I will decide between them."

As before, at the closing examinations the boys stood equal in attainments. They were directed to call the lawyer's office, with no information being given as to the object of the visit.

Two intelligent, well-bred boys they seemed, and the lawyer wondered how he should decide between them. Just then the door opened and an elderly woman of peculiar appearance entered. She was well known for being of unsettled mind, and possessed of the idea that she had been deprived of a large fortune justly hers. As a consequence, she was in the habit of visiting lawyers' offices, carrying in her hands a package of papers which she wished examined. She was a familiar visitor to the office, where she was always received with respect and dismissed with kindly words.

This morning, seeing that the lawyer was occupied with others, she seated herself to wait his leisure. Unfortunately, the chair she selected was broken and had been set aside as useless. As a result, she fell in a rather awkward manner, scattering her papers about the floor. The lawyer looked with a quick eye at the boys, before moving himself, to see what they would do.

Charles, after an amused survey of the fall, turned aside to hide a laugh he could not control. Henry sprang to the woman's side and lifted her to her feet. Then carefully gathering up her papers, he politely handed them to her. Her profuse and rambling thanks served only to increase Charlie's amusement.

After the lady told her customary story, to which the lawyer listened with every appearance of attention, he escorted her to the door, and she departed.

Then he turned to the boys, and after expressing pleasure at having found their acquaintance, he dismissed them. The next day the teacher was informed of the occurrence and told that the scholarship would be given to Henry, remarking:

"No one so well deserves to be fitted for a position of honor and influence as he who feels it his duty to help the humblest and lowliest."[141]

Learning Questions

1. How did Henry show honor to the elderly lady?
2. How was Henry rewarded for his efforts?
3. Name one way young people can honor their parents.

You Show Honor When You:

- Live the values you believe by making good choices every day.
- Are respectful, kind, obedient, and honest.

---

[141] Author Unknown, *Especially for M*, V 2, 159-160.

- Set a good example for others.
- Are not ashamed of your good choices.
- Choose the right no matter what other people say or do.
- Take advantage of every opportunity to develop the possibilities within you.

HOPE

Hope

Definition Hope: Looking forward to something you want.

Quotes

"Hope for the best but prepare for the worst."

English Proverb[142]

"Hope is like the sun, which, as we journey towards it, casts the shadow of our burden behind us."

Samuel Smiles[143]

Explanation

Hope is looking forward to something. When you have hope you do not give up or get discouraged. Instead, you believe that at some point, someday, you'll be who you want to be, get what you want to get, and reach the goals you have set for yourself.

Here are some examples of people in history who had hope:

1. Christopher Columbus hoped he'd find a water route to India, and he discovered America!
2. Thomas Edison hoped he'd invent the electric light bulb. He invented the light bulb and many other new products.
3. Michael Jordan hoped he'd play on a professional basketball team, and he became one of the best basketball players in history.
4. Walt Disney hoped his creation — Mickey Mouse — would be a success. Mickey is now known and loved by children around the world.
5. Martin Luther King hoped for racial equality. His efforts made a significant difference.

There are many people today who are not well known but who are remarkable examples of hope. If you look around and notice the people in your life, you'll probably recognize many who exemplify this value. How about your mother and father? They hope that you will be kind,

---

[142] *Five thousand Quotations for All Occasions.* 1945. Edited by Lewis C. Henry. Garden City, New York: Doubleday & Company, Inc., 124

[143] Stevenson, Burton. 1934. *The Home Book of Quotations: Classical and Modern.* Binghamton, New York: Vail-Ballou Press, 925

obedient and respectful. They also hope you'll be healthy, safe, and become a happy, loving person who will contribute to the world in meaningful ways.

Story for Young Children

<u>Flying Above the Storm</u>

Did you know that an eagle knows when a storm is approaching long before the storm breaks? The eagle will fly to some high spot and wait for the winds to come.

When the storm hits, the eagle sets its wings so that the wind will pick it up and lift it high above the storm.

While the storm rages below, the eagle is soaring high above it, gliding with ease.

The eagle does not escape the storm; it just simply uses the storm to lift it higher. It rises on the same winds that bring the storm.

When the storms of life come upon us, and all of us will experience them, we can rise above them. Storms do not have to overcome us. We can soar above them.

Remember, it is not the burdens of life that weigh us down, but it is how we handle them that counts.[144]

Learning Questions

1. What is one thing you hope for?
2. What do you think your teachers hope for?
3. What do you hope to be when you grow up?

Story for Older Children

<u>Shining Down</u>

One dark morning while driving to work, my dad, Layton Kavalinas, swerved to avoid a deer in the road. His car skidded on black ice, hit a guardrail and spun into an oncoming truck. He died in the crash. My dad was only thirty-five years old.

Streetlights could have helped prevent the accident, but there were no lights on that stretch of highway called the Marquis of Lorne Trail on the outskirts of Calgary, Canada.

I was only eleven when he died. I was devastated over the loss of my father, especially when I realized that his death could have been avoided. In a two-year period, my father and one other

---

[144] Author Unknown, http://www.skywriting.net/

driver were killed, and twenty-nine accidents happened on that area of the highway. Time and again I thought, *"How can I find a way to make my dad's short life really count?*

I felt triumphant when I figured out what I could do. I decided that I would try to get some lights put up in that area to help other drivers see better.

Once I figured out what I had to do, I fought as hard as I could to get new lights on that road. But I didn't realize what a big deal that would be! I was determined and very motivated. I didn't want what happened to my father to happen to anyone else.

I was studying government in school, and I tried to find a way to increase public pressure on City Hall to install lights. With help from my classmates, I handed out flyers at homes and shopping malls, and obtained over three hundred signatures on the petition needed to grab the attention of the politicians in charge of road safety issues. I contacted them, too, and told them what I was trying to do. I was pretty amazed when some of the politicians actually listened to a kid! Finally, there was a meeting at City Hall about the need for new lights.

Before the meeting, the local media found out what I was trying to do and reported on the problem. The reporters helped people in the area "see the light" and acknowledge the danger on Marquis of Lorne Trail.

With TV, radio stations, and newspapers covering it, more people understood why lights were needed; they also learned what it was like for a child to lose a father. A lot of people told me they were touched and they decided to help. The public pressure began to rise and within four months from the morning my dad lost his life on that highway, the city council agreed to spend $290,000 for new lights.

Sometimes, going through the accident over and over, in order to make a point, was a hard thing to do emotionally. At times I had hard nights and I cried. But at other times, I would be really happy and proud that my dad's life was the one that made the difference in helping to save many other lives from fatal accidents.

I was never so proud in my life as I was on September 16, 1996, nearly a year after I lost my dad. Speaking through a walkie-talkie at the side of the road, I gave a city worker instructions to turn on the lights for the first time. During the same lighting ceremony, I was given a plaque from the City of Calgary honoring me for my public service efforts. Since then, the number of collisions on Marquis of Lorne Trail has been drastically reduced.

While helping many people I'll never even meet, I think I also helped my mother, my younger brother, Shaun, and my little sister, Kaitlin, become determined to continue to enjoy life. I helped lift their spirits, and they were there to support me. We all cried together. We all laughed together. We all thought about life together.

My dad's death brought us closer together as a family, making something positive come out of the situation and helping ease our grief.

But it was really my dad who ended up teaching me a lot about determination, courage and faith. In his own way, through this project, he helped me grow up. I learned that if you're determined, if you put your heart into something, you can overcome any obstacle. You can accomplish anything.

Life goes on now. The cameras have stopped filming and the civic leaders focus on other problems. But the streetlights will always be there to help me get through difficult times.

I know that I will always be reminded of the terrible accident and I will still suffer grief from losing my dad, but I gain comfort knowing that area of the highway is now a safer place.

I feel my dad's presence there, and I'll always have the comfort of knowing that every night, a little bit of Dad is shining down.[145]

Learning Questions

1. What did Layton Kavalinas' son do to help overcome the grief of losing his father?
2. What is one thing that frustrates you in your life?
3. Name how you can turn your frustration into an experience that brings hope.

You Show Hope When You:

- Look forward to something.
- Don't give up or stay discouraged.
- Believe that someday you'll become what you want to be or get what you want to get.
- Set goals and work toward reaching them.

---

[145] Michael Kavalinas as told by Monte Stewart, "Shining Down," *Chicken Soup for the Preteen Soul*, 33-35

HUMILITY

Humility

Definition Humility: Belief that you are no more important than other people; you are willing to serve others gladly.

Quotes

"Get someone else to blow your horn and the sound will carry twice as far."

Will Rogers[146]

"The proud man counts his newspaper clippings; the humble man, his blessings."

Bishop Fulton J. Sheen[147]

Explanation

Humility means thinking of others before yourself. Humble people don't believe they are more important than others. Their focus is not on themselves.

When you are humble, you care about serving others cheerfully. You give of yourself freely, with no thought of receiving anything in return.

Humble people are a joy to be around because you don't feel like you have to impress them. They like you just the way you are.

When you are humble you are teachable. You enjoy learning and improving yourself. You focus on continued growth and try to learn from past mistakes.

When you show humility, you don't compare or compete with others. You respect and appreciate people's abilities, and you don't spend time trying to impress them.

When you are humble you ask for help when you need it. You are full of thankfulness for your many blessings. You enjoy life's gifts and you willingly learn from life's challenges.

Story for Young Children

---

[146] Glenn Van Ekeren. *Speaker's Sourcebook II*. 1994. Paramus, New Jersey: Prentice Hall, 196
[147] Glenn Van Ekeren. *Speaker's Sourcebook II*. 1994. Paramus, New Jersey: Prentice Hall, 196

<u>Tyler Learns Humility</u>

Kelly yelled, "Wow! That was a great hit you got, Tyler! How did you learn to do that? I wish you were on my team!"

"Thanks," Tyler said a little shyly as he wondered what else to say. He was happy to hit the ball into right field, in a place that made the outfielder run to get it so Tyler could get on first base. But best of all, it got Josh to third base and he was able to make it home to break the tie and win the game for the Pelicans!

Later that evening, Dad told Tyler how proud he was that their team had won. "But what made me even more pleased was the humble way you acted, Tyler." Dad said.

"What does humble mean, Dad?" Tyler asked.

"Well, it means that you realize it wasn't only what *you* did to get that ball out there. Many people helped you along the way," said Dad. "For instance, I saw Jim out there practicing with you a couple of times, and Mom let you wait on your chores when you practiced with the team." Dad recalled.

"And you too, Dad! You taught me how to wait until a pitch came right where I could hit it." Tyler added.

"You're getting the idea now, Tyler," Dad said smiling. "Can you think of anyone else who helped you be successful today?"

"Well, my coach taught us all the rules and watched how I was holding the bat and told me how to hit the ball," said Tyler.

"That's right, son. An important part of humility is giving other people credit and appreciation for helping you be successful. I think you understand humility now." Dad smiled as Tyler gave him a big hug.[148]

Learning Questions

1. How did Tyler show humility in this story?
2. Why was his dad so pleased with him?
3. Who has helped you in your life?

Story for Older Children

<u>Humility</u>

---

[148] Paula Noble Fellingham

Shortly after Booker T. Washington became Director of the Tuskegee Institute in Alabama, he was walking past the house of a wealthy family. The woman of the house, assuming Washington was one of the yard workers her husband had hired, asked him if he would chop some wood for her. Professor Washington smiled, nodded, took off his coat, and chopped the wood. When he carried the armload of wood into the woman's kitchen, a servant girl recognized him and rushed to her mistress to tell her of his identity.

The next morning, the woman appeared in Washington's office. Apologizing profusely, she said repeatedly, "I did not know it was you I put to work."

Washington replied with great humility, "It's entirely all right, madam. I like to work and I'm delighted to do favors for my friends."

The woman was so taken with his manner and his willingness to forgive that she gave generous gifts to the institute and persuaded many of her wealthy acquaintances to do likewise. In the end, Washington raised as much money for the institute from this one act of chopping wood as he did from any other fund-raising event!

A great leader is never beyond hard work. Willingness to serve others is the essence of true leadership.[149]

Learning Questions

1. How did Professor Washington show humility?
2. How did the woman react to Washington's humility?
3. Name two ways you can show humility.

You Show Humility When You:

- Think of others' needs before your own.
- Don't believe you're more important than others.
- Serve others cheerfully.
- Give with no thought of receiving.
- Don't try to impress others, you don't boast.
- Are teachable. You enjoy learning.
- Try to grow from your mistakes and learn from life's challenges.
- Don't compare or compete with others.
- Ask for help when you need it.
- Have an attitude of gratitude.

---

[149] God's Little Devotional Book for Leaders, p. 43.

HUMOR

Humor

Definition Humor: Things that are funny, amusing.

Quotes

"If you could choose one characteristic that would get you through life, choose a sense of humor."

Jennifer James[150]

"Imagination was given to the man to compensate for what he is not. A sense of humor was provided to console him for what he is."

Horace Walpole[151]

Explanation

Humor is the ability to notice and appreciate the funny things about ourselves, our circumstances, and our world.

Humor means that you can laugh at yourself and the things that happen in your life. For example, what if you were walking along (with no umbrella) and it started to rain on you? You can either enjoy the rain and laugh at how wet you're getting, or you can get upset. Which is better?

What if you drank some chocolate milk and your friend started laughing because you had a chocolate mustache? Would you get angry or laugh with your friend? When you can laugh at yourself and the funny things that happen in your life, people say that you have a good sense of humor.

It's much more fun to be around people who can find the humor in life than to be around people who are so serious that they hardly ever laugh. Did you know that it takes 72 muscles to frown, and only 13 muscles to smile?

Charles Schultz, author of the "Peanuts" cartoon said, "Laughter is not just a pleasure, it's a necessity. I believe that one of the things that has enabled man to survive is the ability to laugh.

---

[150] Glenn Van Ekeren. *Speaker's Sourcebook II*. 1994. Paramus, New Jersey: Prentice Hall, 201

[151] Glenn Van Ekeren. *Speaker's Sourcebook II*. 1994. Paramus, New Jersey: Prentice Hall, 200

If I could present a gift to the next generation, it would be the ability for each individual to learn to laugh at himself."[152]

So, what can you do to have a good sense of humor? Don't be so serious, and don't worry a lot. Instead, look on the bright side of things, find the fun, and be happy!

Story for Younger Children

"<u>Melinda Mae</u>"

Have you heard of tiny Melinda Mae,
Who ate a monstrous whale?
She thought she could,
She said she would,
So she started in right at the tail.

And everyone said, "You're much too small,"
But that didn't bother Melinda at all,
She took little bites and she chewed very slow,
Just like a little girl should...

...and eighty-nine years later she ate that whale
Because she said she would!!![153]

Learning Questions
1. Do you think Melinda really ate a whale?
2. Who is someone you like to laugh with?
3. Do you like to be around people who say funny things?

Story for Older Children

"<u>The Sitter</u>"

Mrs. McTwitter the baby-sitter,
I think she's a little bit crazy.
She thinks a baby-sitter's supposed
To sit on the baby. [154]

Learning Questions

1. What did Mrs. McTwitter think baby-sitting meant?
2. How does having a sense of humor help you in life?

---

[152] Glenn Van Ekeren. *Speaker's Sourcebook II*. 1994. Paramus, New Jersey: Prentice Hall, 218

[153] http://www.geocities.com/Paris/LeftBank/1619/granny.html

[154] http://www.geocities.com/Paris/LeftBank/1619/bbysttr.html

3. Who is the funniest person you know?

You Show Humor When You:

- Notice the funny things in life.
- Laugh at yourself.
- Can laugh at the funny things that happen in the world.
- Choose to look on the bright side of things and be happy.
- Aren't serious all the time.
- Realize people enjoy being around you when you have a sense of humor.

IMAGINATION

Imagination

Definition Imagination: The picturing power of your mind; fantasy.

Quotes

"The most interesting people are the people with the most interesting pictures in their minds."

Earl Nightingale[155]

"The man who has no imagination has no wings."

Muhammad Ali[156]

Explanation

Imagination is being able to "see" pictures in your mind of things that you don't see with your eyes. Like this: pretend right now that you are lying in the grass looking up at the sky. The sun is shining brightly and far up in the sky you see a big, white, puffy cloud. Next, you see a bird flying across the sky in front of the cloud. Can you see that in your mind? What you are doing is imagining. You are using your imagination.

Now, let's do this. Pretend you are in your kitchen at home and your mom is standing at the counter cutting a lemon. You say, "Mom, can I taste that lemon?" She gives you a slice of lemon and you squeeze the juice right onto your tongue. Oh, my! How sour that tastes!

When you were thinking about the lemon, you were making pictures in your mind. Again, you were using your imagination.

Some people use their imaginations to create new things. For example, people who invent things - like artists, musicians, and writers - all use their imaginations to do their work.

Mr. Robert Collier remarked, "The great successful men of the world have used their imagination. They think ahead and create their mental picture in all its details."[157]

Successful people imagine the things they want to accomplish *before* they begin to work. Experiments have shown that the goals we imagine in great detail will very likely be achieved.

---

155 Glenn Van Ekeren. *Speaker's Sourcebook II.* 1994. Paramus, New Jersey: Prentice Hall, 209
156 Glenn Van Ekeren. *Speaker's Sourcebook II.* 1994. Paramus, New Jersey: Prentice Hall, 210
157 Glenn Van Ekeren. *Speaker's Sourcebook II.* 1994. Paramus, New Jersey: Prentice Hall, 210

Walt Disney was an expert with his imagination. When he was a young father, on Saturdays Disney took his daughters to a local park to ride the merry-go-round and play. While sitting on a bench watching his children enjoy their rides, Disney imagined an elaborate family park filled with happy families. He put every detail into place. From the Pirates of the Caribbean to Main Street USA, Disneyland is the result of Walt Disney's ability to create the future in his mind. This pioneer of family amusement had no similar facilities to draw ideas from. He used his imagination to design the original plan.[158]

Curtis Carlson, the wealthy inventor of Gold Bond Stamps said, "I think my success is the result of my ability to see...to imagine how things *can* be. I'm not distracted by how things *are*."[159]

My dear mother, Gwenavere Noble, taught her children that whenever we were in a situation that wasn't pleasant, we could just close our eyes and take ourselves away from it - to anywhere we chose - like to a warm beach or a beautiful room with a lovely big bed to rest on, or to a colorful circus, or high up on top of a mountain. Try it - using your imagination is fun!

Story for Young Children

Covering All the Bases

A little boy was overheard talking to himself as he strode through his backyard, baseball cap in place and toting ball and bat. "I'm the greatest baseball player in the world," he said proudly. Then he tossed the ball in the air, swung and missed.

Undaunted, he picked up the ball, threw it into the air, and said to himself, "I'm the greatest player ever!" He swung at the ball again, and again he missed.

He paused a moment to examine the bat and ball carefully. Then once again he threw the ball into the air and said, "I'm the greatest baseball player who ever lived." He swung the bat hard and again missed the ball.

"Wow!" he exclaimed. "What a pitcher!"[160]

Learning Questions

1. What did the little boy imagine himself doing?
2. How did his imagination make him feel?
3. Name one thing you imagine yourself doing in the future.

---

[158] Glenn Van Ekeren. *Speaker's Sourcebook II*. 1994. Paramus, New Jersey: Prentice Hall, 210-211

[159] Glenn Van Ekeren. *Speaker's Sourcebook II*. 1994. Paramus, New Jersey: Prentice Hall, 210

[160] Author Unknown, "Covering All the Bases," *Chicken Soup for the Soul*, 74

Story for Older Children

<u>Did the Earth Move for You?</u>

Eleven-year-old Angela was stricken with a debilitating disease involving her nervous system. She was unable to walk, and her movement was restricted in other ways as well.

The doctors did not hold out much hope of her ever recovering from this illness. They predicted she would spend the rest of her life in a wheelchair. They said that few, if any, were able to return to normal after contracting this disease.

The little girl was undaunted. There, lying in her hospital bed, she would vow to anyone who'd listen that she was definitely going to be walking again someday.

Angela was transferred to a specialized rehabilitation hospital in the San Francisco Bay area. Whatever new therapies could be applied to her case were used.

The physical therapists were charmed by her undefeatable spirit. They taught her about *imaging* – about seeing herself walking. If it did nothing else, it would at least give her hope and something positive to do in the long waking hours in her bed.

Angela worked as hard as possible in physical therapy, in whirlpools and in exercise sessions. But she worked just as hard lying there faithfully doing her imaging, visualizing herself moving, moving, moving!

One day, as she was straining with all her might to imagine her legs moving again, it seemed as though a miracle happened: The bed moved! It began to move around the room! She screamed out, "Look what I'm doing! Look! Look! I can do it! I moved, I *moved*!"

However, at that very moment *everyone* in the hospital was moving - running for cover. People were screaming, equipment was falling, and glass was breaking. You see, just at that moment there was a huge earthquake in San Francisco.

But Angela was convinced that she moved her legs all by herself. And now, only a few years later, she's back in school on her own two legs. No crutches, no wheelchair. You see, Angela believed that anyone who can shake the earth between San Francisco and Oakland can conquer a little disease.[161]

Learning Questions

1. What did Angela imagine herself doing?
2. How did Angela's imagination help her recover?

---

[161] Hanoch McCarty, "Did the Earth Move for You?", *Chicken Soup for the Soul*, 171-172

3.   What is one thing you can imagine right now, that will help you in the future?

You Show Imagination When You:

- See pictures in your mind that you don't see with your eyes.
- Pretend.
- Create new things.
- Make mental pictures in great detail before you begin to work.
- Think about things as they can be, not as they are.
- Take yourself away from unpleasant situations by traveling to interesting places in your mind.

INDIVIDUALITY

Individuality

Definition Individuality: Things that make you unique and different from other people.

Quotes

"Individuality is everywhere and respected as the root of everything good."

Jean Paul Richter[162]

"Every individual thing in nature has its own beauty."

Ralph Waldo Emerson[163]

Explanation

Your individuality is everything about you that makes you different from other people.

Everyone is special. Each person in the world has something that makes him or her unique…one of a kind. Did you know that there is no one exactly like you? Of all the billions of people who have lived on the earth, or who will ever live on the earth, there has never been someone just like you, and there never will be someone just like you. You're an individual, and you are very important.

Even people who have a twin brother or sister are different from their twin. They might look just alike, but they don't think exactly alike, and each twin has his (or her) individual strengths and weaknesses.

Having individuality means that when you're with your friends and they begin to do something you don't think is right, you can speak up and suggest the right way to act. When you have individuality, you don't try to always "fit in" just to be accepted. You understand that strong leaders usually are strong individuals who set good examples for others.

Another way to show individuality is this: suppose your teacher drew a flower on the board and told all the students to "draw a flower." Some would draw a flower that looked exactly like the teacher's flower on the board. However, students with individuality and creativity wouldn't copy the teacher; they would draw flowers that were different.

---

[162] Edwards, Tyron. 1977. *The New Dictionary of Thoughts*. Stanbook, Inc., 302
[163] Edwards, Tyron. 1977. *The New Dictionary of Thoughts*. Stanbook, Inc., 302

Become an individual of strong character and high morale values and develop your unique talents and gifts. Then take pride in your individuality.

Story for Young Children

<u>Be the Best</u>

If you can't be a pine on the top of the hill
Be a scrub in the valley –
But be the best little scrub by the side of the hill.
Be a bush if you can't be a tree.

If you can't be a bush be a bit of the grass
And some highway happier make.
If you can't be a musky then just be a bass—
But the liveliest bass in the lake!

We can't all be captains, we've got to be crew.
There's something for all of us here.
There's big work to do, and there's lesser to do,
And the task you must do is near.

If you can't be a highway then just be a trail,
If you can't be the sun be a star;
It isn't by size that you win or you fail-
Be the best of whatever you are![164]

Learning Questions

1. What did you learn from this poem?
2. What do you like about yourself?
3. How are you working to be better?

Story for Older Children

<u>A Samurai and a Zen Master</u>

A Samurai, a very proud warrior, came to see a Zen Master one day. The Samurai was very famous but looking at the beauty of the Master and the powerful grace of the man, the Samurai suddenly felt inferior.

He said to the Master, "Why am I feeling inferior? Just a moment ago everything was okay. As I entered your court, suddenly I felt inferior. I have never felt like that before. I have faced death many times, and I have never felt any fear. Why am I now feeling frightened?"

---

[164] http://home.earthlink.net/~dbffxcon/reverent.html

The Master said, "Wait. When everyone has gone, I will answer."

People continued the whole day to come and see the Master, and the Samurai was getting more and more tired waiting. By evening the room was empty, and the Samurai said, "Now, can you answer me?"

The Master said, "Come outside."

It was a full moon night; the moon was just rising on the horizon. And he said, "Look at these two trees. One tree is tall and the other is small. They both have existed beside my window for years, and there has never been any problem.

The small tree has never said to the big tree, 'Why do I feel inferior before you?' This tree is small, and that tree is big -- why have I never heard a whisper of it?"

The Samurai said, "Because they can't compare."

The Master replied, "Then you need not ask me. You know the answer."[165]

Learning Questions

1. Why can't the trees compare?
2. Do people compare themselves with others?
3. What makes you different from other people in your life?

You Show Individuality When You:

- Understand that each person is special…one of a kind.
- Choose the right even when your friends don't.
- Set a good example for others.
- Don't try to "fit in" just to be accepted.
- Understand that each person has great value. Everyone is important.

---

[165] Author Unknown, http://www.cyberquotations.com/stories

INTEGRITY

Integrity

Definition Integrity: When your words and actions match the values you believe in; choosing the right.

Quotes

"Real integrity is doing the right thing, knowing that nobody's going to know whether you did it or not."

Oprah Winfrey[166]

"Integrity is the first step to true greatness."

Charles Simmons[167]

Explanation

Integrity is when your words and actions match what you believe. When you have integrity, you make good choices because it's the right thing to do, not because you're afraid of getting in trouble.

People with integrity know the difference between right and wrong. They know what a lie is and what the truth is. When you have integrity, you don't tell a lie just because you're afraid you will be punished, you tell the truth every time - no matter what. Thomas McCauley wrote, "The measure of a man's real character is what he does when he knows no one will ever find out."[168]

When you have integrity your family and friends know they can count on you to make good choices. For example, if you don't know the answer on a test at school, when you have integrity you don't look at another student's paper for the answer. You never cheat. If you don't know the answer you just get that problem wrong. It's much better to get a poor grade than to be dishonest. People with integrity have peace in their hearts because they are honest with themselves.

Everyone likes to be around people with integrity because they can be trusted. And when you are trustworthy others can depend on you because they know you will always be obedient, truthful, and responsible.

---

[166] http://www.quotationspage.com

[167] Edwards, Tyron. 1977. *The New Dictionary of Thoughts.* Stanbook, Inc., 315

[168] http://www.placervillevet.com/jon/thought.htm

The American President Abraham Lincoln spoke about this value when he said, "I am not bound to win, but I am bound to be true. I am not bound to succeed but I am bound to live up to what light I have. I must stand with anybody who stands for right; stand with him while he is right and part with him when he goes wrong."[169]

Story for Young Children

George Washington and the Colt

George Washington's mother had some fine horses, and the finest of all was a young colt. No one had ever ridden it, and it was allowed to gallop about the pasture, doing no work until it should grow to its full size. The colt was to be the best horse on the farm.

One day George and some other boys were playing down in the pasture. They were catching the horses and riding them. They all rode well, but George rode best of all. He was very proud of his riding. "I can ride any horse on the farm," he boasted. "No horse can throw me."

"You can't ride that colt," one of the boys said, pointing to his prized horse.

"Of course I can ride him," George answered, "but my mother allows no one to get on his back."

"How could you hurt him?" they jeered. "He is almost full grown, and you are not heavy. The only reason you won't try is because you know you *can't* ride him."

George's face flushed angrily, and as the colt galloped past him, he sprang out and caught him by the mane. Then he swung up on his back. The colt was frightened, and rushed around the field, kicking and jumping. George clamped his knees tight to the colt and clung to him. The colt at last reared in the air and fell over backward.

George jumped clear of him as he fell, and then stood, waiting for the colt to get up. The colt didn't move. George began to feel frightened. He went over to the horse and tried to make him stand up, but he could not. The colt was dead; he had burst a blood vessel.

As George stood looking at the colt, he began to think of how sorry his mother would be that he had disobeyed her.

"She'll never trust me again, either," George thought miserably. "I should have known better than to be so foolish. I was afraid to have the boys laugh at me. How can I tell my mother?"

The more he thought of it, the harder it seemed. At last, he turned and walked away toward the woods. "I can't tell her," he thought.

But suddenly he lifted his head and said, "Nonsense! I'm not a coward! I can tell my mother anything!"

---

[169] http://www.hoosierhoofprints.com/Hot_News/FYI's/Quotes.htm

He quickly walked to the house. When he came into his mother's room, she looked up from her sewing and smiled at him. "Where have you been, George?" she asked.

"Down in the pasture, mother," he answered.

"Did you see our young colt? I think we must begin training him soon."

George did not answer for a moment. His mother looked at him and said, "What's the matter, my son?"

"Mother," he said, "the colt is dead."

"Dead?" Mrs. Washington exclaimed. "Why, I saw him just this morning, and he was not sick then."

"It was my fault, mother," George said. Then he told her all that had happened.

Mrs. Washington listened without saying a word. When George had finished, she walked to the window and stood looking out until she had controlled her indignation and disappointment. Then she came over to George.

"My son," she said, "I'm glad you came and told me. Remember, you can always tell your mother anything. You were foolish to mind what the boys said. Never let the remarks of anyone affect you. Do the thing you know to be right, but if you do make a mistake, be brave enough to admit it."[170]

Learning Questions

1. How did George show integrity?
2. Can you talk about a time that you showed integrity?
3. Is it sometimes hard to tell the truth?

Story for Older Children

<u>A Heart at Work</u>

Several years ago, a man named Reuben Gonzolas was in the final match of his first professional racquetball tournament. Reuben was playing the perennial champion for his first shot at a victory on the pro circuit.

At match point in the fifth and final game, Gonzolas made a super "kill shot" into the front corner to win the tournament. The referee called it good, and one of the linesmen confirmed the shot was a winner. But after a moment's hesitation, Gonzolas turned and declared that his shot

---

[170] Author Unknown, *Especially for M*, V 5, pp. 17-18.

had skipped into the wall, hitting the floor first. As a result, the serve went to his opponent, who went on to win the match. When Reuben Gonzolas walked off the court everyone was stunned. The next issue of a leading racquetball magazine featured Gonzolas on its cover.

The lead editorial searched and questioned for an explanation for this first ever occurrence on the professional racquetball circuit. Who could ever imagine it in any sport or endeavor? Here was a player with everything officially in his favor, with victory in his grasp, who disqualified himself at match point and lost. When asked why he did it Gonzolas replied, "It was the only thing I could do to maintain my integrity."[171]

Learning Questions

1. What does this story tell us about Reuben Gonzolas?
2. Do you think that if Reuben had not told the truth he would have regretted it later?
3. Have you ever had your integrity tested? What did you do?

You Show Integrity When:

- Your words and actions match what you believe.
- You make good choices because it's the right thing to do, not because you're afraid of getting in trouble.
- You know the difference between right and wrong, and you choose the right.
- You never cheat or lie.
- You have peace in your heart because you are honest with yourself.
- You can be trusted.
- Your family and friends know they can count on you to make good choices.

---

[171] Author Unknown

JOYFULNESS

Joyfulness

Definition Joyfulness: Full of happiness; gladness.

Quotes

"Joy is not in things; it is in us."

Richard Wagner[172]

"The joy of a spirit is the measure of its power."

Ninon de Lenclos[173]

Explanation

Joyfulness is happiness and a little bit more. Joyfulness is often a feeling inside that we are loved and life is good. It is a peaceful feeling of well-being that helps us love others more easily.

Joyful people smile and laugh often. They see the goodness in others and in life. When you are joyful you look on the bright side of things; you don't complain, whine, worry or pout. For example, you notice how the rain is watering flowers instead of how it is keeping you inside. You notice how the road is getting fixed instead of how long the detour is. Even when there is trouble and sadness, when you have a joyful heart, you try to look for ways to help others deal with their problems.

No matter what is happening in your world, you can choose how you respond to it. You can choose to have a joyful heart on the inside, no matter what is happening on the outside.

Being joyful begins with believing that you are loved and very special… that there is no one just like you on the whole planet. You need to know that you have wonderful gifts and talents. Many people's lives can be touched and improved because of you. So decide today to love much, laugh often, serve others gladly, choose the right, and develop your talents. If you do this, you can have a joyful heart throughout your whole life.

---

[172] http://www.quotationspage.com

[173] http://www.quotationspage.com

Story for Young Children

The Matching Shoes

A well-respected kindergarten teacher once shared a story. One day, a boy in her class came to school with an extra jovial, cheerful attitude. He seemed to jump higher than usual at recess and he walked through the halls with an extra bounce. But, most evident of all, a jubilant smile lit up his face throughout the entire day. No disappointment, no discouraging word, nor any snide comments could dampen his spirits.

Curious as to the reason behind his new joyful countenance, the teacher pulled the child aside and asked him why he was so happy. She was fully expecting him to describe a shiny new bike or perhaps tell her about a special toy. However, his response forever touched her. Pointing to his feet he exclaimed with a smile, "I have matching shoes today!" And with that he turned and ran off to join the other children.

You see, this boy came from a home of very meager circumstances. Usually, he only had two second-hand shoes for the right foot, or two previously discarded shoes for the left foot. But today his feet fit comfortably in both shoes.

The greatest lesson taught that day was not found in any book. It came from a small boy who taught about the source of pure joyfulness.

Truly, a thankful heart is a joyful heart.[174]

Learning Questions

1. Why was the boy so joyful?
2. How does thinking about what we *do* have rather than what we *don't* have make us joyful?
3. Share three things you are joyful about.

Story for Older Children

A World of Smiles

About ten years ago when I was an undergraduate in college, I was working as an intern at my university's Museum of Natural History. One day while working at the cash register in the gift shop, I saw an elderly couple come in with a little girl in a wheelchair.

---

[174] Michelle Ashton

As I looked closer at this girl, I saw that she was kind of perched on her chair. I then realized she had no arms or legs, just a head, neck and torso. She was wearing a little white dress with red polka dots.

The couple wheeled her up to me as I was looking down at the register. I turned my head toward the girl and gave her a wink. As I took the money from her grandparents I looked back at the girl, who was giving me the biggest, cutest smile I have ever seen. All of a sudden, her handicap was gone and all I saw was a beautiful girl, whose smile just melted me and almost instantly gave me a completely new sense of what life is all about.

She took me from a poor, unhappy college student and brought me into her world; a world of smiles, love, and warmth.

That was ten years ago. I'm a successful business person now and whenever I get unhappy and begin to think about my troubles, I remember that precious little girl in a red-and-white polka dot dress, and the remarkable life lesson she taught me.[175]

Learning Questions

1. Even though the little girl was handicapped, how did she show joyfulness?
2. How can we follow her example and have a joyful heart?
3. What makes you joyful?

You Show Joyfulness When You:

- Have a peaceful feeling of well-being and love for others.
- Smile and laugh often.
- Look for the goodness in others and in life.
- Help others through difficult times.
- Choose to respond positively to negative things in your life.
- Understand that the people who love you want the best for you.
- Believe you are special and unique, with gifts and talents which can help others.

---

[175] Author Unknown, http://www.cyberquotations.com/stories

KINDNESS

Kindness

Definition Kindness: Being gentle and good to others.

Quotes

"Lead the life that will make you kindly and friendly to everyone about you, and you will be surprised what a happy life you will lead."

Charles M. Schwab[176]

"Two important things are to have a genuine interest in people and to be kind to them. Kindness, I've discovered, is everything in life."

Isaac Bashevis Singer[177]

Explanation

Kindness is caring about others and having concern for their well-being. Kindness has four parts: kind thoughts; kind words; kind tone of voice; kind actions.

<u>Kind thoughts</u> are pleasant ideas that lift the soul. How we think determines how we speak and act. Kind people think positive, uplifting thoughts. When negative or bad thoughts enter your mind, you should try to quickly replace them with good thoughts. For example, if you think, "He's such a jerk!" Stop and replace it with, "Maybe if I knew him better, I'd understand why he did that." We should try to think about others in the same kind way we'd like them to think about us.

<u>Kind words</u> have great power. They make people feel good and show them that you care. Mother Teresa said, "Kind words can be short and easy to speak, but their echoes are truly endless."[178] This means that long after you speak kindly, people remember what you said and it makes them happy.

Using a <u>kind tone of voice</u> helps create the loving atmosphere we all want in our homes, our schools and at work. It's not always *what* we say but *how* we say it that makes all the difference. When you speak gently and kindly you send messages of love and respect and you'll probably have others speak kindly to you.

---

[176] Glenn Van Ekeren. *Speaker's Sourcebook II*. 1994. Paramus, New Jersey: Prentice Hall, 217
[177] Glenn Van Ekeren. *Speaker's Sourcebook II*. 1994. Paramus, New Jersey: Prentice Hall, 217
[178] Glenn Van Ekeren. *Speaker's Sourcebook II*. 1994. Paramus, New Jersey: Prentice Hall, 217

<u>Kind actions</u> are anything you do to make a person's life easier or happier without expecting a reward. Kind actions show concern and caring. They can be very simple – a smile, a pat on the back, helping with a chore or just listening when someone needs you.

The more often you are kind in thought, word, tone of voice, and action, the faster you will become a truly kind person. And do you know what else will happen? Folks will be nicer to you, and they'll want to be your friend because everyone loves to be around kind people!

Story for Young Children

<u>The Man with Big Shoes and a Big Heart</u>

It was an unseasonably hot day. Everybody, it seemed, was looking for some kind of relief, so an ice cream store was a natural place to stop.

A little girl, clutching her money tightly, entered the store. Before she could say a word, the store clerk sharply told her to get outside and read the sign on the door, and to stay out until she put on some shoes. She left slowly, and a big man followed her out of the store.

He watched as she stood in front of the store and read the sign: No Bare Feet. Tears started rolling down her cheeks as she turned and walked away. Just then the big man called to her. Sitting down on the curb, he took off his size 12 shoes, and set them in front of the girl saying, "Here, you won't be able to walk in these, but if you sort of slide along, you can get your ice cream cone."

Then he lifted the little girl up and set her feet into the shoes. "Take your time," he said. "I get tired of moving them around, and it will feel good to just sit here and eat my ice cream." The shining eyes of the little girl could not be missed as she shuffled up to the counter and ordered her ice cream cone.

He was a big man, all right. Big body, big shoes, but most of all, he had a big heart.[179]

Learning Questions

1. Why did the man give his shoes to the little girl?
2. Do we sometimes think of doing kind things, but we don't because we're afraid people will laugh at us?
3. What is one kind thing you can do today?

---

[179] Anonymous, Canfield et al., eds., *A 4th Course of Chicken Soup for the Soul,* 85-86.

Story for Older Children

A Lesson on Kindness

Jonathan, a university student, took a walk one afternoon with his professor. This kind teacher was a friend to many students. As they were walking, they noticed a pair of old shoes lying in the path. The shoes belonged to a poor man employed in a field nearby — a man who had nearly finished his day's work. The student turned to the professor, saying, "Let's play a trick on that man. We'll hide his shoes, and then we'll get behind the bushes and watch him. It'll be funny when he comes out and can't find his shoes!"

The professor used this moment to teach Jonathan a lesson he'd never forget. The professor said, "Jonathan, years ago a man named Etienne de Grellet said something that I'll never forget. Mr. Grellet said, *"I shall pass through this world but once. If, therefore, there be any kindness I can show, or any good thing I can say, let me not defer it or neglect it, for I shall not pass this way again."* Then the professor suggested, "Instead of tricking the man, why don't we do an act of kindness? Put a dollar in each shoe, and then we'll hide."

The student did so, and then hid with the professor in the bushes nearby. The laborer soon came across the field to the path where he had left his coat and shoes. While he put on his coat, he slipped one foot into a shoe — but feeling something there, he stooped down and found the dollar. Astonishment and wonder swept across his face. He gazed at the dollar, turned it over in his hand, and looked at it again and again. He then looked around him but could see no one. Finally, with a big smile on his face, he placed the money in his pocket and proceeded to put on his other shoe. How great was his surprise when he found another dollar!

His feelings overcame him; he fell upon his knees and uttered a loud, fervent thanksgiving in which he spoke of his wife, sick and helpless…and his children, without any bread, whom this timely bounty would save from hunger. The worker then gave thanks for the kind, unknown person who left two dollars in his shoes.

The young student, deeply moved, stood watching the man with tear-filled eyes. Motionless, the student watched the worker until the poor man was far down the path. Then the professor spoke softly. "My young friend," he said, "today you've seen the power of one simple act of kindness." The student had indeed learned a lesson that was perhaps the most important one the professor ever taught.[180]

Learning Questions

1. How does it make you feel when you are kind?
2. Who should you be kind to?
3. What is one kind thing you can do for a member of your family?

---

[180] Author Unknown, *Especially for M*, V 5, pp. 156-157.

You Show Kindness When You:

- Care about others and have concern for their well-being.
- Think kind thoughts.
- Speak gently and positively in ways that lift others.
- Help others with no thought of reward.
- Overlook others' mistakes; have patience with imperfections.
- Forgive easily and quickly.
- Listen patiently.
- Set a good example.

LEADERSHIP

Leadership

Definition Leadership: Guiding and teaching others.

Quotes

"The function of leadership is to produce more leaders, not more followers."

Ralph Nader[181]

"A leader is one who knows the way, goes the way, and shows the way."

John C. Maxwell[182]

Explanation

Leaders guide and direct people. Leaders are usually followed because people believe in their honesty and competence.

An important quality of a leader is his or her ability to make others feel good about themselves. Most good leaders love people and know how to bring out the best in them. They expect the best, and they treat those who willingly follow them with kindness and fairness.

One successful leader, Lieutenant General Zais, said, "I give you one piece of advice which I believe will contribute more to making you a better leader and will bring you greater happiness…than any other advice I can provide you. And it doesn't call for any special personality…anyone can do it. And that advice is: You must care."[183]

Effective leaders also have enthusiasm, positive attitudes, and workable plans. They let people know that they care about them through encouraging words, and they help people do their best.

One of the most important things you need to do when you're a leader is to be a good example. The best way to teach people how to do anything is to show them through your actions how to do it. For example, if you want others to be kind, be kind to them. If you want them to be punctual, or honest, or cheerful, you lead them best by being punctual, honest or cheerful.

---

[181] http://www.quotationspage.com

[182] https://www.brainyquote.com/topics/leadership

[183] Glenn Van Ekeren. *Speaker's Sourcebook II*. 1994. Paramus, New Jersey: Prentice Hall, 226

Story for Young Children

Learning to Lead

Years ago, in one of my classes at school, there was a boy named Ben who liked to push, shove, and call people names. I don't know why he did the things he did. It was hard for me to like him because of how he treated people, especially my friends and me. He did mean things almost every day.

One day, right before recess, something happened that changed things. Ben was playing with a boy named Andrew, and they accidentally spilled a bunch of corn kernels and dried beans on the classroom floor. The teacher told them that they needed to pick up everyone before they could go to recess.

I felt sorry for them and didn't want them to miss recess, so I offered to help clean up the mess. Once I started helping, two of my friends came along and helped too. We all worked together and were able to finish in time to go to recess. The next day, I noticed that Ben was nicer to my friends and me. And from then on, he was more of a friend. I'm glad that I helped Ben. Even though Ben had often been mean to me before, I felt good inside while I was helping him.[184]

Learning Questions

1. How was the boy in this story a leader?
2. What happened after he decided to help?
3. Name one way you can be a leader.

Story for Older Children

Decisions

Former U.S. President Ronald Reagan enjoyed telling the following story about himself. He claimed it was how he learned, early in life, to make firm and resolute decisions.

According to the story, a kindly aunt once took him to a cobbler to have a pair of shoes custom-made for him. The shoemaker asked, "Do you want a square toe or a round one?" The young Reagan hemmed and hawed, so the cobbler said, "Come back in a day or two and tell me what you want."

A few days later the cobbler saw Reagan on the street and asked what he had decided about the shoes. "I haven't made up my mind," Reagan answered.

"Very well," the cobbler said, and then he announced to his customer, "Your shoes will be ready tomorrow." When Reagan got the shoes, one had a round toe and the other a square toe!

---

[184] Anderson, James Levi. "Ye Have Done It Unto Me," *Friends*, June 1998, 48.

Reagan concluded, "Looking at those shoes every day taught me a lesson. If you don't make your own decisions, somebody else will make them for you."

Remember always that no decision is a decision![185]

Learning Questions

1. What did Reagan learn about making decisions?
2. Why is it important to make good decisions in order to be a good leader?
3. What are two things, right now, that you can do to be a leader?

You Show Leadership When You:

- Guide and direct people.
- Believe in your own abilities, skills, and talents.
- Help other people feel good about themselves.
- Have enthusiasm, a positive attitude, and a workable plan.
- Truly care about people and know how to bring out the best in them.
- Expect the best and treat people with kindness and fairness.
- Are a good example of the qualities you desire others to live.

---

[185] God's Little Devotional Book for Leaders, 1997. Honor Books, Inc: Tulsa, Oklahoma, p. 223.

LEARNING

Learning

Definition Learning: Finding out about things; understanding facts or skills and remembering them.

Quotes

"The question to ask is not whether you are a success or a failure, but whether you are a learner or a non-learner."

Benjamin Barber[186]

"The best of all things is to learn. Money can be lost or stolen, health and strength may fail, but what you have committed to your mind is yours forever."

Louis L'Amour[187]

Explanation

Learning is finding out about your world from books, from others, and from your own life experiences.

People who enjoy learning are usually open-minded to most things in life. They listen carefully and want to know more about their world. People who learn usually don't repeat their mistakes again and again. And when they do something that works well, they do it even better the next time.

Reading books is a wonderful way to learn. Mark Twain remarked, "The man who does not read good books has no advantage over the man who can't read them."[188] To be a high achiever you should read many good books. Walt Disney said, "There is more treasure in books than in all the pirate's loot on Treasure Island…and the best of all, you can enjoy these riches every day of your life."[189] Through books you can instantly be traveling in a different country, learning mathematics, discovering new inventions, or living in the middle of a fairy tale.

---

[186] Glenn Van Ekeren. *Speaker's Sourcebook II*. 1994. Paramus, New Jersey: Prentice Hall, 231
[187] Glenn Van Ekeren. *Speaker's Sourcebook II*. 1994. Paramus, New Jersey: Prentice Hall, 232
[188] Glenn Van Ekeren. *Speaker's Sourcebook II*. 1994. Paramus, New Jersey: Prentice Hall, 234
[189] Glenn Van Ekeren. *Speaker's Sourcebook II*. 1994. Paramus, New Jersey: Prentice Hall, 232

Another way to learn is from other people. Parents, teachers and others in your life can teach you things. Adults have walked down the path you are now walking. Listen to their advice and learn from their wisdom.

A third way you learn is from your own life experiences. For example, what happens at your house when you don't take care of your special things? Do they ever get lost or broken? Sometimes we learn the right way to act by doing things wrong the first time. However, it's usually better to prevent problems than to try and fix them later.

One more thought on learning: When bad things happen in your life, instead of thinking, "Why did this happen to *me*?" You should think, "What can I *learn* from this to help me be a better person?"

Story for Young Children

<u>The Cracked Pot</u>

A water bearer in India had two large pots, one hung on each end of a pole, which he carried across his shoulders. One of the pots had a crack in it, but the other pot was perfect, and always delivered a full portion of water at the end of the long walk from the stream to the master's house. The cracked pot arrived only half full.

For a full two years this went on daily, with the bearer delivering only one and a half pots full of water to his master's house. Of course, the perfect pot was proud of its accomplishments, perfect to the end for which it was made. But the poor cracked pot was very ashamed of its imperfection, and was miserable that it could only do half of what it had been made to do — or so it thought.

The cracked pot, after two years of what it perceived to be a bitter failure, spoke to the water bearer one day by the stream. "I am very ashamed of myself, and I want to apologize to you."

"Why?" asked the water bearer. "What are you ashamed of?"

"For the past two years, I have only been able to deliver half of my real capacity, because this crack in my side allows water to leak out all the way back to the master's house. Because of my flaws, you have to do all of this work, and you don't get full value from your efforts," the cracked pot said.

The water bearer felt sorry for the old cracked pot, and compassionately said, "As we return to the master's house, I want you to notice the beautiful flowers along the path."

As they went up the hill, the old cracked pot did notice the sun shining on the beautiful wild flowers growing along his side of the path, and this cheered it some. However, at the end of the trail, it still felt bad because it had again leaked out half its load, and apologized to the water bearer for its failure.

The bearer said to the pot, "Did you notice that there were flowers only on your side of the path, but not on the other pot's side? That's because I have always known about your flaw and put it to good use. I planted flower seeds on your side of the path (for the return trip), and every day while we walk back from the stream, you've watered them. For over two years I have been able to pick these beautiful flowers to decorate my master's table. If you weren't the way you are, he wouldn't have flowers for his house."

Each of us has our own unique flaws. We're all cracked pots. But if we recognize our flaws and learn from them, we can improve our lives and try to bless the lives of others.[190]

Learning Questions

1. Was the cracked pot sad because he thought he wasn't as good as the other pot?
2. How did the cracked pot make others happy?
3. Name one mistake you made in your life. What did you learn from it?

Story for Older Children

To Succeed, We Must Read

After experiencing many failures in business and in politics, Abraham Lincoln still maintained his daily habit of reading. A critic scoffed, "What good is all that education? It has never earned you a decent living."

Lincoln replied, "Education is not given for the purpose of earning a living; it's learning what to do with a living after you earn it that counts."

One of America's greatest reading advocates is Jim Trelease. He devoted nearly two decades to promoting what he considers the most important social factor in our lives today. "The more you read," he says, "the smarter you grow. The smarter you grow, the longer you stay in school. The longer you stay in school, the more money you earn. The more you earn, the better your children will do in school. So, if you hook a child on reading, you influence not only his future but also that of the next generation."

Reading researchers agree. They have long seen a correlation between the time a person spends reading and the number of his or her innovative ideas and creative solutions. Reading affects a person's ability to reason, and his ability to communicate, by providing an extended and accurate vocabulary.

Spend some time reading today. It will be time well spent. Investing in your personal growth affects your future success. As the poster often seen hanging in libraries and classrooms says, "Succeed- Read!"[191]

Learning Questions

---

[190] Author Unknown, http://www.skywriting.net/

[191] God's Little Devotional Book for Leaders, p. 77

1. What do you enjoy about reading?
2. Name one new thing you learned during the past week.
3. What can you do to make learning a life-long pursuit?

You Show Learning When You:

- Find out about your world from books, from others, and from your own life experiences.
- Read many good books.
- Listen to adults' wise advice and counsel.
- Use your own life experiences to improve and mature.
- Understand the importance of preventing problems.
- Ask, "What can I learn from my life experiences that can help me be a better person?"

LISTENING

 Listening

Definition Listening: Hearing and paying attention.

Quotes

"A good listener is not only popular everywhere, but after a while he knows something."

Wilson Mizner[192]

"We have two ears and only one tongue in order that we may hear more and speak less."

Epictetus[193]

Explanation

Listening is hearing and paying attention to what is being said. Listening is trying to understand a person's message and their feelings. When we listen, it shows we care.

How does it make you feel when you're talking to someone and he or she doesn't look at you, or they walk away? It makes you feel unimportant, and you may believe that what you're saying doesn't matter.

People who don't listen well send the message that they don't care about the person speaking. You don't want people to feel like that; you want to help people feel appreciated.

You should want others to believe that you care about how they feel…that what they have to say is important. When you listen carefully you can learn much, and you can help others be happy.

Edward Richard wrote a short poem called "A Wise Old Owl" that helps us think about the value of listening:

> A wise old owl lived in an oak
> The more he saw the less he spoke
> The less he spoke the more he heard
> Why can't we all be like that bird?[194]

---

[192] *Five thousand Quotations for All Occasions.* 1945. Edited by Lewis C. Henry. Garden City, New York: Doubleday & Company, Inc., 158

[193] *Five thousand Quotations for All Occasions.* 1945. Edited by Lewis C. Henry. Garden City, New York: Doubleday & Company, Inc., 118

[194] *Especially for M,* V11, p. 277

In the article "Family Communications" Marvin J. Ashton wrote, "Listening is more than being quiet. Listening is much more than silence. Listening requires undivided attention. The time to listen is when someone needs to be heard. The time to deal with a person with a problem is when he has the problem. The time to listen is the time when our interest and love are vital to the one who seeks our ear, our heart, our help, and our empathy."[195]

Story for Young Children

Listen Louder

A man realized he needed to purchase a hearing aid, but he felt unwilling to spend much money. "How much do they run?" he asked the clerk.

"That depends," said the salesman. "They run from $2.00 to $2,000."

"Let's see the $2.00 model," he said.

The clerk put the device around the man's neck. "You just stick this button in your ear and run this little string down to your pocket," he instructed.

"How does it work?" the customer asked.

"For $2.00, it doesn't work," the salesman replied. "But when people see it on you, they'll talk louder!"

As you know, most communication problems are not the result of people speaking too softly. The problem is, unfortunately, we are not always good listeners. Do you know that some people pay hundreds of dollars an hour just for someone to listen to them?

Psychologist Carl Rogers said, "A person's real need, a most terrible need, is for someone to listen…not as a 'patient' but as a human soul." People yearn to be heard and understood.[196]

Learning Questions

1. How did the $2.00 hearing aid work?
2. Who is someone who listens to you carefully?
3. How does it make you feel when someone listens to you?

Story for Older Children

Taking the Time

---

[195] Marvin J. Ashton, "Family Communications," *Ensign,* May 1976, 52
[196] Author Unknown

I vividly remember when I was caught in the undertow of too many commitments in too few days. It wasn't long before I was snapping at my wife and our children, choking down my food at mealtimes, and feeling irritated at those unexpected interruptions throughout the day. Before long, things around our home started reflecting the pattern of my hurry-up style. It was becoming unbearable.

I distinctly recall after supper one evening the words of our younger daughter, Colleen. She wanted to tell me about something important that had happened to her at school that day. She hurriedly began, "Daddy, I 'wanna tell you somethin' and I'll tell you really fast."

Suddenly realizing her frustration, I answered, "Honey, you can tell me, and you don't have to tell me really fast. Say it slowly."

I'll never forget her answer. My little girl said, "Then listen slowly, Daddy."[197]

Learning Questions

1. Why did the daughter feel she had to ask her Daddy to 'listen slowly'?
2. How do you know when someone else is really listening to you?
3. Are you a good listener?

You Show Good Listening When You:

- Show you're listening by facing the person and looking in their eyes while they talk.
- Show interest in what the person is saying. Have a pleasant look on your face, look in their eyes, and concentrate on their words.
- Never interrupt (Don't talk while they're talking).
- Watch the speaker's body for clues about how he's feeling. For example, does he have an excited, happy face, or a sad look on his face?
- Check to see if you understand by repeating what the speaker says or by asking questions.
- Talk kindly when it's time to speak. Say things that will help the person if he needs your help.

---

[197] Charles R. Swindoll, *Chicken Soup for the Father's Soul*, 181

LOVE

Love

Definition Love: Deep feelings of caring and concern.

Quotes

"Love is to the heart what the summer is to the farmer's year. It brings to harvest all the loveliest flowers of the soul."

Billy Graham[198]

"Mature love involves growing from a state of receiving much and giving little toward a state of cheerfully giving everything and demanding nothing in return."

Dr. Richard Strauss[199]

Explanation

Love is a special feeling in your heart of deep caring and concern for a person, or for an animal, a thing, or a place.

When you love someone, you want to share your deep, heartfelt thoughts and feelings with them. You want to be with that person, and you will sacrifice your comfort or safety to ensure his or her comfort and safety.

When you love someone, or an animal, you want him (or her) to be happy and fulfilled. You want to contribute to their happiness, and you willingly share your things and yourself.

When you're a loving person you think loving thoughts and your heart smiles inside whenever you think about the people (or things) you love. When you are loving you also speak loving words and show your love with frequent acts of kindness.

When you love others, you are kind and thoughtful, and this makes them feel good. When people and animals show love to you, you feel happy and it's easier to love others.

Love is wonderful because it's contagious. It can spread easily and quickly. One of the most important things we need to learn in this life is how to love others.

---

[198] Glenn Van Ekeren. *Speaker's Sourcebook II*. 1994. Paramus, New Jersey: Prentice Hall, 244
[199] Glenn Van Ekeren. *Speaker's Sourcebook II*. 1994. Paramus, New Jersey: Prentice Hall, 244

It is also very important to love yourself. You should feel confident in your heart that you are of great worth, because you are. You are a very valuable, precious person.

You show love to yourself by thinking kind thoughts about yourself and by developing your special talents and skills. As you grow and learn more, you'll be able to help many people. Serving others is a wonderful way to spread love.

Story for Young Children

<u>One at a Time</u>

A friend of ours was walking down a deserted Mexican beach at sunset. As he walked along, he began to see another man in the distance. As he grew nearer, he noticed that the local native kept leaning down, picking something up, and throwing it out into the water. Time and again he kept hurling things out into the ocean.

As our friend approached even closer, he noticed that the man was picking up starfish that had been washed up on the beach and, one at a time, he was throwing them back into the water.

Our friend was puzzled. He approached the man and said, "Good evening, friend. I was wondering what you are doing."

"I'm throwing these starfish back into the ocean. You see, it's low tide right now and all of these starfish have been washed up onto the shore. If I don't throw them back into the sea, they'll die up here from lack of oxygen."

"I understand," my friend replied, "but there must be thousands of starfish on this beach. You can't possibly get to all of them. There are simply too many. And don't you realize this is probably happening on hundreds of beaches all up and down this coast. Can't you see that you can't possibly make a difference?"

The local native smiled, bent down and picked up yet another starfish, and as he threw it back into the sea, he replied, "Made a difference to that one!"[200]

Learning Questions

1. Who is someone who makes you happy because you know they love you?
2. Say the name of one person, or animal, that you love.
3. Name three ways you can show love to people in your family or to your friends.

---

[200] Jack Canfield and Mark V. Hansen. *Chicken Soup for the Soul,* 1993. Deerfield Beach, Florida: Health Communications, Inc., p. 22-23

Story for Older Children

<u>Brotherly Love</u>

The violent grinding of brakes suddenly applied, and the harsh creaking of skidding wheels gradually died away as the big car came to a stop. Eddie quickly picked himself up from the dusty pavement where he had been thrown and looked wildly around.

Linda! Where was the little sister he had been holding by the hand when they started to cross the street? The next moment he saw her under the big car that had run them down. With one bound, the boy was under the car, trying to lift the child.

"You'd better not try, son," said a man gently. "Someone has gone for help."

"She's not...dead, is she?" Eddie begged.

The man stooped and felt the limp little pulse. "No, my boy," he said slowly.

A policeman came, dispersed the collecting crowd, and carried the unconscious girl into a nearby store. Eddie's folded coat made a pillow for her head until the ambulance arrived. He was permitted to ride in the ambulance with her to the hospital. Something about the sturdy, shabbily dressed boy, only ten years old, and his devotion to his little sister, touched the hearts of the hospital attendants.

"We must operate at once," said the surgeon after a brief preliminary examination. "She has been injured internally and has lost a great deal of blood." He turned to Eddie who stood close by. "Where do you live?"

Eddie told him that their father was dead and that their mother did day work. He didn't know where.

"We can't wait to find her," said the surgeon, "because by that time it might be too late."

Eddie waited in the sitting area while the surgeons worked on Linda. After what seemed like an eternity, a nurse emerged from the operating room.

"Eddie," she said kindly, "your sister is doing very badly, and the doctor wants to give her a transfusion. Do you know what that is?" Eddie shook his head. "Linda has lost so much blood she cannot live unless someone gives her his. Will you do it for her?"

Eddie's face grew paler, and he gripped the knobs of the chair hard. For a moment he hesitated; then gulping back his tears, he nodded and stood up.

"That's a good boy," said the nurse.

She patted his head, and led the way to the elevator which took them to the operating room. No one spoke to Eddie except the nurse, who directed him in a low voice how to prepare for the ordeal. The boy bit his quivering lip and obeyed.

"Are you ready?" asked a man dressed in white, turning from the table over which he had been working. For the first time Eddie noticed Linda, lying so still on the table. His little sister… and he was going to make her well!

Eddie stepped forward quickly. Two hours later the surgeon looked up with a smile into the faces of the young interns and nurses who were engrossed in watching the great man work.

"Fine," he said. "I think she will live."

After the transfusion Eddie had been told to lie quietly on a cot in the corner of the room. In the concern for the delicate operation Eddie had been forgotten.

"It was wonderful, Doctor!" exclaimed one of the young interns. "A miracle!" Nothing, he felt in his enthusiastic recognition of the marvels of surgery, could be greater than the miracles of science.

"I am well satisfied," said the surgeon with pride.

There was a tug at his sleeve, but he didn't notice. In a little while there was another tug, and the great surgeon glanced down to see a pale-faced boy looking steadily up into his face.

"Doctor," said Eddie timidly, "when do I die?"

The interns laughed and the great surgeon smiled.

"Why, what do you mean, my boy?" he asked kindly.

"I thought—when they took somebody's blood—he died," muttered Eddie.

The smiles faded from the lips of the doctors and nurses, and the young intern who had thought there was nothing greater than the miracles of science, caught his breath suddenly. This young boy had climbed to the very height of nobility and sacrifice and had shown them a glimpse of the greatest miracle of all — unconditional love.

There was a long pause before the surgeon answered softly, "You will both get well, Eddie - you and your little sister."

All who witnessed Eddie's act of selfless giving would never forget him.[201]

---

[201] http://www.willoughbyontheweb.com/christmas/story_miracle.htm

Learning Questions

1. How did Eddie show that he loved his little sister?
2. Have you ever had to give up something for someone you love?
3. Name one person who loves you. How do they show they love you?

You Show Love When You:

- Have a deep caring and concern for a person, animal, thing, or place.
- Want to share your deep, heartfelt thoughts and feelings with someone.
- Would sacrifice your comfort or safety to ensure their comfort or safety.
- Want to contribute to his or her happiness and fulfillment.
- Think loving thoughts, speak loving words and frequently perform acts of kindness.
- Love your fellowman, no matter how different they are than you.

LOYALTY

Loyalty

Definition Loyalty: Being faithful to someone or something.

Quotes

"No more important duty can be urged upon those who are entering the great theater of life than simple loyalty to their best convictions."

Edwin Hubbel Chapin[202]

"An ounce of loyalty is worth a pound of cleverness."

Elbert Hubbard[203]

Explanation

Loyalty is being unwaveringly steadfast in your commitment to your family, friends, cause, or country.

When you are loyal you don't change your mind when your values are questioned or laughed at because when you believe in something, it should not matter how other people react. When you believe something is right, you shouldn't change your beliefs because people don't agree with them, or because people make fun of you.

Loyalty means standing up for what you believe is right. For example, if someone laughs at your religious beliefs, don't get angry. Instead, listen politely and keep an open mind. If you don't agree with their beliefs, say, "You may believe what you wish; my beliefs work for me." Remember to speak courteously.

If someone makes fun of your sister or brother, you can say something like this: "Please don't talk about my family that way. He is my brother and that wasn't kind."

Loyalty is standing up for your beliefs and for what you care about. You are loyal when you stand firm during good times and bad times. When people threaten to harm the things, you are loyal to, you try to protect them. You do whatever is necessary to protect them, even when it is difficult.

---

[202] http://www.quotationspage.com
[203] http://www.quotationspage.com

Most people will trust you and admire you when you are loyal and committed to your family, friends, country, and good causes.

Story for Young Children

My Biggest Fan

A famous singer was once contracted to appear at a Paris Opera House. Ticket sales boomed and the night of the concert found the house full and every ticket sold.

A feeling of anticipation and excitement was in the air as the House Manager stepped out on the stage and announced, "Ladies and gentlemen, thank you for your enthusiastic support, but I have news that may be disappointing to some. An accident, not serious in nature but serious enough, will prevent the man you have come to hear from performing tonight." He went on to give the name of the understudy who would step into the role, but the crowd's groans drowned him out. The excitement in the audience turned to bitter disappointment and frustration as the opera began.

The stand-in artist gave the performance everything he had. Throughout the evening, there had been nothing but an uneasy silence. Even at the end, no one applauded.

Then from the balcony, the voice of a little girl broke the silence. "Daddy," she called out, "I think you were wonderful!"

The crowd broke into appreciative applause.[204]

Learning Questions

1. How did the daughter of the performer show her loyalty for her dad?
2. Have you ever shown loyalty for someone you love? How?
3. Have you had to stand firm when someone questioned one of your beliefs? Tell about it.

Story for Older Children

Loyalty

Few sights evoke as much attention and awe as that of a large flock of Canadian geese winging their way in their V-formation to the north or south. They speak of the changing seasons, and also of the value of teamwork.

What many don't know is that when a goose gets sick or perhaps is wounded by a shot, it never falls from formation by itself. Two other geese also fall out of formation with it and follow the ailing goose down to the ground. One of them is very often the mate of the wounded bird, since geese mate for life and are extremely loyal to their mates.

---

[204] Bits and Pieces, "My Biggest Fan," *Chicken Soup for the Father's Soul*, 173

Once on the ground, the healthy birds help protect him and care for him as much as possible, even to the point of throwing themselves between the weakened bird and possible predators. They stay with him until he is either able to fly, or until he is dead. Then, and only then, do they launch out on their own. In most cases they wait for another group of geese to fly overhead and they join them, adding to the safety and flying efficiency of their numbers.

If only we human beings would care for one another this well! Stick with your friends, and more importantly, stick by them.[205]

Learning Questions

1. How do geese take care of each other?
2. How can we show loyalty like the geese?
3. Name one way you can show loyalty to a family member or to a friend.

You Show Loyalty When You:

- Are unwavering in your commitment to family, friends, causes or country.
- Don't change your mind when your values are questioned or laughed at.
- Stand up for what you believe is right, no matter what.
- Stand firm during good times and bad times.
- Protect the things you love when they are threatened.

---

[205] God's Little Devotional Book for Leaders, p. 17

MERCY

Mercy

Definition Mercy: Being kind and forgiving to someone who has made a mistake.

Quotes

"The quality of mercy is not strain'd,
It droppeth as the gentle rain from heaven
Upon the place beneath: it is twice blest;
It blesseth him that gives and him that takes:
It is an attribute to God himself"

William Shakespeare[206]

"The greatest attribute of heaven is mercy."

Francis Beaumont and John Fletcher[207]

Explanation

Mercy is compassion and forgiveness. When you are merciful you care about other people's welfare. You overlook their weaknesses and forgive their mistakes.

When you are merciful you give people many chances to learn what they need to learn in order to "get it right." You are patient and long-suffering.

Merciful people are usually loving, tender, and kind, even to those who treat them unkindly. They care about humanity in general and each individual particularly.

One of the best things about being merciful is the true principle that everything we send into the lives of others comes back into our own, both good and bad. Since merciful people lovingly forgive others, when you show mercy, you'll probably be easily forgiven when you need forgiveness.

Is it easy to overlook hurtful things people do? Not usually. Should you treat others the way you'd like to be treated? Always!

---

[206] William Shakespeare, "The Merchant of Venice, Act 5, Scene 1, lines 184-195
[207] Edwards, Tyron. 1977. *The New Dictionary of Thoughts*. Stanbook, Inc., 404

Be quick to forgive and to forget the mistakes of others. When you can do this, you will have joy and many friends throughout your life.

Story for Young Children

<u>The Rattlesnake</u>

There is a true story about a group of teenagers who were out in the Arizona desert having a party. During their activities a girl was bitten on the leg by a rattlesnake. Everyone was horrified. They all were angry and ran after the rattlesnake to kill it. They wanted revenge, but they never caught the snake.

When they ran back to see how the injured girl was, her leg was swelling up quickly. Soon it was so swollen that it almost looked like an elephant's leg. The youth could tell that it was too late to try and suck the poison out of the leg. They knew that the poison was beginning to spread, so they quickly put her in a car and drove her to the nearest hospital.

The party was far out in the desert, so it took a while to finally get her medical help. She was put in the hospital and treated by the doctors and nurses there. Her leg was elevated to try and bring down the swelling from the rattlesnake's bite, but there was too much poison. Her leg needed to be amputated in order to save her life from the poison penetrating the rest of her body. The doctors told the youth that it was too bad they had spent precious time chasing the rattlesnake when they should have been using the time to remove the poison out of her leg.

This story is about choosing between forgiveness and revenge.

When someone strikes out at us and hurts our feelings or hurts someone we love, we might want to chase after them to get revenge, just like the teenagers in this story chased after the rattlesnake. A better choice is to have mercy. Instead of seeking revenge for what others have done to us, we should focus on removing the bad feelings we have. We should cleanse ourselves inside, just as the teenagers should have sucked out the poison in the girl's leg. We should think about forgiving the person who has hurt us and focus on eliminating our own weaknesses.[208]

Learning Questions

1. Why did the teenagers chase after the snake?
2. What might have happened if the teenagers had immediately sucked the poison out of the girl's leg instead of chasing after the snake?
3. What is one way you can show mercy when someone wrongs you?

---

[208] Retold by Rebecca Ashton

Story for Older Children

He Took My Lickin' for Me

Once upon a time, long ago, during the Great Depression, in the mountains of Virginia, there was a one-room schoolhouse and a pack of rowdy students that no teacher could handle. The boys were so rough that they had sent four teachers packing that very year.

A young, gray-eyed college graduate answered the ad for a new teacher and was given the job. The old School Director looked him up and down and warned him, "I don't want to mislead. You're in for a beatin', ain't no bones about it. Every teacher has took it and you'll take it, too."

"I'll risk it," said the young man.

The next morning the newly hired teacher stood before the class. "We're here to conduct school," he said. The boys in the class screamed and hooted. One of the boys, Big Tom they called him, leaned over to the others and said, "I won't need no help. I can chase this little bird myself."

"Now I want a good school, but I admit I don't know how to do that without your help. Suppose we have a few rules. You tell me what rules we should have, and I'll write them on the blackboard."

"No stealin'!" someone shouted, and the teacher wrote it on the board.

"On time!" came another. Soon there were ten rules written out neatly on the board.

"Now a rule is not much good without a punishment attached," said the teacher. "What should we do if someone breaks the rules?"

"Ten licks with the rod without his coat on!" someone yelled.

The teacher looked up at the rod hanging on the wall. "Ten licks. That's pretty severe, boys. Are you ready to stand by it?" The class agreed.

Not long after, Big Tom came into class very upset. Someone had stolen his lunch. The teacher interviewed the boys one by one and soon discovered the thief - a little scrawny fellow, scarcely ten years old.

The teacher called the boy forward to receive his punishment. "Take off your coat," he instructed.

"I deserve it. I'm guilty. I'll take the ten licks, but please don't make me take off my coat."

"Were you here the day we made the rules?"

The boy nodded, and the teacher took the rod down from its hook.

"You agreed to live by it. Take off your coat."

"Please don't make me," the boy pleaded. But slowly his fingers began to work at the buttons on his jacket, and what did his teacher see? He had no shirt on underneath, and the bones in his bare back stuck out all over. The boy's face was red with shame.

"Why have you come to school without your shirt, Jim?" the teacher asked.

"My daddy's dead and my momma's poor. I only got but one shirt, and it's in the wash today. I wore my brother's coat to keep warm."

The teacher looked down at the rod in his hand. He hesitated, unsure of what to do.

Suddenly Big Tom jumped to his feet. "I'll take his lickin' for him," he said.

"Very well," said the teacher. "There is a certain law that provides for a substitute, if you're all agreed."

Big Tom ripped off his coat and stood next to the boy. The teacher started the lashings, but after the fifth stroke the rod broke across Tom's back. The whole class was sobbing.

Little Jim reached up and caught Tom with both arms around his neck. "I'm sorry I took your lunch, Tom," he cried. "I was awful hungry. I'll love you forever for takin' my lickin' for me. Yes, I will love you forever!"[209]

Learning Questions

1. How did Tom show mercy to Jim?
2. Have you ever loved someone so much that you were willing to do something that showed mercy, even if it was hard for you?
3. In your own words, explain what mercy means to you.

You Show Mercy When You:

- Sincerely care about the welfare of others.
- Overlook weaknesses and hurtful things people do.
- Quickly forgive mistakes.
- Give people many chances to learn how to get it right.
- Are patient and long-suffering.
- Are loving and kind, even to those who treat you unkindly.

---

[209] Retold by Timothy Robinson, *He Took My Lickin' for Me*. (2003). Deseret Book Company, Publisher: Shadow Mountain

MODERATION

Moderation

Definition Moderation: Not too much or too little.

Quotes:

"To climb steep hills requires slow pace at first."

Shakespeare[210]

"The choicest pleasures of life lie within the ring of moderation."

Martin Farquhar Tupper[211]

Explanation

Moderation is using self-discipline to achieve a balance in the different areas of your life.

If you are a person who practices moderation, you aren't excessive. For example, you don't overeat, or work too hard, or sleep too long, or watch too much television, or stay on the Internet too long.

If you practice moderation, you understand that if you want to live a balanced life you need to eat healthfully, exercise regularly, sleep enough, play, work, and learn. But you should do all these things (and more) in a balanced way. That means that you should not spend so much time on one part of your life that you ignore other important areas of your life.

You live moderately by getting enough of what you need but not too much. For example, you should sleep enough to be healthy but sleeping too much is not good for you. (What is too much or too little is often different for different people).

The first part of practicing moderation is learning what is best for your body. The second part is to exercise enough self-discipline to be sure that you get what you need (sleep, food, etc.). The third part is stopping yourself before you get too much.

Some things we do are fine if done in moderation, but they are harmful if done in excess. Television watching and Internet use are two of these activities. They can both become negative addictions if you don't use self-discipline and moderation.

---

[210] Edwards, Tyron. 1977. *The New Dictionary of Thoughts.* Stanbook, Inc., 418
[211] Edwards, Tyron. 1977. *The New Dictionary of Thoughts.* Stanbook, Inc., 419

Achieving a balance isn't always consistently possible throughout your whole life. There are times when you may temporarily be unbalanced and focus on only one or two activities. For example, when someone is attending college or training for the Olympics, she or he may be temporarily very focused on achieving their educational or athletic goals. When those goals are accomplished, it will be easier to practice moderation.

Story for Young Children

<u>The Goose That Laid the Golden Egg</u>

Henry and Hilda lived happily in a small pink cottage on a sunny hilltop.

They worked hard from sunrise, when they went out to feed the geese, until sunset.

They had one cow named Violet. Every morning when Henry milked her, she managed to knock his hat off with a swish of her tail. One particularly curious white goose always came to watch. She was fond of Henry and followed him everywhere, even when he went to feed the two fat pigs.

In the evening, when Henry went indoors to have his supper, the white goose went to the barn where she had a nest.

One night Henry asked Hilda if she was happy on the farm. "Of course," answered Hilda. "We may not have much money, but we have all we need. I wouldn't change anything."

The very next morning, Hilda was surprised to see Henry running out of the barn with something shiny in his hand. "Hilda," he cried, "look what I've got! Our goose has laid an egg, a golden egg!" Henry could hardly believe his eyes.

When they examined the egg more carefully Hilda exclaimed, "It is gold! Solid gold! And look at the size of it. It must be worth a fortune!"

"Do you think she'll lay another one tomorrow?" asked Henry. He could see the end of hard work and the beginning of an easy life.

The next morning, they tiptoed into the barn. "I'll milk Violet later," muttered Henry. "We must see what the goose has for us!" And there, in the straw beside the white goose, lay another golden egg.

Now they had two solid golden eggs! Henry decided the white goose needed a better nesting box, so he set to work and gave the box a new coat of paint. The eggs kept coming and coming.

"We are rich," laughed Hilda each day as she put another egg in the growing pile. We can spend, spend, spend. And they did.

They sold Peggy, the faithful old horse who had served them so long and they bought a spritely young shire horse with bows and ribbons in his tail and mane.

"We can't ask this fine horse to pull our old cart," said Henry. "We must burn it." They were rich now, so they bought a fine new cart.

Every day they bought something new and threw away something they had been happy with before.

Then, one morning, there was no golden egg in the nest. There was no egg at all. "She's probably hungry," said Hilda. "Bring her into the kitchen and I'll feed her. We'll soon have plenty more golden eggs."

But they didn't. "Perhaps she's cold," suggested Henry. "Put her near the stove." They did. But the goose still didn't lay a golden egg.

Hilda flew into a terrible rage. "She must be hoarding them up inside herself!" she shrieked. "Kill her, Henry. Let's open her up and get the eggs. I like being rich!"

So, Henry took the white goose from the nesting box and killed it.

But when he cut her up, there were no golden eggs inside. And the beautiful white goose that had followed him everywhere was gone.

The next morning Hilda and Henry sold their fine new shire horse and bought back faithful old Peggy. "We were happy before we got rich and greedy," said Hilda sadly. "All the golden eggs have given us is unhappiness and now our goose is dead."

"We have learned a lesson, though," said Henry, "We will now be content with what we have." As he said this, the sun came out and shone on the little cottage.[212]

Learning Questions

1. What happened when Henry and Hilda became rich?
2. Does that always happen to rich people?
3. Name two things you can do to practice moderation in your life.

Story for Older Children

<u>Just One More</u>

Jason was too busy thinking about his new video game that he didn't even notice when Miss Debbie handed him his spelling test. He was excited to go home from school and start playing his new game. He probably could beat the dragon before the night was over!

---

[212] Aesop

When Jason finally looked down on his desk, he saw a big red **D** staring at him. *Mom and Dad are not going to be happy about this*, Jason thought. When the bell rang Jason stuffed his test in his backpack and headed out the door. On the bus Jason sat by his friend Cody.

"Hey Jason!" said Cody, "Do you want to come over and play catch today? My dad just bought me a new mitt!"

Cody was Jason's best friend, and they used to do things every day after school. However, ever since Jason started playing video games they hadn't been doing much together.

"No, maybe tomorrow I can come over. Today I'm starting a new game and I want to beat it before the night is over. Do you want to come and watch?" asked Jason.

"No way, that wouldn't be any fun. I guess I'll just see you tomorrow," said Cody.

As soon as Jason got home, he ran inside and turned on the T.V. He then put in his new video game and started to play. *I'll just play one game, and then I'll do my homework,* he thought.

Three hours later Jason's mom called him into the dining room for dinner. Jason didn't answer her because he was in the middle of a game. Suddenly the house seemed really quiet. Jason stopped his video game and went into the kitchen. To his surprise there was a note on the table from his mother.

Dear Jason,
  Sorry we couldn't wait for you, we had to leave for the movie or we would be late. Wish you could have come. There is lasagna in the fridge. If you need anything, just call Grandpa. We will be home by eight.
Love,
Mom

Why couldn't my family have waited two more seconds? I was almost past level 12! Jason thought angrily.

Jason had known about the family movie. They had planned on going over a week ago. He didn't think his family would leave without him. *Maybe I should do some homework while they are gone. Then again, it is Friday, and I can do it tomorrow.*

Jason headed to the living room to turn the video game back on.

ZAP! ZING! "Take that you mean old dragon!" Jason exclaimed. He was almost on level 50 which was the very last level of the video game.

On the following Monday evening things weren't much different.

"JASON! It's family night. Please come upstairs," his father called. Jason turned off the television and headed upstairs. His mom and dad and two older sisters were sitting on the couch waiting for him. Jason plopped down in a chair next to them.

"Tonight I thought we would talk about overcoming weaknesses. We all have weaknesses in our life.

"I know that this is true. I just recently overcame a weakness," Mom confessed. "As you children know, I love watching soap operas. Some days I didn't do anything but watch my shows. I didn't do any laundry, dishes, or grocery shopping. All I did was sit in front of the television. It wasn't until I realized it was a problem that I figured out a solution."

Jason squirmed in his chair. He suddenly felt very uncomfortable. Jason wasn't sure he was going to like this lesson.

"When I worked for the candy place on the corner, I would eat candy all the time," said Jason's oldest sister, Sara. "I would almost eat my paycheck each week in candy. I couldn't control myself because the candy tasted so good. Finally, I decided to set the amount of candy I would eat each day. I stuck to that amount, and I felt a lot better."

"Thank you for sharing your experiences," Dad said. "Now we can go on with our activity."

Jason was excited to play the game his sister Sara had planned. But even though he was excited, he felt funny in his stomach. After the game Jason went upstairs to his room and flopped down on his bed. He thought about what his family had said. *Maybe my weakness is video games.* He never saw his friend Cody anymore, and his grades were really bad. Maybe he should apply the lesson in his own life like his family members had.

Jason still had not beaten the dragon, but he decided to stop playing video games for the night. He had some reading and a lot of thinking to do instead.[213]

Learning Questions

1. Did Jason have a problem with video games?
2. Playing video games in moderation isn't a bad thing. How did Jason let it become a bad thing in his life?
3. Name one thing in your life that you should do in moderation.

You Show Preparation When You:

- Achieve balance in your life.
- Use self-discipline and self-control to prevent overdoing it in any one area of your life.
- Learn what is best for your body.
- Get enough of what you need but not too much.

---

[213] Just One More" by Teresa Weaver, *The Friend,* March 1999, p. 40-42

- Understand that some things are fine if done in moderation, but they're harmful if done in excess and can become addictions.

MODESTY

Modesty

Definition Modesty: Being humble and pure; proper.

Quotes

"Modesty is like a shining light; it prepares the mind to receive knowledge and the heart to receive truth."

Francois Guizot[214]

"Make no display of your talents or attainments; for everyone will clearly see, admire, and acknowledge them, so long as you cover them with the beautiful veil of modesty."

Nathaniel Emmons[215]

Explanation

Modesty is two things. It is being humble and not showing off or bragging about yourself. And modesty is acting and dressing properly.

Modest people accept praise, but they don't think they are better than others. They don't tell people how accomplished they are. When you're modest you let your actions speak for you, and you don't seek attention.

Also, modesty is sharing praise with others in a humble way. For example, when you achieve something with another person, you express your appreciation for his or her help. You acknowledge their good work and share the credit.

Modesty and humility are closely related values.

Additionally, when you are modest you don't wear clothes that attract attention to the private parts of your body. Modesty is respecting your body and not allowing others to touch you where they shouldn't.

---

[214] Edwards, Tyron. 1977. *The New Dictionary of Thoughts*. Stanbook, Inc., 419
[215] Edwards, Tyron. 1977. *The New Dictionary of Thoughts*. Stanbook, Inc., 419

Story for Young Children

<u>Washington's Modesty</u>

George Washington hurried home as soon as Fort Duquesne had fallen at the end of the Revolutionary War. General Washington resigned his commission and got married. He certainly seemed to have all that the heart of man could desire.

Just twenty-seven years old, in the first flush of manhood, keen of sense and yet wise in experience, life must have looked very good. He had left the army with well-earned fame and had come home to take the wife of his choice and enjoy the good will and respect of all men.

While away on his last campaign he had been elected a member of the House of Burgesses, and when he took his seat, three months after his marriage, Mr. Robinson, the Speaker, thanked him publicly for his services to the country.

Washington rose to reply, but he was so utterly unable to talk about himself that he stood before the House stammering and blushing until the Speaker said:

 "Sit down, Mr. Washington, your modesty equals your valor, and that surpasses the power of any language I possess."[216]

Learning Questions

1. What kind of man was Washington?
2. What can we learn from his example?
3. What does modesty mean to you?

Story for Older Children

<u>Learning Modesty</u>

Author Glenn Van Ekeren told this story about how he learned to be more modest:

"It took me three years to work up the nerve to take my wife along with me on a speaking engagement. My wife's approval would be the ultimate compliment and encouragement as I endeavored to become a respected public speaker. I feverishly memorized the key points, practiced my illustrations, and worked on voice fluctuation.

When I stepped on the podium that night, I was confident of my ability to deliver a flawless and inspiring speech. Forty-five minutes flew by and the crowd applauded my efforts. The pride swelled up inside of me as individual audience members shook hands and thanked me for a memorable address.

---

[216] Henry Cabot Lodge, Adapted, http://etext.lib.virginia.edu

In the car on the way home, I turned to my wife and asked, 'Sweetheart, how many great speakers do you think there are in the world today?'

She smiled, placed her hand on mine and softly said, 'One fewer than you think dear.' Ouch!

A thin line exists between having confidence in our abilities and being proud or conceited. Sometimes others have a better view of our position than we do. If you can handle their honesty, an objective outsider might be able to help you keep yourself from crossing that thin line."[217]

Learning Questions

1. How did the speaker's wife help him remain modest?
2. When is a time that you saw someone demonstrate modesty?
3. How can you show modesty in your own life?

You Show Modesty When You:

- Accept praise but don't think you are better than others.
- Don't tell people how good you are.
- Let your actions speak for you.
- Praise and appreciate others.
- Share with others.
- Respect your body and wear clothes that cover your private parts.
- Don't allow others to touch you where they shouldn't.

---

[217] Glenn Van Ekeren. *Speaker's Sourcebook II*. 1994. Paramus, New Jersey: Prentice Hall ,197

OBEDIENCE

Obedience

Definition Obedience: Following rules; doing what you're asked.

<u>Quotes</u>

"Obedience alone gives the right to command."

Ralph Waldo Emerson[218]

"Liberty is obedience to the law which one has laid down for oneself."

Jean-Jacques Rousseau[219]

Explanation

Obedience means following rules and keeping laws. It means doing what you are asked.

Your family, your teachers, and other leaders usually ask you to do things so you'll be safe and learn what you need to know. Even if you don't always understand their reasons, you should be respectful of good people with authority and obey what they ask you to do.

What happens when people don't obey rules? Without obedience people often hurt themselves or others. For example, if drivers don't stop at red lights what will happen? Without obedience to rules this would be a dangerous world.

When you keep family rules and do what you are told, things usually run smoothly at home and people are happy. When you obey, people know they can depend on you, and they trust you to make good decisions.

Ask yourself this question: "Do I obey rules just because I don't want to be punished, or am I obedient because it's the right thing to do?" It takes self-discipline and integrity to obey rules when no one is watching, but that's the best test of your strength of character.

---

[218] *Five thousand Quotations for All Occasions.* 1945. Edited by Lewis C. Henry. Garden City, New York: Doubleday & Company, Inc., 193

[219] http://217.11.110.254/quotations/Obedience/1.html

Story for Young Children

The Obedient Kid

In a stable lived a goat that had a pretty little kid, of which she was very fond. This kid was too young to go about without her mother; and the mother was half afraid to leave her by herself. But the goat was obliged to go out to get food.

One day she said to her little kid, "My dear, I am going to fetch a cabbage and a lettuce for your dinner. Mind you, do not go out while I am away. Lock the door of our stable, and do not open it to anyone who knocks, without first looking out of the window to see who it is that wants to come in. Pray, mind what I say to you, and do as I bid you."

"Yes, Mother," said the kid, "do not be afraid, I will do as you bid me."

So, off the old goat went. But she waited outside the door while the little kid shut it, and she looked back very often to see that it was kept shut.

A wolf who lived near, saw the goat pass by. He had often wished to eat up that nice tender young kid, and this day, having had no breakfast, he was very hungry. "Ah! ah! Now the old mother is out, I will go and eat that silly young kid. She will be sure to leave the door open." Away he ran to the stable where the goat lived. He went to the door with a bounce, thinking to push it open. He did not expect to find the door fastened; but he was mistaken, and he could not get in.

"Although you have fastened the door, little kid," growled he to himself, "I will eat you — I will knock, and you will be sure to come and open the door. And then ——"

He was so pleased with the thoughts of eating the little kid that he licked his lips; and lifting up his paw, gave a loud knock at the door.

"Who is there outside?" asked the little kid from within.

"I, my dear," said the wolf, trying to speak like the goat, "I, your mother; open the door quickly; I am in a hurry."

"Oh, no! You cannot be my mother," said the kid.

"Open the door this minute, or I shall be very angry with you," said the wolf.

"If you are my mother," said the little kid, "you will wait while I look out of the window, for my mother told me to do so before I opened the door."

"Open the door directly," called out the wolf. But the wise little kid went up to the window and looked out.

"Oh! You bad wolf," said she, "to try to cheat me! But you will not eat me today; so you may go away - ha! ha! ha!" and the kid laughed. "I take care to mind what my dear mother says to me. Master Wolf, you may go away!"

The wolf gnashed his teeth and growled. He looked very fierce at the little kid, but he could not reach her. The kid went from the window, but the wolf still heard her "Ha! ha! ha!" as she laughed at him safe inside the stable.

The wolf went away, and soon afterward the goat came back. She knocked at the door. The little kid asked, "Who is there?"

"It is I, your Mother, darling," said the goat.

"You speak like my mother; but I will be sure," said the kid, "before I open the door. If you are my mother really, you will not mind waiting while I look out of the window."

So again, the kid looked out of the window, and when she saw it was her own mother, she ran quickly and opened the door.

"Dear Mother," said she, "such a large, cruel wolf has been here; but I did as you bade me. I looked out of the window before I opened the door."

"Dear kid," said the goat, and she licked her with her tongue; "good kid, wise little kid. If you had not obeyed me, that cruel, greedy wolf would have eaten you up, and you would never have seen your mother again. Good child, to do as I bade you."

And then the goat gave the kid the fine lettuce and cabbage she had brought home with her.[220]

Learning Questions

1. What happened when the mother goat left the stable?
2. Was the kid obedient to his mother?
3. Why should we obey our parents?

Story for Older Children

The Bridge at Willow Creek

Every afternoon after school, twelve-year-old Marcus and his friends rode their bikes along the dirt road that followed Willow Creek. It was their favorite place in the whole town.

The creek twisted through tall trees, and the air smelled like pine and wet earth. Sometimes they skipped stones across the water. Sometimes they raced their bikes along the trail. Other days they

---

[220] Anna Pettit Broomell, Emily Cooper Johnson, Elizabeth W. Collins, Alice Hall Paxson, Annie Hillborn, and Anna D. White, http://www.strecorsoc.org/storygarden/31116_tok.html

simply sat on the old wooden bridge that crossed the creek and talked about school, soccer, and what they wanted to be when they grew up.

But there was one rule Marcus's father had made very clear. One evening at dinner, his father had said, "Marcus, never ride your bike across that bridge. Walk your bike across it. The boards are old, and one of them is loose." Marcus nodded. "Okay, Dad."

At first Marcus obeyed the rule easily. Every time he reached the bridge, he hopped off his bike and walked it carefully across, just like his father had told him. But his friends didn't.

One afternoon Tyler shouted, "Hey, watch this!" Tyler pedaled fast and bounced across the bridge, the wooden boards rattling loudly under his tires. The others laughed and followed him, riding quickly across the bridge.

Marcus stopped at the edge, holding his handlebars. "Come on!" Tyler called from the other side. "It's fine! Your Dad worries too much!"

Marcus looked down at the creek below. It wasn't very deep, but the rocks along the bottom were rough and jagged. He remembered his father's words: *One of the boards is loose.*

Marcus felt a tug inside him. Part of him wanted to ride across like the others and show that he wasn't afraid. But another part of him remembered something his father often said.

"Obedience isn't about control," his father had once explained. "It's about protection. Sometimes the people who love us can see dangers we don't see yet."

Marcus took a deep breath. "I'm walking my bike," he said. Some of the boys rolled their eyes. "You're such a rule follower," Tyler laughed.

Marcus shrugged and stepped onto the bridge, slowly walking his bike across the wooden planks. Behind him, Tyler turned around and started riding back across the bridge again.

Halfway across, there was a loud crack. One of the boards suddenly snapped beneath Tyler's front tire. His bike jerked sideways and he tumbled off, scraping his arm against the wooden rail. "Whoa!" Tyler shouted.

Marcus dropped his bike and ran back toward him. "Are you okay?" he asked.

Tyler sat up slowly, holding his elbow. His arm was scraped and bleeding, but he could still move it. "I think so," he said, looking shaken.

Together the boys carefully walked Tyler and his bike across the rest of the bridge. Later that evening Marcus told his father what had happened.

His father listened quietly and then said, "Marcus, I'm proud of you." Marcus looked surprised. "For what?"

"For choosing to obey, even when your friends didn't."

Marcus thought about the broken board and the loud crack that had echoed across the creek. "I guess you were right about the bridge," Marcus said.

His father smiled gently. "Sometimes obedience isn't easy," he said. "But it helps keep us safe until we're wise enough to see the danger for ourselves."

The next day, when Marcus and his friends reached the bridge again, something had changed. Tyler stopped his bike and looked at Marcus. "Maybe we should walk our bikes this time," he said. Marcus smiled. "Yeah," he said. "That sounds like a good idea."

And one by one, the boys stepped off their bikes and walked carefully across the bridge.

Learning Questions

1. How did Marcus' friends react when he said he wanted to obey his father?
2. When did you think you should obey, even if your friends might laugh at you?
3. What are some ways you can show obedience in your life?

You Show Obedience When You:

- Make good choices, even if others don't.
- Obey your family rules.
- Obey the rules at school.
- Obey safety rules and the rules in your city, state, and country.

OPTIMISM

Optimism

Definition Optimism: Looking on the bright side of things.

Quotes

"Keep your face to the sunshine and you cannot see the shadows."

Helen Keller[221]

"Two men look out through the same bars:
One sees the mud, and one the stars."

Frederick Langbridge[222]

Explanation

Optimism is being cheerful and noticing the good, happy things in life. Mr. W. Clement Stone said, "There is very little difference in people. But that little difference makes a big difference. The little difference is attitude. The big difference is whether it is positive or negative."[223] Having a positive attitude is called optimism.

A person with optimism is called an optimist. This is how optimists think:

1. When it rains, they are grateful that living things are getting a drink, and they look forward to the rainbow that often follows the rain.
2. When it's hot they choose to enjoy the sunshine. When it's cold they choose to enjoy a cozy fireplace.
3. When they see a glass that's half empty they think it's half full.
4. They notice the beautiful rose blossom instead of the thorn on the stem.
5. When bad things happen, they realize it could always be worse.

The truth is, you can choose to be a happy optimist or an unhappy pessimist. You just have to decide how you want to live your life. Robert Louis Stevenson was bedridden much of his life with a disease called tuberculosis. One day his wife heard him coughing loudly and said, "I suppose you still believe it's a wonderful day." Turning toward a window ablaze with sunlight,

---

[221] *Five thousand Quotations for All Occasions.* 1945. Edited by Lewis C. Henry. Garden City, New York: Doubleday & Company, Inc., 197

[222] *Five thousand Quotations for All Occasions.* 1945. Edited by Lewis C. Henry. Garden City, New York: Doubleday & Company, Inc., 197

[223] Glenn Van Ekeren. *Speaker's Sourcebook II.* 1994. Paramus, New Jersey: Prentice Hall, 46

Stevenson said with a cheerful voice, "I do! I will never let a row of medicine bottles block my horizon!" [224]

Many circumstances in our lives are negative and uncontrollable. However, we can choose our responses - our attitudes. Situations may color your view of life, but you have the power to choose what that color will be.

Story for Young Children

The Pebble of Success

In 1942, in Venezuela, South America, a man named Rafael Solano was physically exhausted and mentally defeated. He had begun his quest for diamonds months earlier, with high hopes and great optimism. Rafael was convinced that there were valuable diamonds in the riverbeds he explored.

However, days and months passed with no discovery. Solano had turned over thousands and thousands of rocks, to no avail. As he sat on a boulder in the dry riverbed he announced to his companion, "I'm through. There's no use going on any longer. See this pebble? It makes 999,999 I've picked up without finding one single diamond."

"What's the use?" he questioned. "I quit!"

Solano's friend was still optimistic and encouraged him to examine just one more pebble before he gave up.

And so Rafael Solano bent down and picked up a stone the size of a hen's egg. It was different than the others, and the prospector suddenly realized, to his utter amazement, that he had discovered a diamond…a huge diamond!

Harry Winston, a New York jewelry dealer, paid Solano $200,000 for that millionth pebble. The stone was named "The Liberator" and to date it is the largest and purest diamond ever found. [225]

Learning Questions

1. Can you name someone you know who is an optimistic person?
2. How do you feel when you're around them?
3. Could you be a little more optimistic?

---

[224] Glenn Van Ekeren. *Speaker's Sourcebook II*. 1994. Paramus, New Jersey: Prentice Hall, 47

[225] Adam Khan, http://www.cyberquotations.com/stories

Story for Older Children

<u>You Can Do Anything</u>

My name is Tina Karratti. Many years ago, my Dad was diagnosed with a terminal heart condition. He was put on permanent disability and was unable to work at a steady job. He would be fine for a while but would then fall suddenly ill and have to be taken to the hospital.

My Dad wanted to do something to keep himself busy, so he decided to volunteer at the local children's hospital. He loved children. It was the perfect job for him. Dad ended up working with the terminally and critically ill children. He would talk to them, play with them, and do arts and crafts with them.

Sometimes, one of the children would die. In certain instances, he would tell the grieving parents of these children that he would soon be with their child in heaven and that he would take care of their child until they got there. He would also ask the parent if there was a message they would like to send with him for their child.

My Dad's assurances seemed to help parents with their grieving. One of his children was a girl who had been admitted with a rare disease that paralyzed her from the neck down. I don't know the name of the disease or what the prognosis usually is, but I do know that it was very sad for a girl around eight or nine years old to have such a painful disease. She couldn't do anything, and she was very depressed.

Dad decided to try to help her. He started visiting her in her room, bringing paints, brushes and paper. He stood the paper up against a backing, put the paintbrush in his mouth, and began to paint. He didn't use his hands at all. Only his head would move. Dad would visit her whenever he could and paint for her. All the while he would tell her, "See, you can do anything you set your mind to."

Eventually, she began to paint using her mouth, and she and my dad became friends. Soon after, the little girl was discharged because the doctors felt there was nothing else they could do for her. My Dad also left the children's hospital for a little while because he became ill.

Sometime later after my Dad had recovered and returned to work, he was at the volunteer counter in the lobby of the hospital. He noticed the front doors open. In came the little girl who had been paralyzed, only this time she was walking. She ran straight over to my Dad and hugged him really tightly. She gave him a picture she had painted using her hands. At the bottom it read, "Thank you for helping me walk."

My dad cried every time he told us this story. He explained that love and optimism are sometimes more powerful than doctors. My Dad, who died soon after the little girl gave him the picture, was the most loving and optimistic person I have ever known.[226]

---

[226] Tina Karratti, *Chicken Soup for the Father's Soul*, 179-180

Learning Questions

1. How did her Dad stay optimistic even when he was very ill?
2. How does optimism influence people?
3. Name one way you can be more optimistic.

You Show Optimism When You:

- Are cheerful.
- Notice the good things in life.
- Feel gratitude.
- Realize things can always be worse.
- Choose to respond positively to negative circumstances in your life.

OVERCOMING ADVERSITY

Overcoming Adversity

Definition Overcoming Adversity: Not allowing your problems to discourage you or make you angry.

Quote

"Those who have suffered much are like those who know many languages; they have learned to understand and be understood by all."

Sophie Swetchine[227]

"Good timber does not grow with ease; the stronger the wind, the stronger the trees."

J. Willard Marriott[228]

Explanation

Adversities are the difficulties in life. Overcoming adversity means to courageously keep going when life gets tough. Another way of saying it is this: Overcoming adversity means to not allow adversity to overcome you.

You learn, as you grow older, that sometimes, bad things happen to good people. Sometimes your loved ones get sick and sometimes they die. People in your family might lose their jobs or quarrel with one another. Sometimes your best friends move away, or they get badly hurt.

Every person in the world has to deal with some difficulty - some adversity - in their lives.

The question isn't whether or not you'll experience adversity, but the question is how will you handle it when it comes? You can either be strong and look for ways to help others through the hard times, or you can complain that your life is so hard.

Mr. B.C. Forbes said, "History has demonstrated that the most notable winners usually encountered heartbreaking obstacles before they triumphed. They finally won because they refused to become discouraged by their defeats. Disappointments acted as a challenge. Don't let difficulties discourage you."[229]

---

[227] Edwards, Tyron. 1977. *The New Dictionary of Thoughts*. Stanbook, Inc., 7
[228] Glenn Van Ekeren. *Speaker's Sourcebook II*. 1994. Paramus, New Jersey: Prentice Hall, 20
[229] Glenn Van Ekeren. *Speaker's Sourcebook II*. 1994. Paramus, New Jersey: Prentice Hall, 156

Albert Einstein remarked, "In the middle of every difficulty lies opportunity."[230]

Years ago, every village had a blacksmith who crafted useful tools. As he pumped the bellows, the furnace fire was prepared. Into the intense heat the blacksmith placed a piece of iron until it reached an almost transparent state. The metal was removed from the fire and placed on the anvil, and with a heavy hammer the crafter pounded the iron, which was made bendable by the heat.

The iron was transformed by this repeated process. After the final shape was achieved, the hot iron was placed into water. The drastic temperature change tempered the iron and gave it durability and strength. The heat, hammer, and water together developed strength that could be achieved no other way. [231]

The adversities we encounter in life can strengthen us as we overcome them with wisdom, optimism, faith, and courage.

We are formed, matured, and strengthened through the adversities of life. "If you will call your troubles experiences," wrote John R. Miller, "and remember that every experience develops some latent force within you, you will grow vigorous and happy, however adverse your circumstances may seem to be."[232]

You will learn that as you overcome adversity again and again, you become stronger and better able to meet life's challenges with courage and calmness. Then you can help others do the same.

Story for Young Children

<u>Shake It Off and Step Up</u>

A parable is told of a farmer who owned an old mule. The mule fell into the farmer's well. The farmer heard the mule 'braying' or whatever mules do when they fall into wells. After carefully assessing the situation, the farmer sympathized with the mule but decided that neither the mule nor the well was worth the trouble of saving.

Instead, he called his neighbors together and told them what had happened and asked them to help haul dirt to bury the old mule in the well and put him out of his misery.

At first the old mule was hysterical! But as the farmer and his neighbors continued shoveling and the dirt hit his back, a thought struck him. It suddenly dawned on him that every time a shovel load of dirt landed on his back, he should shake it off and step up! This he did, blow after blow.

"Shake it off and step up... shake it off and step up... shake it off and step up!" he repeated to encourage himself. No matter how painful the blows or distressing the situation seemed, the old

---

[230] Glenn Van Ekeren. *Speaker's Sourcebook II*. 1994. Paramus, New Jersey: Prentice Hall, 22

[231] Glenn Van Ekeren. *Speaker's Sourcebook II*. 1994. Paramus, New Jersey: Prentice Hall, 21-22

[232] http://thewebsage.com/couldyourtroublesreallybeblessings.htm

mule fought panic and just kept right on shaking it off and stepping up.

What do you think happened? That's right - it wasn't long before the old mule, battered and exhausted, stepped triumphantly over the wall of that well! What seemed like it would bury him actually blessed him. All because of the way he handled his adversity.[233]

Learning Questions

1. How did the farmer's old mule get out of the well?
2. What can you shake off in your life so you can step up?

Poem for Older Children

<u>What Do You Do With Your Morsel of Sand?</u>

There once was an oyster whose story I tell -
Who found that some sand had got under his shell
Just one little grain--but it gave him pain,
(For oysters have feelings…they are so plain!)

How did he berate the working of fate
Which had led him to such a deplorable state?
Did he curse out the government?
Call for an election?
And cry that the sea should have given protection?

No! He said to himself as he lay on a shelf—
'Since I cannot remove it—I'll try to improve it'

The years rolled around as the years always do,
And he came to his ultimate destiny—stew!
And the small grain of sand that had bothered him so
Was a beautiful pearl all richly aglow.

The tale has a moral, for isn't it grand
What an oyster can do with a morsel of sand?[234]

Learning Questions

1. Have you ever felt like you had sand under your shell? What was it that bothered you?
2. What's one thing you can do when something bothers you?

---

[233] Author Unknown, http://www.cyberquotations.com/stories
[234] Author Unknown, ESM, Vol 1, p.33

Additional Ideas for Older Children

<u>Examples of People Who Overcame Adversity</u>

- ➤ Walt Disney failed and went bankrupt five times before experiencing success.
- ➤ Beethoven rose above his deafness to compose harmonious music.
- ➤ John Bunyan wrote Pilgrim's Progress while confined to a prison cell for his views on religion.
- ➤ The Greek orator Demosthenes overcame a lifetime of stuttering to rally people with his powerful speeches.
- ➤ Deaf, speechless and blind since early childhood, Helen Keller achieved greatness experienced by few without such handicaps. "The marvelous richness of human experience would lose something of rewarding joy if there were not limitations to overcome," commented Helen Keller. "The hilltop hour would not be half so wonderful if there were no dark valleys to transverse."
- ➤ In the 1952 Olympics, a young Hungarian boy named Karoly Takacs split the bull's eye on the target again and again. His eye-hand coordination with his right arm won him a gold medal. Then disaster struck. His right arm had to be amputated; he lost it. Four years later Karoly returned to the Olympics in Melbourne, Australia, and split the bull's eye as he had done before, using his left arm.
- ➤ As an elementary student actor James Earl Jones stuttered so badly he communicated with friends and teachers using written notes. Today, he is known for the richness and power of his voice.
- ➤ Experiencing a lifetime of personal failures and setbacks, Winston Churchill persevered to become Prime Minister of England at age 62.
- ➤ Adversity can only strip the music of life if we allow it. Washington Irving believed, "Little minds are subdued by misfortunes, but great minds rise above them."[235]

You Show Overcoming Adversity When You:

- Keep going when life gets difficult.
- Learn that sometimes bad things happen to good people.
- Learn that every person has to deal with adversity in life.
- Don't let difficulties discourage you.
- Understand that as you overcome adversity you get better at meeting life's challenges with courage and calmness.
- Help others deal with their challenges.

---

[235] Glenn Van Ekeren. *Speaker's Sourcebook II*. 1994. Paramus, New Jersey: Prentice Hall, 22-23

PATIENCE

Patience

Definition Patience: Waiting without complaining.

Quotes

"To know how to wait is the greatest secret of success."

Joseph De Maistre[236]

"There is no great achievement that is not the result of patient working and waiting."

J.G. Holland[237]

Explanation

Patience is waiting for things you want without complaining. It means staying calm when things go wrong. When you're patient you are kind to others when they make mistakes. You are also gentle with yourself.

Nearly every day we have opportunities to practice patience. Children want to learn quickly how to tie a shoe, ride a bike, or play the piano. Many teenagers want to grow taller faster, drive a car sooner, or find short-cuts in life. Often, adults impatiently want better skills to make more money, or they want to be recognized sooner for their accomplishments. However, since most worthwhile things in life take time, patience is an important value to learn early in life.

Patience is also persevering. It is sticking to a task until it is done, no matter how long it takes. When you have patience, you understand that some things take a long time.

Have you ever planted a seed? You must wait and wait until the seed turns into a flower or a vegetable. When you're patient you wait without getting upset. Did you know it takes many years for trees to grow? Nature seldom seems to be in a hurry.

When you have patience, if something goes wrong and you're hurt or sick, you don't get angry or complain. You understand that everything will be fine eventually. You try to look on the bright side of things and try to discover what you can learn from the experience. For example, if you broke your leg, you could either be angry every day about not playing and running outside or

---

[236] Edwards, Tyron. 1977. *The New Dictionary of Thoughts.* Stanbook, Inc., 469
[237] Edwards, Tyron. 1977. *The New Dictionary of Thoughts.* Stanbook, Inc., 470

you could be patient and enjoy reading and watching good movies while your leg heals. Like all values, practicing patience is a choice.

When we are patient, we use self-control as we calmly endure delay or unpleasant situations without complaining. For example, patient people don't get upset while they're waiting in lines. They don't criticize and blame others when things go wrong. Instead, they have empathy for those who cause their delays. Patient people help others be calm and patient too.

Story for Young Children

The Impatient Monk

There was a monk who was very impatient. You may wonder, why would a monk be impatient? Don't they become monks so that they don't have to deal with the world? Yes, that's true. So, imagine how impatient this monk was…

The more he tried, the more impatient he became, so he decided that he must get away altogether, to learn to be patient. So, he built himself a little home deep in the woods, far away from civilization.

Years later, a man was traveling in those woods and met him. The man was amazed to find anyone living so far away from the rest of the world, so he asked the monk why he was there all by himself.

The monk said that he was there to learn to be patient.

The traveler asked how long he had been there, and the monk replied: seven years. Stunned, the traveler asked, "If there is no one around to bother you, how will you know when you are patient?"

Annoyed, the monk replied, "Get away from me, I have no time for you."[238]

Learning Questions

1. Was the monk really patient?
2. Why should we be patient with others?
3. What can you do to have more patience in your life?

Story for Older Children

The Cab Ride I'll Never Forget

I arrived at the address and honked the horn. After waiting a few minutes, I honked again. Since this was going to be the last ride of my shift I thought about just driving away, but instead I put

---

[238] Carmen Colombo, http://www.wowzone.com/patience.htm

the car in park and walked up to the door and knocked. 'Just a minute', answered a frail, elderly voice. I could hear something being dragged across the floor.
After a long pause, the door opened. A small woman in her 90's stood before me. She was wearing a print dress and a pillbox hat with a veil pinned on it, like somebody out of a 1940's movie.

By her side was a small nylon suitcase. The apartment looked as if no one had lived in it for years. All the furniture was covered with sheets.

There were no clocks on the walls, or anything on the counters. In the corner was a cardboard box filled with photos and glassware.

'Would you carry my bag out to the car?' she said. I took the suitcase to the cab, then returned to assist the woman.

She took my arm and we walked slowly toward the curb.

She kept thanking me for my kindness. 'It's nothing', I told her. 'I just try to treat my passengers the way I would want my mother to be treated.'

'Oh, you're such a good boy, she said. When we got in the cab, she gave me an address and then asked, 'Could you drive through downtown?'

'It's not the shortest way,' I answered quickly.

'Oh, I don't mind,' she said. 'I'm in no hurry. I'm on my way to a hospice.

I looked in the rear-view mirror. Her eyes were glistening. 'I don't have any family left,' she continued in a soft voice. 'The doctor says I don't have very long.' I quietly reached over and shut off the meter.

'What route would you like me to take?' I asked.

For the next two hours, we drove through the city. She showed me the building where she had once worked as an elevator operator.

We drove through the neighborhood where she and her husband had lived when they were newlyweds. She had me pull up in front of a furniture warehouse that had once been a ballroom where she had gone dancing as a girl.

Sometimes she'd ask me to slow down in front of a particular building or corner and would sit staring into the darkness, saying nothing.

As the first hint of sun was creasing the horizon, she suddenly said, 'I'm tired. Let's go now'. We drove in silence to the address she had given me. It was a low building, like a small convalescent home, with a driveway that passed under a portico.

Two orderlies came out to the cab as soon as we pulled up. They were solicitous and intent, watching her every move. They must have been expecting her.

I opened the trunk and took the small suitcase to the door. The woman was already seated in a wheelchair.

"How much do I owe you?" She asked, reaching into her purse.

"Nothing," I said.

"You have to make a living," she answered.

"There are other passengers," I responded.

Almost without thinking, I bent and gave her a hug. She held onto me tightly.

"You gave an old woman a little moment of joy," she said. "Thank you."

I squeezed her hand, and then walked into the dim morning light. Behind me, a door shut. It was the sound of the closing of a life.

I didn't pick up any more passengers that shift. I drove aimlessly lost in thought. For the rest of that day I could hardly talk. What if that woman had gotten an angry driver, or one who was impatient to end his shift? What if I had refused to take the run, or had honked once, then driven away?

On a quick review, I don't think that I have done anything more important in my life.

We're conditioned to think that our lives revolve around great moments.

But great moments often catch us unaware, beautifully wrapped in what others may consider a small one."[239]

Learning Questions

1. How was the cab driver patient?
2. In what ways could patience help you in your life?

You Show Patience When You:

- Wait for things you want without complaining.
- Stay calm when things go wrong.
- Try to discover what you can learn from the experience.

---

[239] Kent Nerburn, https://zenmoments.org/the-cab-ride-ill-never-forget/

- Stick to a task until it is done.
- Understand that some things take a long time and eventually things usually turn out fine.
- Try to look on the bright side of things.
- Are gentle with yourself.
- Are kind to others and forgive others when they make mistakes.

PEACE

Peace

Definition Peace: Being calm; not fighting.

Quotes

"First keep the peace within yourself, then you can also bring peace to others."

Thomas a Kempis[240]

"If you cannot find peace within yourself, you will never find it anywhere else."

Marvin Gaye[241]

Explanation

Peace is an inner feeling of calm. It is the ability to find peaceful solutions to conflict. Peace is the opposite of violence.

Peace helps create agreement between people who disagree. Every family has disagreements occasionally. How we handle them is our choice. To reach peaceful agreements, family members can try this:

1. Listen to each other carefully and sincerely try to understand the needs and wants of the other person.
2. Discuss the conflict with kindness.
3. If possible, agree to compromise so that each person gets at least a portion of what he or she wants. If a compromise isn't possible, consider taking turns.
4. Never be angry or resentful after a final decision has been made.

One effective way of solving family problems is to discuss them during a family meeting. Family members should be encouraged to bring family – related problems to a regularly – held meeting (weekly is ideal). Problems can be discussed in a calm atmosphere where everyone can participate in suggesting possible solutions.

After family members agree on a plan for improvement, the entire family can work on the solution together. Finding peaceful solutions takes self-control and extra effort, but guarantees rich rewards.

---

[240] http://www.quotationspage.com
[241] http://www.quotationspage.com

Peacefulness also means having a peaceful heart. This means that you think kind thoughts about others. You keep an open mind; you listen to, and consider, ideas that are different than yours. When you are peaceful you don't get angry quickly because you are patient with others' mistakes. If someone hurts you, you don't try to get even with them. That's called revenge, and peaceful people are not revengeful. Rather, they let the issue go and get on with their lives.

Peaceful people do all they can to avoid quarreling and fighting. They don't criticize or judge others. If you are peaceful, you speak kindly, gently and softly. That's the language of peace.

Peace comes when people eliminate violence. It comes when we pay attention to the many ways we are alike, rather than focusing on how we are different. Peace comes when people start thinking of one another as friends, no matter how different they are. We will enjoy a peaceful world when men and women learn how to compromise and create peaceful solutions to their problems.

Story for Young Children

Peace

There once was a king who offered a prize to the artist who would paint the best picture of peace. Many artists tried. The king studied all the pictures, but there were only two he really liked. He had to choose which one would win the prize.

One picture was of a beautiful, calm lake. The lake was a perfect mirror; peaceful towering mountains surrounded it. Overhead was a blue sky with fluffy white clouds. All who saw this picture thought that it was a perfect picture of peace.

The other picture had mountains too. The mountains were rugged and bare. Above was an angry sky from which rain fell and in which lightning played. Down the side of the mountain tumbled a foaming waterfall. This did not look peaceful at all. But when the king looked closer he saw behind the waterfall a tiny, green bush growing out of a crack in the rock. In the bush a mother bird had built her nest. There, in the midst of the rush of angry water, sat the mother bird on her nest, perfectly peaceful.

Which picture do you think won the prize?

The king chose the second picture. "Because," explained the King, "peace does not mean to be in a place where there is no noise, trouble, or hard work. Peace means to be in the midst of all those things and still be calm in your heart. That is the real meaning of peace."[242]

Learning Questions

1. What does peace mean to you?

---

[242] Author Unknown, Source Unknown, http://www.inspirationalstories.com

2. How did each picture show peacefulness?
3. What is one thing you can do to have peace in your life?

Story for Older Children

<u>The Splashes of Life</u>

My grandfather took me to the fishpond on the farm when I was about seven, and he told me to throw a stone into the water. He told me to watch the circles created by the stone. Then he asked me to think of myself as that stone. "You may create lots of splashes in your life but the waves that come from those splashes will disturb the peace of all your fellow creatures," he said. "Remember that you are responsible for what you put in your circle, for that circle will touch many other circles. You will need to live in a way that allows the good from your circle to strengthen and add goodness to other circles. The splash that comes from anger or jealousy will send those feelings to other circles. You are responsible for both the good and the bad ripples you send out to others."

That was the first time I realized that each person creates the inner peace or discord that flows out into the world. We cannot create world peace if we are riddled with inner conflict, hatred, doubt, or anger. We radiate the feelings and thoughts that we hold inside, whether we speak them or not. Whatever is splashing around inside of us is spilling out into the world, creating beauty or discord with all other circles of life. "Remember this wisdom," my grandfather added. "Whatever you focus on expands."[243]

Learning Questions

1. How are your thoughts and actions (that ripple out to others), like a stone tossed into a pond?
2. Have you felt the rippling effects of other people's choices splash and spill onto you?
3. What can you do to make sure the circles you create are peaceful?

You Show Peace When You:

- Help create an agreeable solution for people who disagree.
- Have a peaceful heart.
- Think kind thoughts.
- Keep an open mind by listening and considering ideas that are different than yours.
- Don't get angry easily, and don't criticize or judge others.
- Are patient with others' mistakes.
- Don't try to get back at people who upset you.
- Avoid quarreling and fighting.
- Speak the language of peace, which is kindness and gentleness.

---

[243] Author Unknown

PERSEVERANCE

Perseverance

Definition Perseverance: To keep trying no matter how difficult your challenge is.

Quotes

"Keep going and the chances are you will stumble on something, perhaps when you are least expecting it. I never heard of anyone stumbling on something sitting down."

Charles Kettering[244]

"It always seems impossible until it's done."

Nelson Mandela[245]

Explanation

Perseverance means giving full effort to what you're doing and sticking with it until it's finished. An old saying is, "Stick to a task until it sticks to you; starters are many but enders are few." People with perseverance have the courage to hold on and do their best, even when life is difficult.

Many successful people failed at first, but they persevered — they kept trying. Here are some examples:

1. In his first three years making automobiles Henry Ford went bankrupt twice.
2. Charles Goodyear wanted to make a rubber tire that was not affected by temperature, but he failed time and time again. Mr. Goodyear was so poor he was put in prison for not paying his debts. His family and friends ridiculed him, but Goodyear persevered and was finally successful. He invented tires like the ones on cars today, and he became very wealthy.
3. Michael Jordan was cut from his high school basketball team, but he didn't give up. Michael Jordan became perhaps the world's best basketball player.
4. Albert Einstein's university rejected his Ph.D. dissertation saying it was "irrelevant." Einstein persevered and later discovered the Theory of Relativity.
5. David W. Hartman went blind at age eight, but he still wanted to become a doctor. Temple University Medical School told him that no blind person could ever be a doctor. But David Hartman persevered and became the first blind doctor in the world.

---

[244] Glenn Van Ekeren. *Speaker's Sourcebook II*. 1994. Paramus, New Jersey: Prentice Hall, 278
[245] Glenn Van Ekeren. *Speaker's Sourcebook II*. 1994. Paramus, New Jersey: Prentice Hall, 277-278

6. Johnny Unitas loved football and wanted to play on a professional team, but everyone told him he was too little. Johnny worked construction and kept trying out for every team that would let him on the field. Finally, the Baltimore Colts gave him a chance. He became a great quarterback and led the Colts to a world championship. Later, Johnny Unitas was inducted into the Football Hall of Fame.[246]

All of these people and many more have persevered when it would've been easier to give up. John D. Rockefeller said, "I do not think there is any other quality so essential to success of any kind as the quality of perseverance." [247]

Poem for Young Children

Two Frogs in a Bowl

Two frogs fell in a deep bowl,
One was an optimistic soul
But the other took the gloomy view.
"We shall drown!" he cried without adieu.
So, ith a last despairing cry
He flung up his legs and said goodbye.
Quoth the other frog with a merry grin,
"I can't get out, but I won't give in!
I'll just swim around till my strength is spent,
Then will I die the more content."
Bravely he swam until it would seem
His struggles began to churn the cream.
On top of the butter at last he stopped,
And out of the bowl he gaily hopped.
What of the moral? 'Tis easily found:
If you can't hop out, keep swimming around![248]

Learning Questions

1. What did the second frog do to get out of the bowl?
2. If you have a problem, how can you be like the frog?

Story for Older Children

Men Who Persevered

In 1902, an aspiring young writer received a rejection letter from the poetry editor of The Atlantic Monthly. Enclosed with a sheaf of poems the 28-year-old poet had sent was this curt

---

[246] Glenn Van Ekeren. *Speaker's Sourcebook II*. 1994. Paramus, New Jersey: Prentice Hall, 280

[247] Glenn Van Ekeren. *Speaker's Sourcebook II*. 1994. Paramus, New Jersey: Prentice Hall, 277

[248] Author Unknown, EFM, V 1, p. 106

note: "Our magazine has no room for your vigorous verse." He rejected the rejection, however, and went on to see his work published. His name was Robert Frost. One of the most famous and beloved poets of all time.

In 1905, the University of Bern turned down a Ph.D. dissertation as being fanciful and irrelevant. The young physics student, who wrote the dissertation, rejected their rejection and went on to develop some of his fanciful ideas into widely accepted theories. His name was Albert Einstein. Einstein later won the Nobel Prize.

In 1894, a sixteen-year-old found this note from his rhetoric teacher at Harrow, in England, attached to his report card: "A conspicuous lack of success." The young man rejected the rejection and went on to become one of the most famous speakers of the twentieth century. His name was Winston Churchill. Churchill became the Prime Minister of England.

Reject the rejection you receive today, and persevere to achieve success.[249]

Learning Questions

1. What do Robert Frost, Albert Einstein, and Winston Churchill have in common?
2. How can you follow the examples in this lesson to help you achieve your dreams?

You Show Perseverance When You:

- Give full effort to what you're doing and stick with it until it's finished.
- Have the courage to keep doing your best, even when it's difficult.
- Understand that many successful people weren't successful at first.
- Understand that having perseverance is essential for long-term success.

---

[249] God's Little Devotional Book for Leaders, p. 93

PREPARATION

Preparation

Definition Preparation: Getting ready for something.

Quotes

"One of life's most painful moments comes when we must admit that we didn't do our homework; that we are not prepared."

Merlin Olsen[250]

"In all things success depends upon previous preparation, and without such preparation, there is failure."

Confucius[251]

Explanation

Preparation is getting ready for something. You get ready for different things in different ways. For example, if you want to be a great athlete you have to work very hard at your sport, practicing every day to get better. Even on days that you're not "in the mood" or not feeling your very best, you need to practice.

If you want to be an excellent musician — a fine pianist, for example — you need to play the piano, hour after hour, day after day. If you want to be an accomplished scholar, you need to read and study.

Every praiseworthy accomplishment requires preparation. Few people can be successful without hours, days, and sometimes years of preparation.

Basketball star and former Senator Bill Bradley reminds us, "When you are not practicing, remember, someone somewhere is practicing; and when you meet him, he will win."[252] When you diligently prepare, you'll be ready when the opportunity arrives to perform or compete.

---

[250] Glenn Van Ekeren. *Speaker's Sourcebook II*. 1994. Paramus, New Jersey: Prentice Hall, 301

[251] Glenn Van Ekeren. *Speaker's Sourcebook II*. 1994. Paramus, New Jersey: Prentice Hall, 301

[252] http://www.dreamjobcoach.com/practice.shtml

Do you have to enjoy preparation in order to succeed? Former world champion fighter Muhammad Ali would say no. Ali remarked, "I hated every minute of the training, but I said to myself, 'Don't quit. Suffer now and live the rest of your life as a champion.'"[253]

Of course, it's best if you enjoy the process — the journey to success. But understand that there will be days that are difficult no matter how much you like what you're doing. It takes a lot of unspectacular preparation to produce spectacular results.

Story for Young Children

I Can Sleep When the Wind Blows

Many years ago, the old country fair in parts of England was, besides being the place of exhibition for farm products, the place where employer and employee met. A farmer at the fair sought to hire his help for the coming year, and young and old went to the fair to seek employment.

Farmer Smith wanted a boy to work on his farm. He was interviewing some candidates when a thoughtful-looking lad of about sixteen attracted his attention. The gruff old agriculturist asked the boy, "What can you do?" The boy swung back at him in the same style, "I can sleep when the wind blows."

Even though he didn't particularly like the teenager's answer, there was something about his gray eyes that interested the farmer. Smith went to other parts of the fair to look into the faces of other young men who might want a job on his farm – but there was something about the boy's answer that intrigued him.

Before long the farmer returned to the steady gaze of those deliberate eyes of the boy with such an answer. "What did you say you could do?" he thundered for the third time. For the third time, he heard, "I can sleep when the wind blows."

"Get into my wagon; we'll try you out."

One night several weeks later, Farmer Smith awoke about two o'clock in the morning to what sounded like a cyclone. It seemed that gusts from the north had developed with such intensity that they threatened the roof over his head. The trees cracked, and noises outside electrified his nervous system. The speed with which he jumped into his trousers was outdone only by the lightning that split the darkness outside. With shoes half-laced, he rushed out into the farmyard to see if anything on the premises was still intact, and he knew he would need the services of the new boy he had hired. He called up the stairs of the attic where the boy slept, but the response was the healthy lung-heaving of a healthy lad. He went halfway up the stairs and thundered again, but only a snore echoed back. In excitement, he went to the boy's bed and did everything but tear the bedclothes from the youth. The lad slept on.

---

[253] Glenn Van Ekeren. *Speaker's Sourcebook II*. 1994. Paramus, New Jersey: Prentice Hall, 301

With a mixture of desperation and disgust, he faced the gale, and plunged out into the farmyard. He first approached the cow barn. Lo and behold, the milk producers were peacefully chewing their cuds, and inside their abode they were as snug as a mouse under a haystack. It didn't take him long to discover how the boy had chinked up the cracks of the cow abode and fixed the locks and hinges. In the pigpen he discovered the same tranquility, even as the wind howled on.

He turned to the haystack. As he groped in the darkness, it didn't take him long to determine again the preparation of the lad with the gray, steady eyes. Every few feet on that feed stack, wires had been thrown and weighted on each side. With this construction, the alfalfa was peacefully under control.

The farmer was stunned with the revelations he had in a few short minutes on the night of that cyclone. He dropped his head. His mental maneuvers shot like lightning to the boy snoring in the attic. And the farmer remembered the peculiar answer the young man gave him a few weeks ago when he calmly said, "I can sleep when the wind blows."[254]

Learning Questions

1. What did the boy mean when he said, "I can sleep when the wind blows?"
2. How did the boy show preparation?
3. When you have a chore or homework to do, how can you follow the boy's example and prepare yourself?

Story for Older Children

Be Prepared

An engineer of a fast express, as he rounded a bend, suddenly saw a short distance ahead a freight wreck on the track next to his own. Two cars had buckled over and lay in the path of his train. There was no time to slow down; there was not a moment to think. In a flash the engineer pulled the throttle wide open and yelled to the fireman to duck down low. The terrific impetus of the express knocked the wrecked cars from the track amidst splintered debris. The train was brought to a stop a half mile on the other side.

As the passengers crowded around the engineer, one asked him how, in such a moment of crisis, he could think quickly enough to make and to act upon the only decision that could have saved his train from a wreck. He replied, "I did not think. I did not have to think. I had often thought of such a possibility, and I made up my mind ten years ago just what I would do if such a situation ever arose. When it did come, I acted instinctively."[255]

Learning Questions

1. How did preparation help the engineer in this story?

---

[254] Author Unknown, EFM, V 5, p. 214-215
[255] Author Unknown, EFM, V 4, p. 234-235

2. What are some things you should be preparing for?
3. What are you going to start doing today to be more prepared?

You show preparation when you:

- Get ready for something.
- Practice every day.
- Understand that there will be difficult days.
- Keep trying, no matter what.

RELIABILITY

Reliability

Definition Reliability: Being worthy of people's trust.

Quotes

"A man who lacks reliability is utterly useless."

Confucius[256]

"A total commitment is paramount to reaching the ultimate in performance."

Tom Flores[257]

Explanation

Reliability means that when you say you'll do something, you do it without being reminded. For example, if one of your family jobs is to put out the trash, you do it when you're supposed to, without being told again and again.

Reliability is keeping your promises. If you tell someone that you'll do something, you do it, even if later you change your mind and you'd rather not. For example, if you tell someone you'll meet him after school, you keep your promise, no matter what.

When you're reliable you always do your best. Every time you are given an assignment or a job to do, you give it your best effort. Reliable people don't give up when a task is hard, they keep trying.

When you are reliable, you plan ahead. You find out what you're supposed to do, what is expected of you, and you leave enough time to do it well. You start your jobs in plenty of time so that you can do good work and finish on time.

What if something happens while you're working that keeps you from finishing right then? If you're reliable, you come back later and finish your job, without being reminded.

When you are reliable, people can count on you to keep your promises and to do your best. It's nice when people know they can trust you.

---

[256] "The Spoken Word" from Temple Square, presented over KSL and the Columbia Broadcasting System August 8, 1971. © 1971 by Richard L. Evans.

[257] Glenn Van Ekeren. *Speaker's Sourcebook II*. 1994. Paramus, New Jersey: Prentice Hall, 64

Story for Young Children

Bailey the Reliable Dog

Bailey is the most amazing dog you will ever meet. Benjamin is five and is handicapped. Ben's mom bought Bailey to be a companion for her son two years ago. Benjamin is blind and crippled, so he gets around in a wheelchair. Bailey and Benjamin are inseparable; they love and trust one another completely.

Recently, Benjamin was in an accident. He was on top of a short ramp with Bailey. Upon entry to a shop, Benjamin fell backwards and was rolling down the ramp at full throttle. His wheelchair was two meters away from a busy road and Bailey ran as fast as he could to stop and save him. Bailey did just that, but was injured and lost his leg in the process, nearly losing his life. Benjamin was two inches from death but Bailey saved him, putting his own life on the line. Bailey is a true and reliable companion, not to mention a real hero, and as precious as he was then to Ben, he is more precious to Ben now than ever.[258]

Learning Questions

1. What does it mean to be reliable?
2. Name two ways you can show reliability.

Story for Older Children

Optimistic Spirit

The passengers on the bus watched sympathetically as the attractive young woman with the white cane made her way carefully up the steps. She paid the driver and, using her hands to feel the location of the seats, walked down the aisle and found the seat he'd told her was empty. She settled in, placed her briefcase on her lap and rested her cane against her leg.

It had been a year since Susan, age thirty-four, became blind. Due to a medical misdiagnosis, she had been rendered sightless, and she was suddenly thrown into a world of darkness, anger, frustration and self-pity.

Once a fiercely independent woman, Susan now felt condemned by this terrible twist of fate to become a powerless, helpless burden on everyone around her. "How could this have happened to me?" she would plead, her heart knotted with anger. But no matter how much she cried or ranted or prayed, she knew the painful truth - her sight was never going to return.

A cloud of depression hung over Susan's once optimistic spirit. Just getting through each day was an exercise in frustration and exhaustion. And all she had to cling to was her husband Mark.

---

[258] http://www.gettysburgtimes.com/app/nie/trustworthiness.pdf

Mark was an Air Force officer, and he loved Susan with all of his heart. When she first lost her sight, he watched her sink into despair and was determined to help his wife gain the strength and confidence she needed to become independent again.

Mark's military background had trained him well to deal with sensitive situations, and yet he knew this was the most difficult battle he would ever face.

Finally, Susan felt ready to return to her job, but how would she get there? She used to take the bus, but now she was too frightened to get around the city by herself. Mark volunteered to drive her to work each day, even though they worked at opposite ends of the city. At first, this comforted Susan and fulfilled Mark's need to protect his sightless wife who was so insecure about performing the slightest task.

However, Mark soon realized that this arrangement wasn't working. It was hectic and costly. Susan is going to have to start taking the bus again, he admitted to himself. But just the thought of mentioning it to her made him cringe. She was still so fragile, so angry. How would she react?

"I'm blind!" she responded bitterly. "How am I supposed to know where I'm going'? I feel like you're abandoning me." Mark's heart broke to hear these words, but he knew what had to be done. He promised Susan that each morning and evening he would ride the bus with her, for as long as it took, until she got the hang of it.

And that is exactly what happened. For two solid weeks, Mark, military uniform and all, accompanied Susan to and from work each day. He taught her how to rely on her other senses, specifically her hearing, to determine where she was and how to adapt to her new environment. He helped her befriend the bus drivers who could watch out for her and save her a seat.

He made her laugh, even on those not-so-good days when she would trip exiting the bus or drop her briefcase. Each morning they made the journey together, and Mark would take a cab back to his office.

Although this routine was even more costly and exhausting than the previous one, Mark knew it was only a matter of time before Susan would be able to ride the bus on her own. He believed in her, in the Susan he used to know before she'd lost her sight, who wasn't afraid of any challenge and who would never, ever quit.

Finally, Susan decided that she was ready to try the trip on her own.

Monday morning arrived, and before she left she threw her arms around Mark, her temporary bus riding companion, her husband, and her best friend. Her eyes filled with tears of gratitude for his loyalty, his patience, his love. She said good-bye, and for the first time, they went their separate ways.

Monday, Tuesday, Wednesday, Thursday. Each day she went on her own and Susan had never felt better. She was doing it! She was going to work all by herself!

On Friday morning, Susan took the bus to work as usual. As she was paying for her fare to exit the bus, the driver said, "Boy, I sure envy you."

Susan wasn't sure if the driver was speaking to her or not. After all, who on earth would ever envy a blind woman who had struggled just to find the courage to live for the past year?

Curious, she asked the driver, "Why do you say that you envy me?" The driver responded, "It must feel so good to be taken care of and protected like you are."

Susan had no idea what the driver was talking about, and asked again, "What do you mean?"

The driver answered, "You know, every morning for the past week, a fine-looking gentleman in a military uniform has been standing across the corner watching you when you get off the bus. He makes sure you cross the street safely and he watches you until you enter your office building. Then he blows you a kiss, gives a little salute and walks away. You are one lucky lady."

Tears of happiness ran down Susan's cheeks. Although she couldn't physically see him, she had always felt Matt's presence. Susan was lucky, so lucky, for her husband had given her a gift more powerful than sight, a gift she didn't need to see to believe - the gift of love that brings light where there was darkness.[259]

Learning Questions

1. Who is someone in your life who you know you can rely on and trust?
2. Have you thanked that kind person lately?
3. How can you help others by being more reliable?

You Show Reliability When You:

- Say you'll do something and then do it without being reminded.
- Keep your promises.
- Always do your best.
- Don't give up; you keep trying even when it's hard.
- Plan ahead.
- Find out what is expected, and you leave enough time to do it well.
- Act in ways that cause you to be trusted by others.

---

[259] Chaplin Jerry Vintinner, http://www.cyberquotations.com/stories

RESPECT

Respect

Definition Respect: To admire and treat with honor.

Quotes

"Men are respectable only as they respect."

Ralph Waldo Emerson[260]

"If you want to be respected by others, the great thing is to respect yourself. Only by that, only by self-respect will you compel others to respect you."

Fyodor Dostoevsky[261]

Explanation

Respect is having care and concern for other people, their rights, or their property. It is also important to have respect for yourself. You show respect for other people when you treat them kindly, speak politely, and obey the rules.

You respect others' rights when you allow them their privacy and leave them alone when you should. You also respect others when you let them make their own decisions.

You respect people's property by asking permission if you want to use something they own and by taking good care of it when you use it.

When you respect yourself, you would not say, "I'm so stupid! I always make mistakes!" Instead, you'd think, "That's not like me - I usually don't make mistakes like that; I'll do better next time."

You show respect for yourself when you think and speak kindly to yourself in your mind (That is called good self-talk).

When you have self-respect you don't let others use you or harm you. You expect others to value you, just as you value them.

---

[260] Stevenson, Burton. 1934. *The Home Book of Quotations: Classical and Modern.* Binghamton, New York: Vail-Ballou Press, 1705

[261] http://www.quotationspage.com

It is especially important to respect older people. During their lives elderly people have learned many valuable things that they can teach you. Everyone needs to show special respect to elderly men and women. You should always treat them kindly and courteously. Also, you should patiently help them do things they cannot do for themselves. Perhaps your elders helped you when you couldn't do things for yourself.

A good rule to remember is to always treat others with the same respect you want them to show you.

Story for Young Children

<u>The Lion and the Mouse</u>

Once when a lion was asleep a little mouse began running up and down upon him. This soon awakened the lion, who placed his huge paw upon him, and opened his big jaws to swallow him.

"Pardon, O King!" cried the little mouse: "Forgive me this time and I shall never forget it. Who knows but what I may be able to do you a good turn one of these days?"

The lion was so tickled at the idea of the mouse being able to help him, that he lifted up his paw and let him go.

Sometime after, the great lion was caught in a trap, and the hunters desired to carry him alive to the King. So, they tied him to a tree while they went in search of a wagon to carry him.

Just then the little mouse happened to pass by and saw the sad plight of the lion. The mouse hurried to his side and soon gnawed away the ropes that bound the King of Beasts.

"Was I not right?" the little mouse asked the lion. "Little friends may prove to be great friends."[262]

Learning Questions
1. At the beginning of the story, which animal respected the other one?
2. At the end of the story, do you think the lion respected the mouse?
3. What is one thing you can do to show respect to elderly people?

Story for Older Children

<u>Johnny Lingo</u>

"Get Johnny Lingo to help you find what you want and then let him do the bargaining," advised Shenkin as I sat on the veranda of his guest house and wondered whether to visit Nurabandi. "He'll earn his commission four times over. Johnny knows values and how to make a deal."

---

[262] http://www.pacificnet.net/~johnr/cgi/aesop1.cgi?3&TheLionandtheMouse2

"Johnny Lingo." The chubby boy on the veranda steps hooted the name, then hugged his knees and rocked with shrill laughter.

"Be quiet", said his father and the laughter grew silent. "Johnny Lingo's the sharpest trader in this part of the Pacific.

The simple statement made the boy choke and almost roll off the steps. Smiles broadened on the faces of the villagers standing nearby.

"What goes on?" I demanded. "Everybody around here tells me to get in touch with Johnny Lingo and then laughs. It is some kind of trick, a wild-goose chase, like sending someone for a left-handed wrench. Is there no such person or is he the village idiot or what? Let me in on the joke."

"Not idiot," said Shenkin. "Only one thing. Five months ago, at festival time, Johnny came to Kiniwata and found himself a wife. He paid her father eight cows!"

He spoke the last words with great solemnity, and I knew enough about island customs to be thoroughly impressed. Two or three cows would buy a fair-to-middling wife, four or five a highly satisfactory one.

"Eight cows!" I said. "She must have been a beauty that takes your breath away."

"That's why they laugh," my guest said. It would be kind to call her plain. She was little and skinny with no--ah--endowments. She walked with her shoulders hunched and her head ducked, as if she was trying to hide behind herself. Her cheeks had no color, her eyes never opened beyond a slit and her hair was a tangled mop half over her face. She was scared of her own shadow, frightened by her own voice. She was afraid to laugh in public. She never romped with the girls, so how could she attract the boys?"

"But she attracted Johnny?" This is the story Shenkin told me:

"All the way to the Council tent, the cousins were urging Sam to try for a good settlement. Ask for three cows, they told him, and hold out for two until you're sure he'll pay one. But Sam was in such a stew and so afraid that there'd be some slip in this marriage chance for Sarita that they knew he wouldn't hold out for anything. So, while they waited they resigned themselves to accepting one cow, and thought, instead, of their luck in getting such a good husband for Sarita. Then Johnny came into the tent and, without waiting for a word from any of them, went straight up to Sam Karoo, grasped his hand and said, "Father of Sarita, I offer eight cows for your daughter." And he delivered the cows.

"As soon as it was over Johnny took Sarita to the island of Cho for the first week of marriage. Then they went home to Nurabandi and we haven't seen them since. Except at festival time, there's not much travel between the islands." This story interested me so I decided to investigate.

The next day I reached the island where Johnny lived. When I met him, he welcomed me to his home with a grace that made me feel like the owner. I was glad that from his own people he had respect.

I told him what his people had told me about him. "They speak much of me on that island? What do they say?"

"They say you are a sharp trader," I said. "They also say the marriage settlement that you made for your wife was eight cows." I paused, and then went on, coming as close to a direct question as I could. "They wonder why."

"They say that?" His eyes lit up with pleasure. He seemed not to have noticed the question. "Everyone in Kiniwata knows about the eight cows?" I nodded.

"And in Nurabandi everyone knows it, too." His chest expanded with satisfaction. "Always and forever, when they speak of marriage settlements, it will be remembered that Johnny Lingo paid eight cows for Sarita."

So that's the answer, I thought with disappointment. All this mystery and wonder and the explanation is only vanity. It's not enough for his ego to be known as the smartest, the strongest, and the quickest. He had to make himself famous for his way of buying a wife. I was tempted to deflate him by reporting that in Kiniwata he was laughed at for a fool.

And then I saw her. Through the glass-beaded portieres that shimmered in the archway, I watched her enter the adjoining room to place a bowl of blossoms on the dining table. She stood still a moment to smile with sweet gravity at the young man beside me. Then she went swiftly out again. She was the most beautiful woman I have ever seen. Not with the beauty of the girl who carries fruit. That now seemed cheap, common, and earthbound. This girl had an ethereal loveliness that was at the same time from the heart of nature. The dew-fresh flowers with which she'd pinned back her lustrous black hair accented the glow of her cheeks.

The lift of her shoulders, the tilt of her chin, and the sparkle of her eyes all spelled a pride to which no one could deny her the right. And as she turned to leave she moved with the grace that made her look like a queen.

When she was out of sight I turned back to Johnny Lingo and found him looking at me with eyes that reflected the same pride I saw in the lovely young woman.

"You admire her?" he murmured.

"She--she's glorious. Who is she?"

"My wife."

I stared at him blankly. Was this some custom I had not heard about? Do they practice polygamy here? He, for his eight cows, bought both Sarita and this other? Before I could form a question, he spoke again.

"There is only one Sarita." His way of saying the words gave them a special significance. "Perhaps you wish to say she does not look the way they say she looked in Kiniwata."

"She doesn't." The impact of the girl's appearance made me forget tact. "I heard she was homely, or at least nondescript. They all make fun of you because you let yourself be cheated by Sam Karoo."

"You think he cheated me? You think eight cows were too many?" A slow smile slid over his lips as I shook my head. "She can see her father and her friends again. And they can see her. Do you think anyone will make fun of us then?" Much has happened to change her. Much in particular happened the day she went away.

"You mean she married you?"

"That, yes. But most of all, I mean the arrangements for the marriage."

"Arrangements?"

"Do you ever think", he asked reflectively, "what is the lowest price for which she can be bought? And then later, when all the women talk, as women do, they boast of what their husbands paid for them. One says four cows, another maybe six. How does she feel – the woman who was sold for one or two? This could not happen to my Sarita."

"Then you paid that unprecedented number of cows just to make your wife happy?"

"Happy?" He seemed to turn the word over on his tongue, as if to test its meaning. "I wanted Sarita to be happy, yes, but I wanted more than that. You say she's different from the way they remember her in Kiniwata. This is true. Many things can change a woman. Things that happen inside, things that happen outside. But the thing that matters most is what she thinks about herself. Kiniwata, Sarita believed she was worth nothing. Now she knows she is worth more than any other woman on the islands."

"Then you wanted. . ."

"I wanted to marry Sarita; I loved her and no other woman."

"But--," I was close to understanding.
"But," he finished softly, "I wanted an eight-cow wife."[263]

Learning Questions

---

[263] Patricia McCareer, EFM, V 1, p. 396

1. How did Johnny Lingo's act of respect for Sarita affect her?
2. When you are treated with respect, how do you feel about yourself?
3. What can you do to help others feel good about themselves?

You Show Respect When You:

- Show care and concern for other people, their rights, and their property.
- Show care and concern for yourself.
- Speak politely.
- Never interrupt.
- Obey the rules.
- Leave people alone if that is what they want.
- Let others make their own decisions.
- Ask permission to use and take good care of people's things.
- Don't let others use or harm you.
- Treat elders with special kindness and courtesy.

RESPONSIBILTY

Responsibility

Definition Responsibility: Doing things well so people can depend on you.

Quotes

"If you take responsibility for yourself, you will develop a hunger for your dreams."

Les Brown[264]

"I think of a hero as someone who understands the degree of responsibility that comes with his freedom."

Bob Dylan[265]

Explanation

Responsibility has two parts. One part is about being dependable. When you're responsible, you keep your agreements. People know they can count on you to do what you say you'll do, when you say you'll do it.

Being responsible means to do things to the best of your ability. When you are given a job you do it without complaining and you do it well. For example, if you are responsible and your job is to set the table for dinner, you do it cheerfully without being asked. You do it because you understand that it's one of your contributions to the family. We each have a responsibility to help our family be happy. Every family member needs to do his or her part.

Author Joyce B. Maugham wrote, "I don't 'like' to wash the dishes. Maybe I should say it another way. There are many things I'd 'rather' do than wash the dishes. But the dishes have to be washed so I just go ahead and do them. Thomas Huxley, a famous scientist, says that one of the most valuable lessons you will learn is to make yourself do the thing that has to be done when it ought to be done whether you like it or not. So, it seems to me that I am learning an important lesson when I do the dishes."[266]

The second half of responsibility is to take ownership for your thoughts, words and actions. This means that you understand this important fact: *you choose what you think and how you act*. No matter what is happening around you, it is your choice how you respond—you can be happy or sad.

---

[264] Edwards, Tyron. 1977. *The New Dictionary of Thoughts*. Stanbook, Inc., 570

[265] http://www.quotationspage.com

[266] Joyce B. Maugham. "Doing What Has to Be Done," *Talks for Tots,* 1985, p. 103

When you take responsibility for your thoughts, words, and actions, you don't blame anyone, or anything, for your mistakes. For example, you wouldn't say, "You make me angry!" because no one *makes* you angry. You can choose to be in control of your emotions.

You wouldn't say, "It's not my fault, I forgot!" When you're responsible, if something goes wrong you can explain, but you don't make excuses. When you make a mistake, you take responsibility for it by admitting that you're wrong. Then you do your best to make it right.

Responsible people are respected and trusted.

Story for Young Children

Jason Took Responsibility

Just over the six-foot fence in Jason's backyard was a parking lot for an apartment building. Someone had tossed a paper bag of empty beer bottles from the parking lot over the fence into Jason's backyard where he had found them. Jason took the bottles and tossed them, one by one, back over the fence. Since he couldn't see through the fence, he couldn't see them land, but he could hear the crash each time a bottle broke in the parking lot. It was kind of fun.

That evening a man from the apartments rang the doorbell, and Jason, who was downstairs, overheard the man telling his father about a punctured tire. Jason went quietly into his room, quickly put on his pajamas, got in bed, and pretended to be asleep.

His parents, after reassuring the neighbor they would pay for the tire if it turned out to be their son's doing, sat down to decide how to handle the incident. They realized that they had three challenges: (1) to help Jason tell the truth about the matter (they knew him well enough to be pretty sure what the truth was); (2) to help him feel sorry for what he'd done; and (3) to help him feel enough responsibility for his actions that he wouldn't do something similarly irresponsible in the future. As they thought about it, they realized that it was fortunate the whole thing had come to their attention after Jason was in bed when they had time to think it through, rather than in his presence. Otherwise, they might have confronted him without turning it into a learning experience.

When Jason came to breakfast the next morning, Dad said, "Son, I noticed that sack of beer bottles. Whoever tossed them into our yard shouldn't have done it, should he?"

Jason looked up with a little hope in his eyes and answered, "No."

Dad said, "You probably felt like tossing them back over and didn't really stop to think that they might hurt someone or break something." Jason looked down, but said nothing. "Did you throw them over, son?" There was a pause, then a quiet, "Yes."

"We're proud of you for telling the truth, son. A man's car ran over one of those bottles and got a flat tire. We're lucky none of the bottles broke a windshield. But we do need to decide what to do about that flat tire. Do you feel sorry about throwing those bottles and puncturing the tire?"

"Yes." "Are you going to take responsibility for what you did?"

"Yes." Jason cleaned up the rest of the glass. He saved money from working for three weeks to pay for the tire. He apologized to the car's owner. He promised both his parents and the car owner that he would never throw anything over the fence again. Jason made restitution and took responsibility for his actions.[267]

Learning Questions

1. How did Jason take responsibility for his actions?
2. How do you feel when you take responsibility for your words and actions?

Story for Older Children

<u>Responsibility Helped Grandpa</u>

There was once a family of Eastern European refugees, driven from their home by invading soldiers who decided their only chance of escaping the horrors of war was to climb the mountains that surrounded their village. They were sure they'd find safety in a neighboring neutral country, if only they could make it over the pass.

The grandfather was not well, however, and the days of his mountain hiking were long past.

"Leave me behind," he pleaded. "The soldiers won't bother with an old man like me."

"Yes, they will," warned the son. "It will mean your grave." "We can't leave you behind, Grandpa," implored the daughter. "If you won't go, then we won't either."

The old man finally relented, and the family, which numbered some ten people of varying ages, including the daughter's year-old baby girl, set off after dark toward the blue-black mountain range in the distance.

As they walked along silently, each took a turn carrying the baby, whose weight made travel more difficult, as they climbed the steep mountain pass.

After several hours, the grandfather sat down on a rock and hung his head. "Go on without me," he says in a low voice. "I can't make it."

"Yes, you can," his son implored. "You have to."

---

[267] Paula Noble Fellingham

"No," replied the old man. "Leave me here."

"Come on," said the son. "We need you—it's your turn to carry the baby."

The old man looked up and saw the tired faces of the others in the group. He looked at the baby carried in the arms of his thin, thirteen-year-old grandson.

"Yes, of course," said the old man. "It's my turn. Come, give her to me."

He stood up and took the baby in his arms and looked into her small, innocent face. Suddenly, the grandfather felt a renewed strength, and a powerful desire to see his family find safety in a land without war.

"Come on," he called with a note of determination in his voice. "Let's go. I'm fine now. I just needed to rest. Let's keep moving."

They all headed up the hill again with the grandfather carrying the baby.

The family reached safety that night, and everyone who started the long journey through the mountains finished it, including the grandfather.[268]

Learning Questions

1. What helped the grandfather feel more courageous and take responsibility for his family's safety?
2. What is one thing you can do to be more responsible?

You Show Responsibility When You:

- Can be trusted because you're dependable.
- Keep your agreements.
- Do tasks cheerfully and well.
- Do your household chores without being asked.
- Understand that doing your household chores contributes to your family's happiness.
- Take ownership of your thoughts, words, and actions.
- Don't blame anyone or anything for your mistakes.

Don't make excuses; admit your mistakes.

---

[268] Floyd Wickman and Terri Sjodin, "For My Grandson," *Chicken Soup for the Father's Soul*, 264-265

SELF-DISCIPLINE

Self-Discipline

Definition Self-discipline: Being in control of yourself.

Quotes

"Respect your efforts, respect yourself. Self-respect leads to self-discipline. When you have both firmly under your belt, that's real power."

Clint Eastwood[269]

"By constant self-discipline and self-control, you can develop greatness of character."

Grenville Kleiser[270]

Explanation

When you have self-discipline you do what you know you should do without being told. You make good decisions and choose the right with your thoughts, words, and actions.

Having self-discipline with your thoughts means that when unkind or bad thoughts enter your mind you think, "That wasn't kind." Then you replace bad thoughts with good thoughts by thinking kindly about the person or the situation you're in.

Having self-discipline with your words means that when you're angry you don't get out of control and yell. You don't say unkind things to people or about people. Instead, you stay in control and tell people how you feel, without anger. You talk in a regular, calm voice, and you don't call names or quarrel.

Having self-discipline with your actions means that you don't hit people. It also means that you control your body. This means that you treat your body carefully by not eating too much, not watching too much television, not spending too much time on the Internet, or playing too many video games.

People who are self-disciplined don't do things that hurt their bodies or their minds.

---

[269] Les Brown http://www.goodreads.com
[270] http://www.quotationspage.com

When you are self-disciplined you spend time helping other people and improving yourself. You use your time wisely and do things like family chores, exercise, read, practice a musical instrument, play sports, visit, or help others.

Self-disciplined people are usually very productive and successful in life.

Story for Young Children

<u>The Race</u>

"I've swum twenty laps already, and I just can't go another one." Candice shouted to her swimming coach, who was standing near the edge of the pool.

 "Yes, you can!" Coach Baker encouraged confidently. "You're good for at least four more laps."

Candice looked up at the tall thin man and wondered why he expected so much of her.

"Four more!" the coach shouted. "And watch that kick. Your rhythm is off."

Candice pushed off from the bank feeling discouraged and wanting to cry. Carefully she cupped her hands and pulled at the water.

"One, two, three, four, five, six," she counted over and over to herself as she kicked and then rhythmically fit her windmill-like arms into the pattern. Slowly but smoothly, she glided over the water. Her arms and legs ached, and her lungs gasped for air as her head turned in and out of the water.

Candice touched the edge and then sprung backward and began the backstroke. Once more she glided gracefully through the water.

As she neared the edge, she wished she could stop, but even in the water she could hear Coach Baker's voice calling from the deck, "Two more laps. You're looking good, but don't get lazy with those arms. Pull, pull!"

Candice turned on her stomach again and did one more lap freestyle and then tried another lap on her back. Her muscles were so tired she wondered how she could make it.

"The last lap! This is the last lap!" she kept telling herself as she swam. She felt a smile cross her lips when she finished.

 "That was pretty good," Coach Baker said without smiling. "We'll have a short workout tomorrow, and then you'll be ready for the swimming meet on Saturday. Remember what you can eat and what you can't and get to bed early tonight and tomorrow night."

Slowly Candice crawled out of the pool. For a while she sat on the edge of the pool, dangling her feet in the water and breathing fast.

Is all this worth it? She wondered. *Or am I going to all this trouble and work for nothing?*

Then she looked down at the pool and her thoughts changed. "This time I'm going to win!" she whispered. "Every time I practice and every time I lose, I learn something. I can't give up now. I'm going to win!"

She grabbed her towel and sweatshirt and went into the dressing room to change her clothes.

Within fifteen minutes she was on the bus going home. By now her tired muscles were beginning to feel better.

At the first stop a girl about her age got on the bus. Candice watched as the girl walked down the aisle and then stopped next to her seat.

"Hi," the girl said. "May I sit here?"

"Sure," Candice replied.

"My name is Stacey Moyle," the girl said as she sat down.

"I'm Candice Thomas," Candice replied.

"I'm going to visit my grandmother," Stacey said. Then she opened a small sack and pulled out two chocolate bars. "Would you like some candy?" she asked.

Candice looked longingly at the candy. She loved chocolate, but the coach's rules kept ringing in her ears, "Don't eat empty calories. Eat high protein foods."

She looked once more at the candy bar and her mouth began to water. "I'd better not," Candice finally said reluctantly, "but thanks anyway."

"Come on," Stacey urged. "I'll feel silly eating if you don't."

Candice looked once more at the candy. Then she remembered her tired muscles and all the work she had done so she could win.

"No, thank you," she said more firmly. "I really wouldn't care for any. But you go ahead. I don't mind."

During the next two days Candice's thoughts alternated between discouragement and excitement.

But as she climbed onto the starting block Saturday afternoon, she felt only one emotion: a determination to win.

The starter's voice called out, "Judges ready?"

Eight hands at the ends of the pool signaled readiness, and the voice instructed, "Swimmers, take your mark."

Candice stepped up and curled her toes around the edge of the starting block.

"Get set," the starter shouted.

Candice poised herself to make the starting dive.

Bang! The gun rang out and the eight swimmers flew off the blocks.

One girl led the way, with Candice a little behind her and a girl in the next lane just a little farther back.

Candice pulled and kicked down the first lap. As she made the turn, the girl in the next lane caught up with her so Candice let go with all her strength. Halfway down the lap she started gaining on the leader and the two girls raced neck and neck.

When Candice felt she was starting to fall behind, she pushed herself even more. She felt as if her lungs would burst, but the extra push was just enough. She finished two-tenths of a second before the other girl!

Coach Baker ran over to help Candice out of the pool. His face was one big smile.

"Congratulations!" he said. "I knew you had what it takes!"

Candice gasped for breath. Her muscles ached, but she had never felt so good.

"Thanks, coach," she whispered between breaths, "I owe it all to you."

"No, you don't," he said. "You're the only one who can win. I've helped a little, but you're the swimmer!"

While Candice was getting dressed, she thought about what Coach Baker had said. Lots of people are willing to help, but it's up to me to *help myself* she decided with a smile.[271]

Learning Questions

1. How did Candice show self-discipline when she was tempted?
2. How did her self-discipline pay off?
3. Name one of your temptations that require self-discipline to overcome.

---

[271] Sherrie Johnson, "The Race," Friend, May 1974, 17

Story for Older Children

Years ago, in Monterey, California, a crisis arose. Monterey had become a paradise for pelicans. After cleaning their fish, the local fishermen would throw the pelicans the fish entrails. The birds soon became fat and lazy.

Eventually, a new market was found that could use the fish entrails commercially. The pelicans no longer had a free meal. Yet, the pelicans made no effort to fish for themselves. They just waited and waited for the handouts that didn't come.

Many pelicans starved to death. They seemed to have forgotten how to fish for themselves.

The opposite approach was taken by an elderly woman waiting for a bus. She was crippled with rheumatism and loaded down with packages. As the bus door opened, a man offered her a helping hand. The woman smiled and shook her head. "I'd best manage alone," she said. "If I get help today I'll want it tomorrow."

George Bernard Shaw once noted, "People are always blaming their circumstances for what they are. I don't believe in circumstances. The people who get on in this world are the people who get up and look for the circumstances they want, and if they can't find them, make them."[272]

Learning Questions

1. The pelicans suffered because they didn't have any self-discipline. How are people sometimes like these pelicans?
2. How did the old lady show her understanding of self-discipline?
3. Name one way that you use self-discipline in your life.

You Show Self-Discipline When You:

- Make good choices without being told or reminded.
- Control your thoughts by replacing bad thoughts with good ones.
- Control your words by using a calm voice instead of yelling or calling names.
- Control your actions and don't hit.
- Control your body and don't do things that hurt you or other people.
- Help others.
- Improve yourself.
- Use your time wisely.

---

[272] God's Little Devotional Book for Leaders, p. 207

SELF-RELIANCE

Self-Reliance

Definition Self-reliance: Depending only on yourself.

Quotes

"Be yourself; no base imitator of another, but your best self. There is something which you can do better than another. Listen to the inward voice and bravely obey that. Do the things at which you are great, not what you were never made for."

Ralph Waldo Emerson[273]

"Doubt whom you will, but never doubt yourself."

Christian Nestell Bovee[274]

Explanation

Self-reliance is when you do things by yourself without being asked and without being helped.

When you are old enough, you should begin to take care of yourself in as many ways as you can. For example, when you do family chores and help your parents cheerfully, without being told, you're being self-reliant, and your contributions help the family.

If you are self-reliant in just a few ways you can help take some of the burdens of responsibility off your mother and/or father. Life is easier for your parents when you help lighten their load.

Self-reliance also means that you take responsibility for your words and actions. You don't blame others when things go wrong. For example, what if you were at a birthday party and you suddenly realized that you left the gift for your friend at home? Would you blame it on your Mom or Dad? Or would you say, "I'm sorry, I left your present at home. I'll get it to you tomorrow." Then, the next day you would be sure and do what you promised. You would take the present to your friend.

Self-reliant people don't wait for others to do things for them. And they don't expect others to help them do something when they can do it themselves. Self-reliant people see what needs to be done, and they do it. If they need help, of course they ask for it. For example, what if you were ready to get into bed but there were no sheets or blankets on the bed because the sheets were just

---

[273] https://www.goodreads.com/work/quotes/1472936-self-reliance-and-other-essays
[274] Edwards, Tyron. 1977. *The New Dictionary of Thoughts.* Stanbook, Inc., 605

washed? Would you call your mother and expect her to put the sheets on your bed? Or would you do it yourself? Putting them on yourself shows self-reliance. If you try your best and it doesn't work, then ask for help. People are usually happy to help you after you try to do it yourself.

Story for Young Children

<u>Who to Believe?</u>

There was once a little girl who was born into a very poor family in a shack in the backwoods of Tennessee. She was the 20th of 22 children, prematurely born and frail. Her survival was doubtful. When she was four years old, she had double pneumonia and scarlet fever—a deadly combination that left her with a paralyzed and useless left leg. She had to wear an iron leg brace. Yet she was fortunate to have a mother who encouraged her.

Well, this mother told her little girl, who was very bright, that despite the brace and leg, she could do whatever she wanted to do with her life. She told her that all she needed to do was have faith, persistence, courage, and an indomitable spirit.

So at nine years of age, the little girl removed the leg brace and took the step the doctors told her she would never take normally. In four years, she developed a rhythmic stride, which was a medical wonder. Then this girl got the notion, the incredible notion, that she would like to be the world's greatest woman runner. Now, what could she mean—be a runner with a leg like that?

At age 13, she entered a race. The girl came in last—way, way last. But that didn't stop her. She entered every race in high school, and in every race she came in last. Everyone begged her to quit.

However, one day, she came in next to last. And then there came a day when she won a race.

From then on, Wilma Rudolph won every race that she entered.

Wilma went to Tennessee State University, where she met a coach named Ed Temple. Coach Temple saw the indomitable spirit of the girl. He saw that Wilma was a believer who had great natural talent. He trained her so well that in 1960 she went to the Olympic Games in Rome.

There she was pitted against the greatest woman runner of the day, a German girl named Jutta Heine. Nobody had ever beaten Jutta. But in the 100-meter dash, Wilma Rudolph won. She beat Jutta again in the 200 meters.

Wilma had just earned two Olympic gold medals.

Finally came the 400-meter relay. It would be Wilma against Jutta once again. The first two runners on Wilma's team made perfect hand-offs with the baton. But when the third runner handed the baton to Wilma, she was so excited she dropped it, and Wilma saw Jutta taking off down the track. It was impossible that anybody could catch this fleet and nimble girl. But Wilma did just that!

Wilma Rudolph earned her third Olympic gold medal.

That day she made history as she became the first woman ever to win three gold medals in the same Olympic games. And they said she would never walk again![275]

Learning Questions

1. What would have happened if Wilma had listened to the doctors who said she would never walk normally?
2. How did Wilma demonstrate self-reliance when she raced in high school?
3. What can you do to show self-reliance?

Story for Older Children

Pinned!

The clock was running out in my New York high school wrestling match, and the score was 13 to 2. I was behind, and even though I had tried everything, I was no match for my opponent, Glen.

Yet I thought to myself, *I can't afford to lose. Everything depends on my match. If I lose, we can't possibly get enough points in the rest of the matches to win. And there will go our undefeated season.*

This was supposed to be our high school's 99th consecutive wrestling team match win, and the 100th team match was scheduled later that day. It took many years of undefeated seasons to have a school record like that.

Reporters from local newspapers and several radio stations would be at the 100th match because we were about to make Long Island wrestling history. No one ever expected us to lose.

Unfortunately, for publicity's sake, the coaches had decided to save all the first-string wrestlers for the upcoming 100th match and let the second string wrestle the 99th. We watched in horror as many of our teammates lost their individual matches. It became painfully obvious to all of us that everything was going to depend on my bout.

To make matters worse, I was the last-minute substitute for our 165-pound wrestler, and Glen, my opponent, outweighed me by 13 pounds. Throughout each period, I worked extremely hard to leverage speed and skill to put Glen on his back. Instead, I fought most of the time to keep my own back off the mat! I simply could not compete with Glen's size and strength.

---

[275] *Chicken Soup for the Woman's Soul*, 118-119

In the final moments of the match, Glen was on his knees with his chest pressed against my back. He must have figured he could contain me there while he caught his breath and ran out the clock. Meanwhile, my coach sat despairing with his head in his hands.

The roar of the crowd was deafening as they cheered Glen's imminent win and Jefferson's upset.

By chance, my eyes caught sight of the clock. There were only 20 seconds to go. I wondered, *What do I do now?*

Just then, Glen's head dropped to obscure my view. He was exhausted. Instantly, both of my hands grabbed Glen's head. I tucked it into my chest and arched my back. Over he went like a sack of potatoes. "Pin!" shouted the referee as his hand slammed the mat and the buzzer sounded.

I'd pinned Glen before his feet ever hit the mat. Victory was mine! With only seconds left, I had glued Glen, and our high school won its 99th in a row and went on to win the 100th team match.

Over the years, that single event has helped me recognize and deal with many of life's more difficult situations. When the clock has run out and you have done all you can to wear out the opposition, when you have used every skill you ever learned and a few you picked up along the way, when your reputation is at stake with everyone depending on you, and when only a few faithful friends and family are still cheering for you, what do you do?

You don't give up![276]

Learning Questions
1. How was the wrestler able to defeat Glen in the match?
2. How do we help others when we are self-reliant?
3. When was a time that you showed self-reliance?
4.

You are Self-Reliant When You:

- Do things by yourself without being asked and without being helped.
- Begin to take care of yourself in ways that you can.
- Do family chores and help your family cheerfully.
- Help lighten your parents' load.
- Take responsibility for your thoughts, words and actions.
- Don't blame others when things go wrong.
- Don't wait for others to do things for you.
- Don't expect others to do things for you that you can do yourself.
- See what needs to be done and do it.

---

[276] New Era, October 2000, 12

SERVICE

Service

Definition Service: Helping others with no thought of reward.

Quotes

"Be silent as to services you have rendered but speak of favors you have received."

Seneca the Younger [277]

"The service you do for others is the rent you pay for the time you spend on earth."

Mohammed Ali[278]

Explanation

Service is kindness in action. It is giving of yourself to others without expecting anything in return. Having an attitude of service means looking for ways to help rather than waiting to be asked. The needs of others are important to those who unselfishly serve, and they help people because they care about them.

For children, serving others can be as simple as being friendly at school. One teacher said, "Children who have attitudes of service are alert to situations in which classmates are hurting. If they see a student eating alone, they sit with him. They are understanding and caring."[279]

It is true that "self-centered" people aren't as happy as those who are "others-centered." Instead of looking at mirrors to see what you need, you should look through windows to see other people's needs.

In families there are countless ways to serve one another. You can help keep the house clean, the yard clean, help prepare meals, or wash the dishes. If you can't think of ways to serve, just ask your mom or dad what you can do to help.

A wonderful thing about service is that those who help others also benefit.

---

[277] http://www.quotationspage.com

[278] http://www.quotationspage.com

[279] Paula Noble Fellingham. 2000. *Solutions for Families*. Austin, Texas: Families Now, Inc., 83

A Hindu proverb reads, "Help thy brother's boat across, and lo, thy own has reached the shore."[280] Lightening the burdens of others always brings joy and happiness to the one who served.

Story for Young Children

<u>Amanda Learned How to Give</u>

"Evacuate your homes now!" bellowed the loudspeaker on a truck. "The fire is coming! The fire is coming!"

The forest fire raged down the mountain towards the town. Fierce winds fanned the enormous flames. Short of water and help, the firefighters couldn't hold it back any longer. Families were going to lose their homes and belongings. There was nothing anyone could do.

Seven-year-old Amanda sat in her family's living room, watching the news reports. It was hard to believe that the fire was only an hour away. She stared as flames licked through the treetops.

She didn't want to watch, but she couldn't look away. She felt sad and sick.

Amanda went to her room and thought about the fire. Looking around, she wondered what it would be like to leave everything behind. She had lots of prized possessions. The most precious was Ginger, her favorite doll. She looked at her other dolls, her trophies, her toys, even her clothes and shoes. Losing everything was hard to even think about.

When Dad got home, Amanda and her parents ate dinner. They discussed the new evacuations. Tears welled up in Amanda's eyes, and she began to cry.

"What's the matter?" Mom asked.

"Why can't they stop the fire?" Amanda asked. "Where will people live if their houses burn down?"

"Everyone will move into temporary shelters," Mom answered. "They will get food, clothes, and a warm place to sleep until this is all sorted out."

"What about their things? Who's going to help them save their things?"

"The fire is too hot and moving too fast for anyone to think much about saving things," Dad said. "It's more important to make sure the people are safe. Most things can be replaced."

---

[280] http://www.ennea.com/Quotes/quotes.htm

Too upset to finish her supper, Amanda asked to be excused and went to her room and knelt by her bed. "Girls just like me are going to lose everything," she prayed. "Somebody has to help them. I want to help them, but what can I do?"

When she awoke the next morning, Amanda knew exactly what to do. She filled a large shopping bag with clothes, books, and games. Last of all, she put in Ginger. "Mom, I want to give these things," she said. "Can you help me?"

Mom looked through the bag. "You're giving away some of your nicest treasures," she said. "Are you sure you want to give away Ginger?"

Amanda tried to swallow the lump in her throat. "This is what I should do," she said. "I know this will help someone feel better. Will you help me?"

Mom hugged her. "Of course. The church is collecting donations. I was going to take some blankets and canned goods over this afternoon, but I think we should go right now instead."

Waiting in line with other people who were making donations, Amanda began to feel that giving away Ginger was just too hard. She thought longingly about keeping her favorite doll. The line inched forward, giving her time to think some more. When it was her turn, she handed her bag to the volunteers, Ginger and all. Silently saying good-bye, she watched as her bag was carried to the trailer. It was so hard to give up her things! She turned and walked quietly back to the car.

Back home, a television report announced that four hundred homes had been destroyed. But there was good news, too. The fire was nearly under control, and no one had been hurt.

Amanda watched the reports every night. She was worried about the four hundred families without homes. She thought about her shopping bag of treasures and wondered if it had really mattered among the thousands of other donations. And she really missed Ginger.

Suddenly Amanda sat up and looked more closely at the television screen. Something looked familiar. A little girl in a shelter was clutching a doll that looked a lot like—yes, it really was—Ginger!

Amanda jumped up and squealed with delight. Her donation really *had* made a difference.[281]

Learning Questions

1. What made Amanda want to give up her doll Ginger?
2. How was she feeling about the families who lost their homes?
3. What can you do to follow Amanda's example of service?

---

[281] Mary Datwyler, "Giving Up Ginger," *Friend*, June 2002, 38

Story for Older Children

The King's Highway

Once a king had a great highway built for the members of his kingdom. After it was completed, but before it was opened to the public, the king decided to have a contest. He invited as many as desired to participate. Their challenge was to see who could travel the highway best.

On the day of the contest the people came. Some of them had fine chariots, some had fine clothing, fine hairdos, or great food. Some young men came in their track clothes and ran along the highway. People traveled the highway all day, but each one, when he arrived at the end, complained to the king that there was a large pile of rocks and debris left on the road at one spot, and this got in their way and hindered their travel.

At the end of the day, a lone traveler crossed the finished line and wearily walked over to the king. The traveler was tired and dirty, but he addressed the king with great respect and handed him a bag of gold. He explained, "I stopped along the way to clear away a pile of rocks and debris that was blocking the road. This bag of gold was under it all, and I want you to return it to its rightful owner."

The king replied, "You are the rightful owner."

The traveler replied, "Oh no, this is not mine! I've never known such money."

"Oh yes," said the king, "you've earned this gold, for you won my contest. He who travels the road best is he who makes the road smoother for those who will follow."[282]

Learning Questions

1. How did the traveler serve others? Would you do the same?
2. What does it mean to show service?
3. What blessings do you receive from serving others?

You Show Service When You:

- Give of yourself without expecting a reward.
- Look for ways to help rather than wait to be asked.
- Help people because you care about them.
- Are alert to situations where your help is needed.
- Do household chores and other jobs cheerfully.
- Understand that your service strengthens you and your family.

---

[282] Author Unknown, EFM, V 2, p. 289

STEADFASTNESS

Steadfastness

Definition Steadfastness: Continuing to try no matter how hard your task is.

Quotes

"What this power is I cannot say; all I know is that it exists and it becomes available only when a man is in that state of mind in which he knows exactly what he wants and is fully determined not to quit until he finds it."

Alexander Graham Bell[283]

"Be like the cliff against which the waves continually break; but it stands firm and tames the fury of the water around it."

Marcus Aurelius[284]

Explanation

Steadfastness means being so committed to something or someone that you stay with it, or with them, no matter how difficult it is.

For example, what if you had a sister who was very sick for a long, long time? If you were steadfast, you would help your family and your sister without complaining. You would try to be helpful and cheerful day after day, no matter how hard it was. That is being steadfast; you don't give up when things are difficult.

If you are steadfast in learning something new, you keep trying to learn and to do your best. No matter how discouraged you get, you don't quit.

When the going gets tough, steadfast people keep going.

Also, when you're steadfast you move steadily forward. You might be going slowly, but that's okay. Moving forward, even when your progress is slow, will get you where you're going. When people are steadfast, they usually reach their goals, no matter how long it takes.

Being dependable and steadfast sets a good example for others to follow. It gives them the strength and courage to be steadfast too.

---

[283] Glenn Van Ekeren. *Speaker's Sourcebook II*. 1994. Paramus, New Jersey: Prentice Hall, 104
[284] http://www.quotationspage.com

Story for Young Children

The Hare and the Tortoise

The Hare was once boasting of his speed before the other animals. "I have never been beaten," said he. "When I put forth my full speed. I challenge anyone here to race with me."

The Tortoise said quietly, "I accept your challenge."

"That is a good joke," said the Hare. "I could dance around you all the way!"

"Keep your boasting until you've beaten me," answered the Tortoise. "Shall we race?"

So, a course was fixed and a start was made. The Hare darted almost out of sight at once, but soon stopped and, believing that the Tortoise could never catch him, lay down by the wayside to have a nap. The Tortoise never for a moment stopped, but went on with a slow but steady pace straight to the end of the course.

When the Hare awoke from his nap, he saw the Tortoise just near the winning post. The Hare ran as fast as he could, but it was too late. He saw the Tortoise had reached the goal.

Then said the Tortoise: "Slow and steady wins the race."[285]

Learning Questions

1. How did the tortoise beat the rabbit, even though the rabbit was faster?
2. What can you learn from the tortoise?
3. Name one way you can be steadfast in your life.

Story for Older Children

See It Through

When you're up against a trouble,
Meet it squarely, face to face;
Lift your chin and set your shoulders,
Plant your feet and take a brace.

When it's vain to try to dodge it,
Do the best that you can do;
You may fail, but you may conquer—
You can do it! See it through!

---

[285] http://bygosh.com/Aesop/HaT.htm

Black may be the clouds about you
And your future may seem grim,
But don't' let your nerve desert you;
Keep yourself in fighting trim.

Even hope may seem but futile
When with troubles you're beset,
But remember you are facing
Just what other men have met.

You may fall, but fall still fighting;
Don't give up, whate'er you do;
Eyes front, head high to the finish ---
You can do it! See it through![286]

Learning Questions

1. Do you ever feel overwhelmed with the pressures of life?
2. What is one goal you think you might be able to achieve if you are steadfast?
3. Can you think of someone in your life right now who is trying to reach a goal? What can you do to help them?

You Show Steadfastness When You:

- Are so committed to something that you stay with it, no matter what.
- Are helpful and cheerful day after day without complaining.
- Keep trying to do your best even when you're discouraged.
- Don't quit.
- Move steadily forward even if you're going slowly.

---

[286] Author Unknown, EFM, V 4, p. 64

TACT

Tact

Definition Tact: Speaking and acting in a way that doesn't hurt people's feelings.

Quotes

"Talent is something, but tact is everything. Talent is serious, sober, grave, and respectable; tact is all that, and more too."

W.P. Scargill[287]

"Tact is the ability to describe others as they see themselves."

Abraham Lincoln[288]

Explanation

Tact is speaking or acting in a way that doesn't hurt people's feelings or upset them. Being tactful means telling people things in a considerate and kind way.

You may have heard the good advice, "Think before you speak." Since our thoughts always come before our words, it is important that we are aware of our thoughts so we can control our words.

When you don't control your thoughts and words you sometimes blurt things out before you think about how they might hurt someone's feelings. Then after you've spoken, you can't take your hurtful words back. Unkind words are sometimes remembered with sadness for a long, long time.

When you are tactful you don't point out people's differences or weaknesses and you don't say anything to embarrass them.

When you are tactful you say things in a way that will help people and encourage them to improve. For example, if you are with a friend who falls off their bicycle you would not say, "If you weren't so clumsy you wouldn't fall off your bike."

You would say something like this: "I used to fall off my bike too because I'd lean over instead of sitting straight up. Maybe if you try sitting straight, you'll stay on next time."

---

[287] Edwards, Tyron. 1977. *The New Dictionary of Thoughts.* Stanbook, Inc., 653

[288] http://www.quotationspage.com

Tactful people speak with gentleness, kindness, and good timing. Sometimes using tact means not saying anything at all.

Story for Young Children

The Art of being Tactful yet Truthful

A king called three great artists and asked them to paint his portrait. There was a valuable prize for making the best portrait. The king had only one eye.

One artist thought that the king may get angry if he showed him with only one eye. So he made a beautiful portrait with two eyes.

The second artist thought that the portrait should be completely real and so he sketched the picture with only one eye.

The third artist acted tactfully and showed the king with a bow and arrow. An eye was hidden in the posture as the king was aiming to hit the target.

All the portraits were beautiful but the prize for the best portrait went to the third artist as he had succeeded by tactfully showing the truth.

Learning Questions

1. How many artists tried to win the prize?
2. Why did the third artist win?
3. Sometimes, does being tactful require creativity? Why?

Story for Older Children

The Window Washers

A window washing company was washing the exterior windows of a condominium complex one day. One of the crew members mistakenly began to wash the windows of a unit that was not on the schedule.

The owner of the condominium came rushing out and said to the window washer, "I didn't order this service. I have no intention of paying you for this work!"

The man washing the windows thought fast on his feet and replied, "That's okay. Every time we do a condominium complex, we do one extra unit 'on the house' to show owners such as yourself what a fine job we do, and to show you what you are missing.

The owner of the unit was so impressed that he signed on for the service the next time the company visited his complex.

The company executives, hearing of his tact, decided to adopt this approach as a sales gimmick. It turned out to be the best boost to business the company had ever experienced, and the quick-thinking employee earned a raise.[289]

Learning Questions

1. How did the window washer use tact?
2. Have you ever noticed someone being tactful when they speak? If so, who?
3. Can you think of a time you used tact to help in a difficult situation?

You Show Tact When You:

- Speak in a way that doesn't hurt people's feelings.
- Think before you speak.
- Control your thoughts and words.
- Don't point out people's differences or weaknesses.
- Don't say anything to embarrass others.
- Say things in a way that will help people and encourage them to improve.
- Speak with gentleness and kindness.
- Sometimes don't say anything at all.

---

[289] God's Little Devotional Book for Leaders, p. 287.

TEAMWORK

Teamwork

Definition Teamwork: Working well with others.

Quotes

"There are no problems we cannot solve together, and very few that we can solve by ourselves."

Lyndon Johnson[290]

"Ask not what your teammates can do for you. Ask what you can do for your teammates."

Ervin "Magic" Johnson[291]

Explanation

Teamwork is when people work well together. In business it is very important to have teamwork, so the company will reach its goals and be productive.

Likewise, families are happiest when they function like a team — working together to reach the same goals. Each individual member is very important, with special strengths that contribute to the whole. Children and parents each have important positions on the team, and everyone is needed to make it work well.

What happens when teams quarrel and they don't have unity? They usually don't win. Families are the same way. When there is contention and selfishness, no one is happy. On the other hand, when family members are kind and unselfish, there's joy and peace in the home, and it's pleasant to be there.

Some ways you can increase the teamwork in your family are to: help one another cheerfully; do household chores together; set family goals; start and enjoy lots of traditions; eat meals together; create a family flag; sing songs; go on vacations; and take lots of time to be together.

Author H. David Burton wrote, "Once I witnessed a long-standing baseball record broken. A record once thought unbreakable. Tears rolled down my cheeks as I watched this fine athlete who broke the record stand on the field with his family and receive accolades from the public and his team. Although I am impressed with this young man's ability to hit and field a baseball, I am far more impressed with the attributes he displayed in achieving that feat. He demonstrated

---

[290] John C. Maxwell. 2001. *The 17 Indisputable Laws of Teamwork*. Nashville: Thomas Nelson Publishers, p. 4
[291] John C. Maxwell. 2001. *The 17 Indisputable Laws of Teamwork*. Nashville: Thomas Nelson Publishers, p. 203

great perseverance, consistency, sacrifice, courage, and determination in reaching his goal. These are some of the attributes we need to help us be successful."[292]

Story for Younger Children

<u>Teamwork</u>

Rosa was the oldest in the Hart family. She was old enough to read. She had a brother, Randy, and a sister, Joan. They hadn't learned to read yet, so Rosa was reading them a story about an alligator who was a good fisherman. The alligator caught a fish with his sharp pointed teeth. This made Joan think about her loose tooth and she began to wiggle it. After a few minutes of wiggling, Joan cried out, "I pulled it out!"

Rosa and Randy turned to Joan just as she dropped her tooth.

Randy said, "That wasn't very smart. Why didn't you hold it tightly?"

Joan didn't answer because she was crying.

Rosa knew that scolding Joan wouldn't help her feel better, so she asked her brother and sister if they wanted to play the spy game.

"What's that?" Joan and Randy asked at the same time.

"The three of us can look for the tooth. Whoever finds it is the winner," Rosa explained.

The finder was Randy who excitedly pointed to the space between the cushions on the sofa they had been sitting on. All three were happy that they worked together to make Joan smile again, even if it showed where the empty tooth had been.[293]

Learning Questions

1. What happened when all three children worked together?
2. How did it make Joan feel when her brother and sister helped find her tooth?
3. Do you help your family members when they need help?

Story for Older Children

<u>My Chum</u>

He stood at the crossroads all alone,
The sunlight in his face.

---

[292] H. David Burton, "I Will Go," *Ensign*, Nov. 1995, 43
[293] Paula Noble Fellingham

He had no thought for the world unknown-
He was set for the manly race.

But the roads stretched east and the roads stretched west,
And the lad knew not which road was best,

So he chose the road that led him down,
And he lost the race and the victor's crown.

He was caught at last in an angry snare,
Because no one stood at the crossroads there

To show him the better road.
Another day at the self-same place,

A boy with high hopes stood.
He, too, was set for the manly race;

He, too, sought the things that were good.
But one was there who the roads did know,

And that one showed him which way to go.
So he turned from the road that would lead him down,

And he won the race and the victor's crown.
He walks today the highway fair

Because one stood at the crossroads there
To show him the better way.[294]

Learning Questions

1. Why did the second boy do better than the first?
2. Can you think of a time in your life when someone helped you make a good choice?
3. Can you work with your family as a team better? How?

You Show Teamwork When You:

- Work well together.
- Set family goals.
- Understand that each individual is important, with special strengths and talents.
- Understand that parents and children each have important positions on the "family team."
- Are kind and unselfish.

---

[294] *The Little Book of Inspirational Stories*. (2000) Ed. R. Dale Jeffery, Covenant Communications, American Fork, Utah. "My Chum," Anonymous, pg. 65

- Help one another.
- Do chores together.
- Start and enjoy family traditions.
- Eat meals together.
- Create a family flag; sing songs.
- Take vacations; spend time together.

THRIFT

Thrift

Definition Thrift: Being careful with money.

Quotes

"A penny saved is a penny earned."

English Proverb[295]

"It is better to have a hen tomorrow than an egg today."

Thomas Fuller[296]

Explanation

Thrift is being careful with money and with things.

When you are thrifty, you understand how important it is to be thoughtful and careful with your money and with things you own.

Many years ago, during the 1930's, there was a time in America called the "Great Depression" when most people had very little money. When their clothes wore out, they didn't have money to buy new ones. They didn't have money for new furniture or new cars. People learned how to be very careful with their things and with their small amounts of money. They learned to be thrifty.

When you're thrifty you use things over and over again instead of throwing them away or buying new things. You don't waste food, water, or anything. When you're thrifty you don't spend all of your money. You use money carefully and then you take some of it and save it to use another day, when you need it.

Thrifty people are usually grateful for what they have. They count their blessings and think about what they *do* have instead of what they *don't* have.

---

[295] *Five thousand Quotations for All Occasions.* 1945. Edited by Lewis C. Henry. Garden City, New York: Doubleday & Company, Inc., 283

[296] *Five thousand Quotations for All Occasions.* 1945. Edited by Lewis C. Henry. Garden City, New York: Doubleday & Company, Inc., 283

Story for Young Children

Learning Thrift

The Scott family was having their weekly family meeting and the children were curious to know what their parents had planned. There was a tall pile of dollar bills stacked on the dinner table. Mom and Dad had decided that the children needed to learn how the family money was spent. It looked like a lot of money to the three Scott children.

Dad began by taking several bills off the pile to pay for taxes and insurance. Next, he set aside money for their house payment and utilities. The pile became considerably smaller.

Money for food, clothing and medical services came out next.

At that time the family stopped and talked about what their needs were and what their wants were. Carol was in disbelief that the money went so fast. Bill wondered how Mom and Dad paid for Christmas each year. And Jerry wanted to know how they were going to buy his birthday present, since his birthday was only two weeks away.

The Scott family agreed that this had been a real learning experience and everyone felt they should be more careful with their spending and saving. Years later it was fun to remember the night they spent the family income together.[297]

Learning Questions

1. What did the Scott family learn about money?
2. What are the different ways their family spent money?
3. What can you do to save money?

Story for Older Children

The Rich Family

I'll never forget Easter 1946. I was fourteen, my little sister, Ocy, was twelve, and my older sister, Darlene, was sixteen. We lived at home with our mother and the four of us knew what it was to do without. My dad had died five years before, leaving Mom with no money and with children to raise.

One month before Easter, the pastor of our church announced that a special holiday offering would be taken to help a poor family. He asked everyone to save and give sacrificially.

When we got home, we talked about what we could do. We decided to buy fifty pounds of potatoes and live on them for a month. This would allow us to save twenty dollars of our grocery

---

[297] Paula Noble Fellingham

money for the offering. Then we thought that if we kept our electric lights turned off as much as possible and didn't listen to the radio, we'd save money on that month's electric bill.

Darlene got as many house and yard cleaning jobs as possible, and both of us babysat often. For fifteen cents we could buy enough cotton loops to make three potholders to sell for a dollar. We made twenty dollars on potholders. That month was one of the best of our lives.

Every day we counted the money to see how much we had saved. At night we'd sit in the dark and talk about how the poor family was going to enjoy having the money the church would give them. We had about eighty people in church, so we figured that whatever amount of money we had to give, the offering would surely be twenty times that much. After all, every Sunday the pastor had reminded people to save for the sacrificial offering.

The night before Easter, we were so excited we could hardly sleep. We didn't care that we wouldn't have new clothes for Easter; we had seventy dollars for the sacrificial offering. We could hardly wait to get to church!

On Sunday morning, the rain was pouring down. We didn't own an umbrella, and the church was over a mile from our home, but it didn't seem to matter how wet we got. Darlene had cardboard in her shoes to fill the holes. The cardboard came apart, and her feet got wet.

But we sat in church proudly. I heard some teenagers talking about our old dresses. I looked at them in their new clothes.

When the sacrificial offering was taken, we were sitting in the second row from the front. Mom put in a ten-dollar bill, and each of us kids put in a twenty-dollar bill.

We sang all the way home from church. At lunch, Mom had a surprise for us. She had bought a dozen eggs, and we had boiled Easter eggs with our fried potatoes!

Late that afternoon, the minister drove up in his car. Mom went to the door, talked with him for a moment, and then came back with an envelope in her hand. We asked what it was, but she didn't say a word. She opened the envelope and out fell a bunch of money. There were three crisp twenty-dollar bills, one ten-dollar bill and seventeen one-dollar bills.

Mom put the money back in the envelope. We didn't talk, we just sat and stared at the floor. We had gone from feeling like millionaires to feeling poor. We kids had such a happy life that we felt sorry for anyone who didn't have our Mom and our late Dad for parents and a house full of brothers and sisters and other kids visiting constantly. We thought it was fun to share silverware and see whether we got the spoon or the fork that night. We had two knives that we passed around to whoever needed them. I knew we didn't have a lot of things that other people had, but I'd never thought we were poor. But on that Easter day I found out that we were.

The minister had brought us the money for the poor family, so we *must* be poor, I thought. I didn't like being poor. I looked at my dress and worn-out shoes and felt so ashamed — I didn't even want to go back to church. Everyone there probably already knew we were poor!

I thought about school. I was in the ninth grade and at the top of my class of over one hundred students. I wondered if the kids at school knew that we were poor. I decided that I could quit school since I had finished the eighth grade. That was all the law required at the time.

We sat in silence for a long time. Then it got dark, and we went to bed. All that week, we girls went to school and came home, and no one talked much. Finally, on Saturday, Mom asked us what we wanted to do with the money. What did poor people do with money? We didn't know. We'd never known we were poor. We didn't want to go to church on Sunday, but Mom said we had to. Although it was a sunny day, we didn't talk on the way. Mom started to sing, but no one joined in, and she sang only one verse.

At church we had a missionary speaker. He talked about how churches in Africa made buildings out of sun-dried bricks, but they needed money to buy roofs. He said one hundred dollars would put a roof on a church. The minister added, "Can't we all sacrifice to help these poor people?" We looked at each other and smiled for the first time in a week.

Mom reached into her purse and pulled out the envelope. She passed it to Darlene, Darlene gave it to me, and I handed it to Ocy.

Ocy put it in the offering.

When the offering was counted, the minister announced that it was a little over one hundred dollars. The missionary was excited. He hadn't expected such a large offering from our small church. He said, "You must have some rich people in this church." And then it struck us! We had given eighty-seven dollars of that "little over one hundred dollars."

We were the rich family in the church! Hadn't the missionary said so? From that day on, I've never been poor again.[298]

Learning Questions

1. How did the "rich family" show thriftiness?
2. Why were they the richest family in the church?
3. Name some ways you can help others with your money.

You Show Thrift When You:

- Are careful with money and things.
- Understand that you need to be thoughtful about how you use the things you own.
- Use things over and over instead of throwing them away or buying new things.
- Don't waste food, water or anything.
- Don't spend all your money; you save some of it.

---

[298] *Chicken Soup for the Golden Soul,* http://www.chickensoup.com/stories/golden/rich.html

TOLERANCE

Tolerance

Definition Tolerance: Being patient with things that you wish were different.

Quotes

"Tolerance is the best religion."

Victor Hugo[299]

"Live and let live."

Scottish Proverb[300]

Explanation

Tolerance is being flexible and patient when life is challenging.

When you are tolerant of other people you don't let them annoy you. If you disagree with them you think, "That's okay if they don't agree with me. We just don't think the same way about this."

Some people want no changes in their lives. They want everything to stay the same. When you're tolerant you don't get upset with change, you understand that it is part of life and you adapt.

Some people expect others to think and act just like them. When you're tolerant you accept differences and you realize that variety is good.

Tolerant people quickly forgive the weaknesses of others, especially the members of their own family. When you're tolerant you don't criticize others and you don't complain, because you understand that complaining does not make things better.

Sometimes you just have to live with things you cannot change. You can either live miserably or tolerantly. It's up to you.

---

[299] *Five thousand Quotations for All Occasions.* 1945. Edited by Lewis C. Henry. Garden City, New York: Doubleday & Company, Inc., 287

[300] *Five thousand Quotations for All Occasions.* 1945. Edited by Lewis C. Henry. Garden City, New York: Doubleday & Company, Inc., 287

Story for Young Children

Puppies for Sale

A store owner was tacking a sign above his door that read "Puppies For Sale." Signs like that have a way of attracting small children, and sure enough, a little boy appeared under the store owner's sign. "How much are you going to sell the puppies for?" he asked.

The store owner replied, "Anywhere from $30 to $50."

The little boy reached in his pocket and pulled out some change. "I have $2.37," he said. "Can I please look at them?"

The store owner smiled and whistled and out of the kennel came Lady, who ran down the aisle of his store followed by five teeny, tiny balls of fur. One puppy was lagging considerably behind. Immediately the little boy singled out the lagging, limping puppy and said, "What's wrong with that little dog?"

The store owner explained that the veterinarian had examined the little puppy and had discovered it didn't have a hip socket. It would always be limp. It would always be lame. The little boy became excited. "That is the puppy that I want to buy."

The store owner said, "No, you don't want to buy that little dog. If you really want him, I'll just give him to you."

The little boy was quiet. He looked straight into the store owner's eyes, pointing his finger, and said, "I don't want you to give him to me. That little dog is worth every bit as much as all the other dogs and I'll pay full price. In fact, I'll give you $2.37 now, and 50 cents a month until I have him paid for."

The store owner was countered, "You really don't want to buy this little dog. He is never going to be able to run and jump and play with you like the other puppies."

The little boy then reached down and rolled up his pant leg to reveal a badly twisted, crippled left leg supported by a big metal brace. He looked up at the store owner and softly replied, "Well, I don't run so well myself, and this little puppy will need someone who understands!"[301]

Learning Questions

1. Why did the little boy choose the crippled puppy?
2. Why didn't the store owner want to sell the crippled puppy to the boy?
3. What did the little boy say to the store owner that showed he had tolerance for the puppy and for his own crippled leg?

---

[301] Dan Clark, "Puppies for Sale," *Chicken Soup for the Soul*, 66-67

Story for Older Children

<u>The Baby and the Wolf</u>

This is a true story about a trapper who lived in Alaska. His wife had died leaving him with a baby to care for. He had to go out trapping for long hours. He would put the baby in the crib and leave his dog home to watch out and protect the baby.

One cold winter day he came home and saw his dog in a corner with blood all over his mouth. He quickly looked to see if his baby was all right. The crib was empty and he couldn't see the baby.

Angrily the trapper picked up an ax and killed the dog who he thought had killed his baby. Suddenly he heard the baby cry. He was surprised to find the baby on the floor under the crib, safe and sound.

Now he was confused. What had really happened? Looking around a little more he found a dead wolf in another corner of the log cabin. Now he realized what had happened. The dog had saved the baby's life by killing the wolf. The trapper had judged the dog hastily and wrongly. The trapper had killed his loyal friend.

We should be very careful not to judge others. We should try to think positively and kindly about them. We should show tolerance and kindness to our fellowman and to animals.[302]

Learning Questions

1. How would things have turned out differently if the trapper had been tolerant of his dog instead of judging him too quickly?
2. Why is it harmful to judge others?
3. How can you show tolerance for others?

You Show Tolerance When You:

- Are flexible and patient when life is challenging.
- Don't let people annoy you.
- Don't get bothered by people who disagree with you.
- Understand that change is part of life and we need to be flexible and adapt.
- Accept differences and realize that variety is good.
- Quickly forgive the weaknesses of others.
- Don't criticize or complain.
- Accept things you cannot change.

---

[302] Retold by Rebecca Ashton

TRUSTWORTHINESS

Trustworthiness

Definition Trustworthiness: Being the kind of person that others can believe and rely on.

Quotes

"The man who trusts men will make fewer mistakes than he who distrusts them."

Camillo di Cavour[303]

"Trust yourself. You know more than you think you do."

Benjamin Spock[304]

Explanation

Trust is believing in something or someone. It is having confidence that things will turn out the way they should. Trustworthiness is being the kind of person people can trust.

People who are trustworthy keep their promises. When they say they'll do something, they always do it, and they do their very best at whatever it is.

When you are honest and you always finish what you promise to do, people know they can trust you. For example, when you do your household chores each day, even when you don't want to, your parents know they can trust you.

Trustworthy people always tell the truth. Others believe them and trust their word. It is important to be trusted by the people in your life.

When you're trustworthy, if a friend tells you a secret you don't share their secret with anyone.

What if you choose wrongly and share your friend's secret with two or three people and they each tell two or three others? Soon many people will know your friend's secret and then how will your friend feel about you? He or she will probably be sad and disappointed, and they will know you are not trustworthy. After you lose someone's trust it is difficult to get it back. It may take years of telling the truth before your friend will trust you again.

---

[303] Edwards, Tyron. 1977. *The New Dictionary of Thoughts.* Stanbook, Inc., 302
[304] http://www.quotationspage.com

Story for Younger Children

<u>Hans The Shepherd Boy</u>

Hans was a little shepherd boy who lived in Germany. One day he was keeping his sheep near a great forest when a hunter rode up to him.

"How far is it to the nearest village, my boy?" asked the hunter. "It is six miles, sir," said Hans. "But the road is only a sheep track. You might easily lose your way."

"My boy," said the hunter, "if you show me the way, I will pay you well."

Hans shook his head. "I cannot leave the sheep, sir," he said. "They would stray into the woods and the wolves might kill them."

But if one or two sheep are eaten by the wolves, I will pay you for them and I will give you more than you can earn in a year."

"Sir, I cannot go," said Hans. "These sheep are my master's. If they are lost, I should be to blame."

"If you cannot show me the way, will you get me a guide? I will take care of your sheep while you are gone."

"No," said Hans, "I cannot do that. The sheep do not know your voice, and—" Then he stopped.

"Can't you trust me?" asked the hunter.

"No," said Hans. "You have tried to make me break my word to my master. How do I know that you would keep your word?"

The hunter laughed. "You are right," said he. "I wish I could trust my servants as your master can trust you. Show me the path. I will try to get to the village alone."

Just then several men rode out of the woods. They shouted for joy.

"Oh, sire!" cried one. "We thought you were lost!"

Then Hans learned, to his great surprise, that the hunter was a prince. He was afraid that the great man would be angry with him. But the prince smiled and spoke in praise of him.

A few days later a servant came from the prince and took Hans to the palace.

"Hans," said the prince, "I want you to leave your sheep and come to serve me. I know you are a boy whom I can trust."

Hans was very happy with his good fortune. "If my master can find another shepherd to take my place, then I will come and serve you."

So, Hans went back and tended the sheep until his master found another shepherd. After that he served the prince happily for many years.[305]

Learning Questions

1. Why wouldn't Hans do what the prince wanted?
2. How did Hans show he was trustworthy?
3. How was he blessed for his trustworthiness?

Story for Older Children

The Ultimate Trust

In Holland in 1940, many people found it hard to trust each other. The German army had invaded Holland at the beginning of World War II. Germany's leader, Adolf Hitler, had a plan to kill all of Europe's Jews. Jewish families were taken from their homes and sent to work camps. Many Jews died in these camps.

Anne Frank was a Jewish girl living in Holland when the Germans invaded. Her father, Otto, owned a business in a building that had a secret apartment, or annex. The Frank family decided to hide in the annex.

Otto Frank asked a very trustworthy person to help hide his family; his secretary, Miep Gies. She agreed to help. Miep Gies was so loyal that she was willing to risk her family's safety to help the Franks.

For more than two years, Gies and her husband did the shopping for the eight people hiding in their annex. That was very dangerous. If she had been caught, she surely would have been sent to one of the work camps. Only Otto Frank survived.

The diary that Anne Frank kept while in the annex was discovered, preserved, and published after the war. The diary tells about people who had courage, hope, and trust. When asked about her great trustworthiness, Miep Gies said simply, "We did our human duty to help people in need."[306]

Learning Questions

1. How do you think Otto Frank knew that Miep Gies was trustworthy?
2. Name two trustworthy people in your life.

---

[305] Retold by Ella Lyman Cabot, The Moral Compass, pp. 260-261

[306] "The Ultimate Trust," taken from the book *Trustworthiness*, by Emily Lauren, 2002, Raintree Steck-Vaughn Publishers, p. 28-29

3. How can you be like them?

You Show Trust and Trustworthiness When You:

- Believe in something or someone.
- Keep your promises.
- Do your best.
- Finish what you start.
- Do your chores even when you don't want to.
- Keep secrets.
- Tell the truth.

UNDERSTANDING

Understanding

Definition Understanding: Learning and feeling in your heart how other people feel and what they believe.

Quotes

"To love you as I love myself is to seek to hear you as I want to be heard and understand you as I long to be understood."

David Augsburger[307]

"The man who can put himself in place of the other man, who can understand the working of other minds, need never worry about what the future has in store for him."

Owen D. Young[308]

Explanation

There are at least three ways to understand others. First, you think about how the person is feeling — with their life experiences, needs and desires. You try to "be" that person for a moment. Second, you watch their body language (facial expression, posture) for clues that tell you how they are feeling. Third, you listen to them very carefully, concentrating on what they're saying, not on what you are going to say next.

In our families we should try to understand one another *before* we try to be understood. Doing this shows our love for one another. Family members should be able to share their feelings in confidence, knowing they won't be laughed at, and feeling understood. We should never laugh at one another, but rather try to be understanding and kind. Sam Levenson said, "We may not always see eye to eye, but we can try to see heart to heart."[309]

Successful designer Patricia Moore noticed how difficult it was for her grandfather to get around and do the simplest things. Her grandfather had a disease called arthritis. Twenty-five-year-old Patricia wanted to know what it was like to have his challenges.

---

[307] Glenn Van Ekeren. *Speaker's Sourcebook II.* 1994. Paramus, New Jersey: Prentice Hall, 360
[308] Glenn Van Ekeren. *Speaker's Sourcebook II.* 1994. Paramus, New Jersey: Prentice Hall, 360
[309] http://www.jessejamesseminars.com/wanted_poster_jan03.htm

So one day she dressed up like an old woman. She padded her back into a hump and wore contact lenses smeared with Vaseline. To complete her make-over, she wore thick support stockings and a fuzzy wool coat. Then Patricia went into town.

Moore was ignored in stores as she struggled to complete simple tasks, and she was rudely honked at as she crossed the street with difficulty, failing to make it across before the light changed. Patricia Moore discovered what life is like for old people who are in pain and can't see well. She then really understood how they feel.

In the book and movie "To Kill a Mockingbird" Harper Lee said, "If you can learn this simple trick you'll get along a lot better with all kinds of folks: you never really understand a person until you consider things from his point of view…until you climb into his skin and walk around in it."[310]

We should do our best to genuinely understand our family, friends, and everyone we meet.

Story for Young Children

<u>Mountain Goats</u>

One of the famous characteristics of mountain goats is their irritability. I don't know if it's true of all goats, but it's certainly true of mountain goats in the Rockies. These goats are so prickly that if they stay in close proximity they not only hurt each other but have even been known to kill members of their own families.

As puzzling as this behavior may seem to us, there is a good reason for it. Mountain goats live in areas where there is a very limited food supply. If they were to live in groups, they'd all end up dying as none would get enough to eat.

It can be the same with people. Often their behavior is puzzling to us, sometimes downright offensive. They can be cold, prickly, irritable and harsh. Yet if we take the time to look, we'll find that there are usually reasons why people are like this – perhaps they've been hurt themselves, perhaps they're dealing with great stresses. But whatever the reason, there is a reason for their prickliness. Unlike goats, however, it's not healthy for us humans to live apart, and perhaps we need to explore our own prickliness and reach out lovingly to those who are so prickly.[311]

Learning Questions

1. Why don't mountain goats live in groups?
2. Do you know a prickly, irritable person?
3. Name one thing you can do to make that person happier.

---

[310] http://www.picosearch.com

[311] http://storiesforpreaching.com/category/sermonillustrations/understanding-others/

Story for Older Children

<u>The New Kid In Town</u>

Nathan was the homeliest kid I'd ever seen. He was a skinny new student with huge ears and funny-looking hair. So why was this new kid leaning on Amy Miller's locker like they were best friends? Amy was a popular cheerleader and gorgeous beyond belief. And why was she smiling at Nathan instead of ignoring him like she ignored the other boys who weren't popular?

"Weird," John thought. "What's going on?"

By lunchtime John had forgotten about the new kid. He sat down at his usual table in the corner, all alone. John wasn't homely like the new kid—just a little overweight and kind of nerdy. Nobody ever talked to John unless they had to.

Just then John looked up and saw that new kid again. He was holding his lunch tray and standing over Amy, smiling like he'd just won a race. And she was smiling too! Then she moved over and made room on the bench next to her. But what Nathan did next was really shocking. Instead of sitting next to Amy, the new kid turned around and walked over to John's table.

"Care if I join you?" he asked.

Just like that. *Care if I join you? Like the whole seventh grade was fighting to sit at my table!* John thought.

"Sure," John answered. "I mean no. I don't mind."

So the kid sat down. And he came back, day after day, until they were friends. Good friends.

John had never had a real friend before, but Nathan invited John to his house, on trips with his family and they often swam in Nathan's swimming pool.

And kids were talking to him! They were nodding to him in the hallways, and even asking him questions about assignments and things. And John was talking back to them without being embarrassed. It was great!

One day at lunchtime John asked Nathan, "Why did you sit with me that first day? Didn't Amy ask you to sit with her?"

"Sure, she asked. But she didn't need me."

"What?"

"Yes, you needed me. Don't you remember? You were sitting alone looking sad and afraid," Nathan explained.

"Afraid?"

"Uh huh. You see, at my old school I used to be just like you. I used to sit alone, and I was afraid people were laughing at me."

"You - afraid?" John couldn't imagine Nathan by himself because he had such a great personality.

"Yes," Nathan answered. "It took a friend to help me see that I wasn't alone because of how I look. I was alone because I never smiled or cared about other people. I was so worried about myself that I didn't pay attention to anyone else. That's why I sat with you, to let you know someone cares. Amy already knows that."

"Oh, she knows, all right," John said as he watched two guys fighting to sit near her. John and Nathan both laughed. *It felt good to laugh,* realized John.

At that moment John looked across the table at Nathan and was suddenly filled with a deep appreciation for his new friend. John's heart swelled as he smiled at Nathan and said, "Thanks for understanding!"[312]

Learning Questions

1. How did Nathan come to understand the way John was feeling?
2. Can you improve your awareness of other people and their needs?
3. Is there someone you can be a friend to, and then help others understand that person better?

You Show Understanding When You:

- Learn with compassion how other people feel.
- Think about how the other person is feeling, with his life experiences, his needs and desires.
- Try to "be" the other person for a moment.
- Watch people's body language.
- Listen very carefully, concentrating on what is being said.
- Never ridicule or laugh at anyone.

---

[312] Retold by Paula Noble Fellingham

UNSELFISHNESS

Unselfishness

Definition Unselfishness: Sharing with others easily; giving freely.

Quotes

"We must not only give what we have; we must also give what we are."

Desire-Cardinal Mercier[313]

"Success in life has nothing to do with what you gain in life or accomplish for yourself. It's what you do for others."

Danny Thomas[314]

Explanation

Unselfishness means thinking of others before yourself. Since "un" means "not," unselfish means not selfish…not thinking about yourself. When this value becomes a part of you, many of the other values (like love, empathy, gratitude, and kindness) come more easily.

The great scientist Albert Einstein understood the supreme importance of this value. He believed that "only a life lived for others is worth living."[315] This means that success in life is not about what you do for yourself, it's all about what you do for others.

Let's think about some ways to be unselfish. If you are a giving, unselfish person, you:

- Don't get upset when you are asked to help around the house. You help cheerfully because you love your family.
- Don't expect people to do things for you. Instead, you look for ways to help others.
- Smile and are friendly to everyone, no matter who they are and no matter how they treat you.
- Obey the first time you're asked to do something.
- Notice when other people need your help or when they need an act of kindness to perk them up.
- Give other people the biggest piece, the first turn, etc.

---

[313] Glenn Van Ekeren. *Speaker's Sourcebook II*. 1994. Paramus, New Jersey: Prentice Hall, 169

[314] Glenn Van Ekeren. *Speaker's Sourcebook II*. 1994. Paramus, New Jersey: Prentice Hall, 169

[315] http://www.ournet.md/~hi-tech/einstein_life.html

The very best kind of unselfishness is when you don't tell anyone about the acts of kindness you do.

A good way to learn how to be unselfish is to ask yourself this question: "What can I do to make someone happy?" Another way is to imagine what it would be like to *be* the people in your life…then think about what you can do to make their lives easier.

Selfishness is like looking in a mirror — only seeing your own needs. Unselfishness is like looking through windows — seeing the needs of others. You'll be a much happier person if you can learn to look through windows instead of mirrors.

American President George Bush, Sr. said, "We all have something to give. So, if you know how to read, find someone who can't. If you've got a hammer, find a nail. If you're not hungry, not lonely, not in trouble — seek out someone who is."[316]

Story for Young Children

The Unselfish Child

An old story is told about the great famine in England years ago. The entire country suffered from hunger except the rich. One day a kind, wealthy man who loved children sent for twenty of them and said, "Every day until this dreadful famine is over, I will bring you a basket of bread. You may each choose a loaf and take it home to share with your families."

Since the children were very hungry, they seized the basket and struggled with each other to get the largest loaf. Sadly, when the children ran away, clutching their bread, they forgot to thank the man who had been so generous. All except one little girl named Gretchen.

She stood there alone, a little distance from the gentleman. Then, smiling, Gretchen picked up the last loaf, the smallest of all, and thanked him for his kindness before she left.

When the children returned the next day they behaved rudely again – pushing and shoving to get the biggest piece of bread. Again, little Gretchen took the last loaf - scarcely half the size of the others. But when she came home and her mother began to cut the loaf, out dropped five shining silver coins.

"Oh, Gretchen!" exclaimed her mother, "this must be a mistake! These silver coins surely don't belong to us! Now hurry and return them to the kind gentleman."

Gretchen ran back to the man as fast as she could. But when she explained about the mistake he said, "No, my dear child, it was not a mistake. The silver was baked into the smallest loaf by my baker because I wanted to reward you. Please remember this throughout your life: Those who unselfishly think of others before they think about themselves will receive blessings far greater

---

[316] Glenn Van Ekeren. *Speaker's Sourcebook II*. 1994. Paramus, New Jersey: Prentice Hall, 169

than silver. They will find love and happiness, and they'll receive the respect and admiration of all who know them."[317]

Learning Questions

1. How did Gretchen show unselfishness?
2. What is one way you can be unselfish?
3. Name one person in your family for whom you can do something special, that will make them happy.

Story for Older Children

Brotherhood

Abram and Zimri were brothers and tilled their lands in a happy vale together. The same plow turned the sod of both their farms in the Spring, and when Autumn came with its fruitful harvest, they shared equally the bounteous product of their common labor, and each stored his portion in his barn.

Abram had a wife and seven sons, but Zimri lived alone. One evening as Zimri lay upon his lonely bed, he thought of Abram and his family. Within himself, he said, "There is my brother, Abram. He has a wife and seven sons, for whom he must provide, while I have neither wife nor child, and yet we share our crops alike. Surely this is an injustice to my brother. I will arise and go down to the fields and add to my brother's store."

The moon looked out from between the murky clouds, and threw a shimmering light upon the stubbled field, newly reaped. Zimri took a generous third of his sheaves from his own abundant store and carried them to his brother's pile. He returned to his home with a light heart and slept soundly.

As Abram lay upon his bed that night, he thought of his brother. Within himself, he said, "There is my brother, Zimri. He is alone. He has no sons to help him. He does his work without assistance, while I have seven lusty sons who bind my sheaves. Yet we divide our gains equally. Surely this is not right. I will arise and go down to the field and will add to my brother's store."

The trees stood straight in the light of the cold, round moon, and their yellow leaves were shown, then hidden, as the playful moon sported with the clouds. Abram rose and guided by the doubtful light, stole softly to the fertile field. From his ample store he took a generous third and carried it to add to his brother Zimri's pile. He returned to his home with a good heart and slept, for his soul was at peace.

When morning came, and each surveyed his store of sheaves, he wondered how it was that his own store had not decreased, although the night before he had given away a third—but neither of

____

[317] Retold by Paula Noble Fellingham

the brothers spoke in explanation. At length, their day's toil was ended, the sun reclined upon its bed covered by the western hills, and the brothers returned to their homes.

Before the generous Zimri slept that night, he arose—and led by his beneficent thought that Abram's share should be greater than his own, again visited the scene of his exploit the night before. The tall cedars stood up black against the sky, and the moon slivered their high tops with a mellow, slanting light. Again, he carried from his sheaves a third and stored them with his brother Abram's lot. He then retired behind his pile to keep watch.

It was not long before Abram came stealing softly down the silent field. He turned now right, then left, as if he wished not to be seen. He took from his sheaves again the third and placed it in Zimri's store.

The brothers met. Zimri saw it all, but could not speak, for his heart was full. He leaned upon his brother's breast, and they wept.[318]

Learning Questions

1. How do you feel when someone gives you something kindly and unselfishly?
2. What is one unselfish act that you can do for someone in your family this week?

You Show Unselfishness When You:

- Think of others before yourself.
- Help others cheerfully.
- Look for ways to serve others; notice those around you who need an act of kindness.
- Smile and be friendly.
- Obey right away.
- Give other people the biggest piece, the first turn, etc.
- Imagine how it would feel to BE the people in your life, then decide what you can do to make their lives easier.
- Look through windows—seeing the needs of others—instead of mirrors, seeing only your own needs.

---

[318] Author Unknown, EFM, V 5, 175-176

WISDOM

Wisdom

Definition Wisdom: Knowledge plus good judgment.

Quotes

"The intellect of the wise is like glass; it admits the light of heaven and reflects it."

Augustus Hare[319]

"Wisdom is oft-times nearer when we stoop than when we soar."

William Wordsworth[320]

Explanation

Knowledge plus good judgment equals wisdom. Knowledge is knowing something, and using good judgment means behaving well. Here are some examples of people who used wisdom and made wise decisions:

- On a cold, rainy day Jennifer wore a coat and used an umbrella, so she'd stay warm and dry.
- Matt decided to obey his mother and finish his chores before going swimming.
- Diana turned off the television when she saw that the program was not something she should watch.
- When John's friends asked him to do something he knew was wrong, John said "No, thank you."
- The lifeguard at the swimming pool said, "No running." Angela listened and then walked carefully.

Every day you make many choices. For example, you always choose what you think about. You sometimes choose what you eat, what you wear, and where you go. Since life is made up of many choices, it's important to decide if your choices are wise or foolish - good or bad.

Think about today, for example. Have you made good choices today? Good choices include thinking kind thoughts and trying to help other people whenever you can. Another good choice is listening and learning from the wise adults in your life.

---

[319] Edwards, Tyron. 1977. *The New Dictionary of Thoughts*. Stanbook, Inc., 730
[320] Edwards, Tyron. 1977. *The New Dictionary of Thoughts*. Stanbook, Inc., 731

A young man once came to Socrates and said, "Socrates, I have come sixteen hundred miles to talk to you about wisdom and learning." He said, "You are a man of wisdom and learning and I would like to be like you. Would you teach me how to be a man of wisdom and learning?"

Socrates said, "Come, follow me." And he led the way down to the seashore. Then they waded out into the water up to their waists. Then Socrates seized the young man and held his head under the water. The young man struggled, kicked, and tried to get away but Socrates held him down.

Now, if you hold somebody's head under water long enough, he will eventually become fairly peaceable, and when the young man quit kicking, Socrates carried him to the bank, laid him out to dry, and Socrates went back to the marketplace.

After the young man had thawed out a little bit he came back to Socrates to find the reason for this rather unusual behavior. Socrates said to him, "When your head was under water, what was the one thing you wanted more than anything else?" The young man answered, "More than anything else I wanted air."

Then Socrates said, "When you want wisdom and learning as much as you wanted air, you will find a way to get it."[321]

Story for Young Children

<u>The Wise Woman's Stone</u>

A wise woman who was traveling in the mountains found a precious stone in a stream. The next day she met another traveler who was hungry, and the wise woman opened her bag to share her food. The hungry traveler saw the precious stone and asked the woman to give it to him. She did so without hesitation. The traveler left, rejoicing in his good fortune. He knew the stone was worth enough to give him security for a lifetime. But a few days later he came back to return the stone to the wise woman.

"I've been thinking," he said, "I know how valuable the stone is, but I give it back in the hope that you can give me something even more precious. Give me what you have within you that enabled you to give me this precious stone. Tell me how you had the strength within you to give me your valuable stone."[322]

Learning Questions

1. Why did the traveler bring back the stone to the wise woman?
2. What do you think was the wise woman's strength?
3. Can you name someone who is wise?

---

[321] Sterling W. Sill, Excerpt from "Hold Up Your Hands," *Ensign,* July 1973, 102

[322] https://mirthandmotivation.com/2011/10/24/on-wisdom-humor-short-stories-to-make-you-think-smile/

Story for Older Children

<u>The King's Falcon</u>

In the old days of hunting, before gunpowder was invented, when bows and arrows were used, in some parts of Europe falcons were trained to help in the hunt. Falcons are a species of hawk, and are faithful and efficient.

The falcon would soar into the air, survey the country round about, and, if he discovered a deer, with the shriek of his voice or the flap of his wings, he guided his master to the game.

Now the king had been out hunting with his fellow noblemen but he became lost. He had with him his trained falcon who rested on his wrist. The king was starving, as was the bird. However, worse than the call for food was their thirst. The king was so desperate for water that he would have eaten mud.

His tongue was as thick as leather; his eyes were bulging with concern. He had desperately scanned every rock for some sign of moisture. The monarch could hardly pull one foot in front of the other.

But lo, a hundred yards ahead he detected something that looked like dripping water. It was water! New strength came into his veins. He automatically leaped forward with the cup he always carried. The falcon, of course, was ever present on his wrist.

Drip, drip, drip, and the cup was finally full. The king was just putting it to his lips when his falcon knocked the cup from his hands. Had the bird gone crazy? He filled it again. With one eye on the hawk and one on the cup, for the second time he raised it to his lips, but again for the second time it was knocked from his grasp.

The king unsheathed his sword. He spoke angrily to his feathered friend, who had been so faithful to him up to now, "You do that again, and off comes your head!"

Drip, drip, drip for the third time. The falcon was on the job watching his master and the newly filled cup. As the hunter raised the water to his lips, the bird loosed himself, clawed the hands of the king, and knocked the lifesaving, sparkling water to the desert floor.

Out came the king's sword and off came the head of the falcon. As the parched earth absorbed the blood of his precious hawk, the king scratched his forehead and began thinking. What in the world had possessed his faithful servant? He would investigate.

His eyes followed the drops of water as they trickled down the rock. "I'll climb up there," the king decided. It only took a minute, and he was at the source of the miniature spring. He turned a ghastly pale and nearly fainted at what he saw in the hollow rock.

Taking up a great part of the stagnant pool was a coiled poisonous snake that had been dead for weeks. The water, while it sparkled over the rocks, was cankered with the virus of the serpent.

Sadly, the king retraced his steps and now gazed on the lifeless form of his feathered hero. The king tearfully realized that he had allowed his thirst and his temper to overrule his wisdom. The bird had been flying over those hills for two days. His viewpoint was better than the king's, whose experience had been confined to the ground.

The king wept with deep regret and remorse.[323]

Learning Questions

1. What would have happened if the king had been wise and accepted the warnings of the hawk?
2. What is some wise counsel that your parents, teachers, or friends have given you?
3. How can your wisdom help others?

You Show Wisdom When You:

- Add good judgment to your knowledge.
- Behave well.
- Make wise, good choices.
- Evaluate your choices.
- Listen and learn from the wise adults in your life.

---

[323] Marvin O. Ashton, EFM, V 1, 200-201

Paula Noble Fellingham

WORK

Work

Definition Work: Using effort and energy to accomplish something of value.

Quotes

"You may have the loftiest goals, the highest ideals and the noblest dreams, but remember this: nothing works unless you do."

Nido R. Qubein[324]

"Work is love made visible."

Kahlil Gibran[325]

Explanation

Work means using effort and energy to do something that helps you or someone else.

Your attitude has a lot to do with how well you work. You can either be cheerful as you work, or you can be grumpy and upset. Here are three ideas that can help you have a good attitude about work:

1. Be thankful that your body is strong and healthy enough to work.
2. Understand that work is part of life. There are certain things that have to be done each day, and helping with the work is part of being alive.
3. Remember that your attitude is your choice — you can choose to be either cheerful or upset as you work. However, it makes you and everyone around you happier when you choose to work cheerfully. In the story of Snow White she told the elves to "whistle while you work!" That's a good idea because it's hard to be upset while you're whistling or singing.

Also, you should always try to do your best work. No matter what the chore is - big or small - you should give it your best effort. Martin Luther King Jr. said, "If you are called to be a street sweeper, sweep streets even as Michelangelo painted, or Beethoven composed music, or Shakespeare wrote poetry. Sweep streets so well that all the hosts of heaven and earth will pause to say, 'Here lived a great street sweeper who did his job well!'"[326]

---

324 Glenn Van Ekeren. *Speaker's Sourcebook II*. 1994. Paramus, New Jersey: Prentice Hall, 391
325 Glenn Van Ekeren. *Speaker's Sourcebook II*. 1994. Paramus, New Jersey: Prentice Hall, 390
326 Glenn Van Ekeren. *Speaker's Sourcebook II*. 1994. Paramus, New Jersey: Prentice Hall, 391

Sometimes you get discouraged when work is hard. If that happens, try to remember that if you keep going, if you don't give up, soon the work will be finished and then you'll feel good about it.

Story for Young Children

<u>Beauty and the Day's Work</u>

There was once a young man who took an unusual view of work. He was given a job in a stone quarry, facing with chisel and hammer the rough blocks that were to form the foundation for a temple.

"You must face ten of these blocks each day," said the foreman, "but you need not be too careful about how they look, since they are to be buried in the earth."

When the young man had finished the first day's work, he stood for a while and looked down on what he had done. The stones were roughly square, to be sure, but everyone was ugly and uneven. The youth, loving beauty, seized his hammer and chisel and went to work again, smoothing the rough places and running a straight line along each edge.

Every morning and evening the youth spent an extra hour or two adding form to blocks that he knew were to be buried deep in the earth.

Now it happened that the chief architect came one day to the quarry. His trained eye noted the beauty of the pile of foundation stones, and he said to the youth, "I suppose you know that these stones will never be seen again by men?"

The youth hung his head, for he thought the great man was angry with him. At last, he raised his eyes and said, "The extra work has cost my master nothing. I have done it on my own time and for my own pleasure."

The next day the architect came again and sat where he could look down into the quarry without being seen. An hour before the other men arrived, the youth came and the ring of his hammer sounded clear in the crisp dawn. The architect smiled. "Here is a labor of love for the cause of beauty," he said to himself. "The boy has a noble nature. This day shall he drop his chisel and come with me as an apprentice in the sacred task of temple building."

Years later, when the youth of the stone quarry was fashioning a great amphitheater in a far-distant city, a young man came to him and asked, "Sir, what must I do to succeed? I am about ready to begin my life's work."

The boy of the stone quarry smiled. "There is no recipe for success," he said, "but I can open for you the door to happiness. Add beauty to your day's work, whatever that may happen to be!"[327]

---

[327] Author Unknown, *Especially for M*, V 3, 142-143

Learning Questions

1. What were the rewards of the boy's hard work?
2. Do you ever do extra work that is not required?
3. Does having a cheerful attitude make work more enjoyable?

Story for Older Children

The Baskets

The story is told about a minister in Africa who called the natives to him one day and asked them to help him harvest his crop. He asked them to each bring a basket to carry the crop to market in the town.

At the end of the day, the minister let each worker fill his basket for himself as a wage. Those who had brought big baskets had a great salary. But those who had purposely brought small baskets so they would not have to work as hard were disappointed when their salary was small.[328]

Learning Questions

1. What happened to those who brought big baskets to carry the crops?
2. Has there ever been a time when you were blessed because you worked hard?
3. What kind of work do you enjoy doing?

You Show Work When You:

- Use energy and effort to accomplish your goals.
- Do things that help others.
- Understand that work is part of life.
- Do your best, have a good attitude as you work, and don't give up.

---

[328] Author Unknown, *Especially for M*, V 3, 328

About the Author

Recipient, Doctorate of Education (Ed.D.) in Human Relations. Author of 8 books, including the best-selling ***Believe It! Become It! How to Hurdle Barriers and Excel Like Never Before.***

Recipient of the "Points of Light Award" given by U. S. President George W. Bush. Recipient of the "President's Volunteer Service Award" given by U.S. Presidents Barack Obama and Donald Trump.

Recipient of the "Lifetime Achievement Award" by President Biden.

Honored as Washington State Young Mother of the Year and Utah State Woman of the Year.

Dr. Paula Fellingham was the Founder and CEO of the Win Win Women Network, the world's largest live-streaming and social network for women, and global community of women. Dr. Paula's former Women's Information Network (WIN) hosted the largest gathering of women in history for the 100th anniversary of International Women's Day: 377 live events in 152 countries.

Paula is the Founder of the non-profit Global Prosperity and Peace Initiative (GPPI). Dr. Fellingham and her team work with Peace Ambassadors worldwide to fulfill their mission "to increase the love, prosperity, and peace on Earth." See www.ProsperityandPeace.org and www.WomensGlobalAlliance.org. Dr. Fellingham is also the Founder of the International Youth Parliament: www.InternationalYouthParliament.com and the Women of the Middle East Network: (W.O.M.E.N.) www.WomenOfTheMiddleEast.org, launched in Israel.

Paula's comprehensive "Total Life Excellence" curriculum is taught globally to strengthen people mentally, physically, emotionally, socially, spiritually, financially, and in their relationships.

Paula has given presentations to delegates at the United Nations, for the World Movement of Mothers in Paris, and at many other conferences worldwide. Paula participated in the World Congress on Families, and at the World Movement of Mothers Conference at NATO Headquarters.

For years Paula hosted a daily two-hour family-strengthening radio show called "Solutions for Families".

Producer of the Fellingham Family musical group, Paula's eight-member family band performed across America and internationally for twelve summers. During their final season they presented 273 shows. Paula received her Bachelor of Arts in 1971, and her Doctorate in 2004. Dr. Gilbert Fellingham (University Professor of Statistics) and Paula are the parents of 8 grown children.

Dearest Reader,

I invite you to contact me and/or participate in some of the wonderful projects that strengthen individuals and families worldwide. Email pfellingham@gmail.com

To learn more, visit these websites...

www.PaulaFellingham.com - www.SolutionsforFamilies.com

www.WomensGlobalAlliance.org - www.TotalLifeExcellence.com

www.ProsperityandPeace.org - www.InternationalWomensDay.org

My Family

It is my sincere hope that you will use the messages and stories in this book to strengthen your family. And, if you wish, I invite you to participate with me as we strengthen others. I would love to connect with you!

With so much love,

Paula Noble Fellingham